P9-CEI-323

The *Best* of COUNTRY COOKING
2010

Editor in Chief: Catherine Cassidy
Vice President, Executive Editor/Books: Heidi Reuter Lloyd
Creative Director: Ardyth Cope
Food Director: Diane Werner RD
Senior Editor/Books: Mark Hagen
Editor: Krista Lanphier
Art Director: Gretchen Trautman
Content Production Supervisor: Julie Wagner
Design Layout Artist: Kathy Crawford
Graphic Design Associate: Heather Meinen
Proofreaders: Linne Bruskewitz, Amy Glander
Recipe Asset System Manager: Coleen Martin
Premedia Supervisor: Scott Berger
Recipe Testing & Editing: Taste of Home Test Kitchen
Food Photography: Taste of Home Photo Studio
Administrative Assistant: Barb Czysz

U.S. Chief Marketing Officer: Lisa Karpinski
Vice President/Book Marketing: Dan Fink
Creative Director/Creative Marketing: Jim Palmen

THE READER'S DIGEST ASSOCIATION, INC.

President and Chief Executive Officer: Mary G. Berner
President, U.S. Affinities: Suzanne M. Grimes
SVP, Global Chief Marketing Officer: Amy J. Radin

Taste of Home Books
©2010 Reiman Media Group, Inc.
5400 S. 60th St., Greendale WI 53129

International Standard Book Number (10): 0-89821-803-9
International Standard Book Number (13): 978-0-89821-803-9
International Standard Serial Number: 1097-8321

All rights reserved. Printed in U.S.A.

Taste of Home is a registered trademark of
The Reader's Digest Association, Inc.

For other Taste of Home books and products, visit
www.ShopTasteofHome.com.

THE WORLD'S #1 COOKING MAGAZINE

PICTURED ABOVE AND ON FRONT COVER:
Roasted Chicken with Garlic-Sherry Sauce (p. 46), Roasted Veggie Medley (p. 160) and Layered Strawberry Shortcake (p.114).
Photography by Jim Wieland. Food styled by Diane Armstrong. Set styled by Stephanie Marchese.

Classic Recipes from the Heart of the Country

YOUR FAVORITE RECIPES can be found right here in *The Best of Country Cooking 2010*. Just like the wonderful classic cookbooks that lined the shelves of generations before you, this cookbook has traditional, reliable recipes that are a perfect addition to your collection.

This latest edition in our popular series has a total of 321 recipes, old-fashioned and modern, that were created by readers of our rural- and nostalgia-based magazines. That includes hundreds of home-style dishes that have been featured in recent issues of *Country Woman*, *Country*, *Country EXTRA*, *Reminisce* and *Reminisce EXTRA*.

What's more, every dish has been sampled and approved by some of the toughest critics around—hungry families! In addition, our Test Kitchen tried out every recipe in this book, so you can be confident each dish is a "keeper."

This book begins with an appealing variety of Snacks & Beverages. You'll find perfect party bites such as Asparagus Snack Squares (p. 7), Olive Zucchini Spread (p. 8) and Crab-Stuffed Mushrooms (p. 15). And you'll be able to whet your whistle with yummy beverage concoctions such as Orange Julius (p. 6) and Mocha Morning Drink (p. 9).

You can't go wrong with the Soups, Salads & Sandwiches chapter…particularly when you need a fast meal. Just mix and match the recipes for easy menu planning. We've even highlighted four hearty, convenient wraps (pp. 26-27) that make eating on the run a snap. They're so good, you simply have to try them.

You can also take your pick of this beautiful book's 53 recipes included in the Main Dishes chapter. It's filled with wonderful comfort foods like Irish Beef Stew (p. 43) and Four-Cheese Baked Ziti (p. 51). If you're looking for a robust breakfast, take a look at the morning recipes, such as Sausage Johnnycake, on pages 48-49. For a supper with international flair, such as Wasabi Beef Fajitas, take a peek at the recipes on pages 64-65 which use unique spices and flavors from various corners of the globe.

Round out dinners with any of the heart-warming items in Side Dishes & Condiments. You won't want to wait to try cheesy potato bakes, fresh vegetables and zesty condiments. You can count on tried-and-true recipes that fill hungry tummies, such as Vidalia Onion Bake (p. 74), Grandma's Scalloped Corn (p. 76), Zippy Cranberry Mustard (p. 80) and a host of robust side dishes.

And because nothing represents a country kitchen like oven-fresh loaves and biscuits, the comforting chapter Breads, Rolls & More offers plenty of golden baked goods, including coffee cake, quick breads, sweet rolls and more.

Speaking of baking, you'll want to check out the 23 recipes in Cookies, Bars & Brownies. Whether you're looking for classroom snacks, bake-sale items or Christmas cookies, this is one chapter you'll turn to time and again. Caramel Candy Bars (p. 99) and Coconut Brownies (p. 109) will become household favorites.

In addition, *The Best of Country Cooking 2010* features more than 45 impressive sweets. See Dazzling Desserts for delectable finales like Spiced Plum Pie (p. 112), Blueberry Citrus Cake (p. 125) and Chocolate Shoofly Pie (p. 127). A special section featuring fancy and fun cupcakes (pp. 118-119) is included as well.

You'll also find all of the standbys you've come to expect from this handy collection:

Cooking for Two—Dishes and dinners that are sized right for a pair.

Meals in Minutes—Four full suppers that require a minimum of prep work.

Most Memorable Meals—A total of 24 recipes divided into six delightful menus.

Be sure to watch for the blue ribbon symbol, left, as you thumb through *The Best of Country Cooking 2010*. It identifies prize-winning recipes that earned high honors in national cooking contests sponsored by one of our magazines.

So what are you waiting for? Grab a fork and dig in! It won't be long before you realize why these dishes are simply the best in the country.

CONTENTS

HERE'S A SUPER WAY *to start out a supper! Or, for a treat any time of day, turn to these satisfying appetizers, snacks, sweets and refreshing beverages.*

LOVE AT FIRST BITE. Appetizer Chicken Kabobs (p. 5).

Snacks & Beverages

APPETIZER CHICKEN KABOBS
(Pictured at left)

Gail Ponak, Viscount, Saskatchewan

These little chicken kabobs are a perfect appetizer. They're quick and easy to prepare, which means I can spend more time visiting with guests.

- 3/4 cup soy sauce
- 1/4 cup sugar
- 1 tablespoon canola oil
- 1/4 teaspoon garlic powder
- 1/2 teaspoon ground ginger
- 2 boneless skinless chicken breasts, cut into 1-inch chunks
- 6 to 8 green onions, cut into 1-inch pieces
- 1/2 pound medium fresh mushrooms, stems removed

In a large bowl, combine first five ingredients. Pour half into a large resealable plastic bag; add the chicken. Seal bag and turn to coat. Pour the remaining marinade into another large plastic bag; add onions. Seal the bag and toss to coat. Marinate for 30 minutes.

Drain and discard marinade from chicken. Drain and reserve marinade from onions. On soaked wooden skewers, thread a piece of chicken, onion, mushroom and another chicken piece.

Place kabobs on a broiler rack. Broil 5 in. from the heat, turning and basting with reserved marinade after 3 minutes. Broil for 3 minutes longer or until chicken is no longer pink. **Yield:** 20-24 appetizers.

WARM PERCOLATOR PUNCH

Janet Crawford, Ashland, Kentucky

It smells like Christmas all through my house when I serve up this pleasantly spicy punch. It can also be made in a Dutch oven.

- 6 cups unsweetened apple juice
- 6 cups cranberry juice
- 3 cups water
- 2/3 cup packed brown sugar
- 1/4 teaspoon salt
- 1 tablespoon whole cloves
- 2 cinnamon sticks (3 inches)

In a 24-cup percolator, combine the juices, water, brown sugar and salt. Place cloves and cinnamon sticks in the percolator basket; cover and begin perking. When cycle is complete, discard spices. **Yield:** 15 servings (about 3-1/2 quarts).

SAUCY MEATBALLS

Trish Berg, Dalton, Ohio

Mini meatballs in a sweet, tangy sauce are definitely family friendly. They're a hit as a party-starter or for supper. Try them served over noodles.

- 2 eggs, lightly beaten
- 1 cup dry bread crumbs
- 2 teaspoons salt
- 1/4 teaspoon pepper
- 2 pounds ground beef
- 1 bottle (14 ounces) ketchup
- 1 jar (12 ounces) grape jelly
- 1 medium onion, finely chopped

In a large bowl, combine the eggs, bread crumbs, salt and pepper. Crumble beef over mixture and mix well. Shape into 1-in. balls.

Place on a greased rack in a shallow baking pan. Bake, uncovered, at 350° for 20 minutes or until no longer pink. Drain on paper towels. Transfer to a greased 13-in. x 9-in. baking dish.

In a large saucepan, combine the ketchup, jelly and onion. Cook and stir over medium heat for 3-5 minutes or until jelly is melted. Pour over meatballs. Bake, uncovered, 20 minutes longer or until sauce is bubbly. **Yield:** 12 servings.

DRY BREAD CRUMBS

Dry bread crumbs may be purchased or made from very dry bread or Zwieback crackers. Place in a plastic bag and crush with a rolling pin. Spoon into a measuring cup.

FROSTY CHOCOLATE MILK

Monica Crandall, Battle Creek, Michigan

Kids don't need to be coaxed to drink their milk the way I serve it. I like to dress it up with chocolate and strawberry syrup, whipped cream and sprinkles. This way there isn't any problem with kids getting their daily servings of dairy. The milk treat can also be served as a dessert.

> 1 cup 1% chocolate milk
> 4 tablespoons chocolate syrup, *divided*
> 2 tablespoons strawberry syrup
> **Whipped cream in a can**
> 1 tablespoon colored sprinkles
> 2 fresh strawberries

In a small bowl, combine the milk, 2 tablespoons chocolate syrup and strawberry syrup. Cover and freeze for 5 minutes.

Drizzle the remaining chocolate syrup on the sides and bottom of each of two chilled glasses. Fill with the chocolate milk mixture. Top each with 1 tablespoon whipped cream; garnish each with sprinkles and a strawberry. **Yield:** 2 servings.

ORANGE JULIUS

(Pictured above)

Rita Swanson, Three Hills, Alberta

This is a refreshing drink year-round, but it also is a festive beverage to serve at special occasions. It's a good alternative to sugared soft drinks, too.

> 1 can (6 ounces) frozen orange juice
>   concentrate, thawed
> 1 cup milk
> 1 cup water
> 1/4 cup sugar
> 1 teaspoon vanilla extract
> 10 to 12 ice cubes

In a blender, combine the orange juice, milk, water, sugar and vanilla. Cover and blend until smooth. With blender running, add ice cubes, one at a time, through the opening in lid. Blend until smooth. Serve immediately. **Yield:** 4-5 servings.

APPETIZER COUNT

For an appetizer buffet that serves as the meal, offer five or six different appetizers and plan on eight to nine pieces per guest. If you'll also be serving a meal, two to three appetizers per person is sufficient.

PUMPKIN PIE DIP

Kari Egger, Portland, Oregon

This pumpkin dip is particularly yummy when served with cinnamon-sugar cutouts that I make from extra pie crust dough. It's good with gingersnaps and sugar cookies, too. The dip is a nice break from savory appetizers, and goes over well during the holidays.

> 1 package (8 ounces) cream cheese,
>   softened
> 2 cups confectioners' sugar
> 1 can (15 ounces) solid-pack pumpkin
> 5 teaspoons ground cinnamon, *divided*
> 1/2 teaspoon ground ginger
> 4 sheets refrigerated pie pastry
> 4 teaspoons sugar

In a large bowl, beat the cream cheese until fluffy. Add confectioners' sugar, pumpkin, 1 teaspoon cinnamon and ginger; beat until smooth. Cover and refrigerate until serving.

Roll out pie pastry on a lightly floured surface to 1/4-in. thickness. Cut with a floured 2-1/2-in. autumn-shaped cookie cutter. Place on an ungreased baking sheet. Reroll scraps if desired. Combine the sugar and remaining cinnamon; sprinkle over cutouts.

Bake at 425° for 6-8 minutes or until firm. Remove to wire racks. Serve with pumpkin dip. **Yield:** 3-1/2 cups (about 4-1/2 dozen cutouts).

CRAB WONTON CUPS
(Pictured below)

Connie McDowell, Greenwood, Delaware

These tasty little crab tarts make excellent appetizers served warm and crispy from the oven. You can add them to your list of holiday finger food as well. They're real crowd-pleasers.

    32 wonton wrappers
Cooking spray
     1 package (8 ounces) cream cheese,
         softened
   1/2 cup heavy whipping cream
     1 egg
     1 tablespoon Dijon mustard
     1 teaspoon Worcestershire sauce
     5 drops hot pepper sauce
     2 pouches (3.53 ounces *each*) premium
         crabmeat, drained
   1/4 cup thinly sliced green onions
   1/4 cup finely chopped sweet red pepper
     1 cup grated Parmesan cheese

Press wonton wrappers into miniature muffin cups coated with cooking spray. Spritz wrappers with cooking spray. Bake at 350° for 8-9 minutes or until lightly browned.

Meanwhile, in a small bowl, beat the cream cheese, cream, egg, mustard, Worcestershire sauce and pepper sauce until smooth. Stir in the crab, green onions and red pepper; spoon into wonton cups. Sprinkle with Parmesan cheese.

Bake for 10-12 minutes or until filling is heated through. Serve warm. Refrigerate leftovers. **Yield:** 32 appetizers.

ASPARAGUS SNACK SQUARES
(Pictured above)

Judy Wagner, Chicago, Illinois

We have asparagus almost every day during the short Midwest growing season, and this simple pizza-like dish is great for a party-starter or as the main course at a friendly luncheon.

     1 cup chopped sweet onion
     3 tablespoons butter
     2 garlic cloves, minced
     1 pound fresh asparagus, trimmed
   1/4 teaspoon pepper
     2 tubes (8 ounces *each*) refrigerated
         crescent rolls
     1 cup (4 ounces) shredded part-skim
         mozzarella cheese
     1 cup (4 ounces) shredded Swiss cheese

In a large skillet, saute the onion in butter until tender. Add garlic; cook 1 minute longer.

Cut the asparagus into 1-in. pieces; set the tips aside. Add remaining asparagus to skillet; saute until crisp-tender. Add the asparagus tips and pepper; saute 1-2 minutes longer or until the asparagus is tender.

Press dough into an ungreased 15-in. x 10-in. x 1-in. baking pan; seal seams and perforations. Bake at 375° for 6-8 minutes or until lightly browned. Top with asparagus mixture; sprinkle with cheeses. Bake 6-8 minutes longer or until cheese is melted. Cut into squares. **Yield:** 3 dozen.

Olive Zucchini Spread

(Pictured above)

GaleLynn Peterson, Long Beach, California

This spread is a great way to use up extra zucchini from the garden. The flavors are wonderful, and it makes enough to satisfy a crowd. I like to serve it at receptions, potlucks or casual get-togethers.

> 2 packages (8 ounces *each*) reduced-fat
>   cream cheese
> 3 cups shredded zucchini
> 1 jar (7-1/2 ounces) marinated artichoke
>   hearts, drained and finely chopped
> 1/4 cup pimiento-stuffed olives, chopped
> 1 can (4-1/4 ounces) chopped ripe olives
> 18 garlic cloves, minced
> 3 tablespoons chopped red onion

> 2 tablespoons minced fresh cilantro
> 2 tablespoons lime juice
> 2 tablespoons olive oil
> 1 green onion, chopped
> 1 French bread baguette, sliced

In a large bowl, combine the first 11 ingredients; beat until blended.

Transfer to a serving bowl; cover and chill for at least 4 hours or overnight. Serve with baguette slices. **Yield:** 6 cups.

Iced Almonds

Susan Marie Taccone, Erie, Pennsylvania

My mother-in-law gave me this recipe some 15 years ago. I've made well over 100 batches since then!

Snacks & Beverages

1/4 cup butter
2-1/2 cups whole unblanched almonds
1 cup sugar
1 teaspoon vanilla extract

In a heavy saucepan, melt butter over medium-high heat. Add almonds and sugar. Cook and stir constantly for 7-8 minutes or until syrup is golden brown. Remove from the heat; stir in vanilla.

Immediately drop by clusters or separate the almonds on a greased pan. Cool. Store in an airtight container. **Yield:** 4 cups.

MOCHA MORNING DRINK
(Pictured below)

Jill Rodriguez, Gonzales, Louisiana

When I'm sipping this delicious coffee, I almost feel like I've been to my favorite coffeehouse.

6 cups hot brewed coffee
3/4 cup half-and-half cream
6 tablespoons chocolate syrup
7 teaspoons sugar
6 cinnamon sticks (3 inches)
Whipped cream in a can, optional

In a large saucepan, combine the coffee, cream, chocolate syrup and sugar. Cook and stir over medium heat until sugar is dissolved and mixture is heated through. Ladle into six large mugs. Stir with a cinnamon stick. Garnish with whipped cream if desired. **Yield:** 6 servings.

VEGGIE CHEESE SPREAD
(Pictured above)

Sue Fraser, Grande Prairie, Alberta

This easy cheese spread is one of my family's favorite snacks. To make it a bit fancier, sprinkle tiny shrimp over the seafood sauce. It can be made ahead of time and is an ideal addition to an appetizer table.

1 package (8 ounces) cream cheese, softened
1/2 cup sour cream
1/4 cup mayonnaise
1 cup seafood cocktail sauce
2 cups (8 ounces) shredded part-skim mozzarella cheese
1 medium green pepper, chopped
3 green onions, chopped
1 medium tomato, chopped
Assorted crackers or tortilla chips

In a small bowl, beat cream cheese, sour cream and mayonnaise until smooth. Spread onto a serving plate; top with seafood sauce. Sprinkle with half of the cheese and vegetables; repeat layers.

Cover and chill until serving. Serve with the crackers or tortilla chips. **Yield:** 6-1/4 cups.

CAESAR SALSA BAGUETTE SLICES
(Pictured below)

Jodie Gharbi, Shreveport, Louisiana

I love throwing themed get-togethers. This appetizer was the hit of "Mediterranean Night." The fresh garden flavors in the tomato-packed salsa are outstanding with a crusty, chewy baguette.

> 2 cups chopped seeded tomatoes
> 3 tablespoons minced fresh chervil *or*
>   1 tablespoon dried chervil
> 1 tablespoon minced fresh cilantro
> 1 tablespoon minced fresh parsley
> 1 tablespoon capers, drained
> 1/2 teaspoon hot pepper sauce
> 2 tablespoons plus 1-1/2 teaspoons
>   olive oil
> 4-1/2 teaspoons lemon juice
> 2-1/2 teaspoons red wine vinegar
> 1 shallot, finely chopped
> 1 garlic clove, minced
> 1/2 teaspoon anchovy paste
> 1/8 teaspoon grated lemon peel
> 1 loaf (10-1/2 ounces) French bread
>   baguette, cut into 1/2-inch slices and
>   toasted

Combine the tomatoes, chervil, cilantro, parsley, capers and hot pepper sauce. In another bowl, whisk the oil, lemon juice, vinegar, shallot, garlic, anchovy paste and lemon peel. Drizzle over the tomato mixture; toss to coat. Serve with toasted baguette slices. **Yield:** 32 appetizers.

CRAB CRESCENT LOAF
(Pictured above)

Maureen Dongoski, Petersburg, West Virginia

Golden crescent roll slices are scrumptious filled with dilled cream cheese and tender pieces of crab. You're sure to appreciate the rich flavor and easy preparation.

> 1 tube (8 ounces) refrigerated crescent
>   rolls
> 2 packages (3 ounces *each*) cream cheese,
>   softened
> 1/3 cup chopped onion
> 1/2 teaspoon dill weed
> 1 cup chopped imitation crabmeat *or*
>   1 can (6 ounces) crabmeat, drained,
>   flaked and cartilage removed
> 1 egg yolk, lightly beaten

On a greased baking sheet, unroll the crescent dough into one long rectangle; seal seams and perforations. In a small bowl, beat the cream cheese, onion and dill until blended. Spread the mixture lengthwise over half of the dough to within 1/2 in. of edges. Top with crab.

Fold dough over filling; pinch seam to seal. Brush top with egg yolk. Bake at 375° for 18-22 minutes or until golden brown. Cut into slices. **Yield:** 1 loaf (12 slices).

SUMMERTIME COOLER

Taste of Home Test Kitchen

When the mercury rises, this pick-me-up punch will cool you down in no time. The pairing of ginger and lemon flavors makes for a perfect marriage.

> 1/2 cup sugar
> 4 cups cold water

2 tablespoons lemon juice
1/2 teaspoon minced fresh gingerroot
1/2 teaspoon cider vinegar

In a 1-1/2-qt. pitcher, combine all ingredients; chill. Stir before serving. **Yield:** 4 servings.

HOT GINGER COFFEE
(Pictured below)

Audrey Thibodeau, Gilbert, Arizona

This warm drink is wonderful after shoveling, skiing or sledding. You can also try the crystallized ginger in baked goods or over ice cream.

6 tablespoons ground coffee (not instant)
1 tablespoon grated orange peel
1 tablespoon chopped crystallized ginger
1/2 teaspoon ground cinnamon
6 cups cold water
Whipped cream, cinnamon sticks *and/or*
    additional orange peel, optional

Combine the coffee, orange peel, ginger and cinnamon; pour into a coffee filter. Brew with water according to manufacturer's directions.

Pour into mugs; garnish with whipped cream, cinnamon sticks and orange peel if desired. **Yield:** 6 servings.

Editor's Note: Look for crystallized or candied ginger in the spice or baking section of your grocery store.

POPCORN ALMOND BRITTLE
(Pictured above)

Ruth Peterson, Jenison, Michigan

With popcorn, almonds and candied cherries tossed together in a sweet crisp coating, this is a festive favorite we enjoy every year.

6 cups popped popcorn
1 cup slivered almonds
1/2 cup *each* red and green candied cherries,
    chopped
1-1/2 cups sugar
1/2 cup corn syrup
1/2 cup water
1/2 teaspoon salt
2 tablespoons butter
1 teaspoon vanilla extract

In a greased 13-in. x 9-in. baking pan, combine the popcorn, almonds and cherries. Bake at 350° for 10 minutes. Turn oven off and keep mixture warm in the oven.

Meanwhile, in a large heavy saucepan, combine the sugar, corn syrup, water and salt; cook and stir over low heat until sugar is dissolved. Cook over medium heat, without stirring, until a candy thermometer reads 305°-310° (hard-crack stage).

Remove from the heat; stir in the butter and vanilla. Immediately pour over popcorn mixture; toss gently. Spread onto a greased baking sheet. When cool, break into small pieces. **Yield:** about 1-1/2 pounds.

Editor's Note: We recommend that you test your candy thermometer before each use by bringing water to a boil; the thermometer should read 212°. Adjust your recipe temperature up or down based on your test.

CREAM CHEESE DEVILED EGGS

(Pictured above)

Abi McMahon, Sherman Oaks, California

Peas and bacon give this traditional appetizer a nice little twist. A family favorite, these deviled eggs are always first to disappear from the table.

  8 hard-cooked eggs
  1 package (8 ounces) cream cheese, softened
  2 teaspoons Dijon mustard
  1/4 teaspoon salt
  1/4 teaspoon pepper
  1/4 cup frozen peas, thawed
  3 bacon strips, cooked and crumbled

Cut the eggs in half lengthwise. Remove yolks; set whites aside.

In a small bowl, mash yolks. Add cream cheese, mustard, salt and pepper; beat until blended. Stir in the peas.

Stuff or pipe the mixture into the egg whites. Sprinkle with bacon. Refrigerate until serving. **Yield:** 16 appetizers.

LEMON CIDER

Annette Engelbert, Bruce Crossing, Michigan

With a quick wave of your kitchen "wand," you can conjure up a beverage that's ripe with flavor. You can serve it cold as a refreshing punch for a party or warm on a chilly fall day.

  1 gallon apple cider *or* juice
  1 can (12 ounces) frozen lemonade concentrate, thawed
  1 lemon, thinly sliced *or* cinnamon sticks

In a punch bowl, combine cider and lemonade. Float lemon slices on top.

To serve warm, heat the cider and lemonade; garnish individual servings with a cinnamon stick. **Yield:** 4-1/2 quarts.

CREAMY FETA-SPINACH DIP

(Pictured below)

Elissa Armbruster, Medford, New Jersey

Garlic and feta make a powerfully tasty pair in this addictive dip. I first tried it at a party and had to drag myself away from the bowl!

  1 cup (8 ounces) fat-free plain yogurt
  3/4 cup crumbled feta cheese
  2 ounces reduced-fat cream cheese, cubed
  1/4 cup reduced-fat sour cream
  1 garlic clove, minced
1-1/2 cups finely chopped fresh spinach
  1 teaspoon dill weed
  1/8 teaspoon pepper
Fresh vegetables *and/or* sliced bread

Line a strainer with four layers of cheesecloth or one coffee filter; place over a bowl. Place the yogurt in prepared strainer; cover the yogurt with edges of cheesecloth. Refrigerate for 2 hours or until yogurt has thickened to the consistency of whipped cream.

Transfer the yogurt to a food processor (discard liquid from bowl). Add the feta cheese, cream cheese, sour cream and garlic; cover and process until smooth.

Transfer to a small bowl. Stir in the spinach, dill and pepper. Cover and refrigerate until chilled. Serve with vegetables and/or sliced bread. **Yield:** 2 cups.

▗▖▗▖▗▖▗▖▗▖▗▖▗▖▗▖

CHICKEN TACO RING

(Pictured above)

Kathy Martinez, Enid, Oklahoma

If you want to wow your guests with Southwestern zest, try this eye-catching appetizer. I serve it with salsa, sour cream and other toppings served in small homemade tortilla bowls.

- 2 tubes (8 ounces *each*) refrigerated reduced-fat crescent rolls
- 2/3 cup finely crushed tortilla chips, *divided*
- 2 cups finely chopped rotisserie chicken
- 3/4 cup shredded reduced-fat Mexican cheese blend
- 1/2 cup reduced-fat mayonnaise
- 1 can (4 ounces) chopped green chilies, undrained
- 1/4 cup chopped pitted ripe olives
- 1 plum tomato, seeded and chopped
- 1 tablespoon taco seasoning
- 1 tablespoon lime juice

GARNISH:

- 1 cup (8 ounces) reduced-fat sour cream
- 1 cup salsa
- 2 plum tomatoes, sliced
- 1 medium lime, halved and sliced

Grease a 12-in. pizza pan. Unroll crescent dough. Sprinkle with 1/4 cup tortilla chips; press down gently. Separate into 16 triangles.

Place wide end of one triangle, chip side down, 3 in. from edge of prepared pan, with the point overhanging edge of pan. Repeat with remaining triangles, overlapping the wide ends (dough will look like a sun when complete). Lightly press wide ends together.

In a small bowl, combine the chicken, cheese, mayonnaise, chilies, olives, tomato, taco seasoning, lime juice and remaining tortilla chips. Spoon over wide ends of dough. Fold points of triangles over filling and tuck under wide ends (filling will be visible).

Bake at 375° for 20-25 minutes or until golden brown. Garnish with sour cream, salsa, tomatoes and lime. **Yield:** 16 servings.

NUTTY CARAMEL CORN
(Pictured below)

Jacque Castillo, Brookings, Oregon

Plain microwave popcorn becomes irresistible when it's yummied up with molasses, peanut butter and nuts. This awesome snack never lasts long around our house, because it's hard to eat just one bite.

> 3 packages (3-1/2 ounces *each*)
>   microwave popcorn
> 1 cup salted peanuts
> 1 cup salted roasted almonds
> 1 cup packed brown sugar
> 3/4 cup butter, cubed
> 3/4 cup corn syrup
> 3/4 cup peanut butter
> 1/2 cup molasses
> 1 teaspoon vanilla extract
> 1/2 teaspoon baking soda
> 1 cup pecan halves

Pop the popcorn according to manufacturer's directions. Meanwhile, in a large heavy saucepan, combine the peanuts, almonds, brown sugar, butter, corn syrup, peanut butter and molasses. Bring to a boil over medium heat; cook and stir for 5 minutes.

Remove from the heat; stir in the vanilla and baking soda (mixture will foam). In a very large bowl, combine popcorn and pecans. Add hot syrup mixture and toss to coat. Spread onto greased baking sheets.

Bake at 250° for 1 hour or until dry, stirring every 15 minutes. Remove from pans to waxed paper to cool. Break into clusters. Store in airtight containers or plastic bags. **Yield:** 6 quarts.

MUSHROOM CHEESE BREAD
(Pictured above)

Lori Stefanishion, Drumheller, Alberta

I serve this satisfying bread as a side with meat, fish and main-dish soups and salads. The savory slices are lifesavers when you need a last-minute appetizer or brunch item.

> 6 cups sliced fresh mushrooms
> 1 tablespoon butter
> 4 green onions, chopped
> 1 loaf (1 pound) French bread
> 1 carton (8 ounces) spreadable garlic and
>   herb cream cheese
> 2 cups (8 ounces) shredded Italian cheese
>   blend
> 1 cup mayonnaise
> 1 cup grated Parmesan cheese

In a large skillet, saute the mushrooms in butter until tender. Add the onions; cook and stir until liquid has evaporated. Set aside.

Cut French bread in half lengthwise and then widthwise; spread cut sides with herb cream cheese. Combine the Italian cheese, mayonnaise and Parmesan cheese; spread over bread. Top with mushroom mixture.

Place on a baking sheet. Bake at 350° for 20 minutes or until cheese is melted. If desired, broil 4-6 in. from the heat for 2-4 minutes or until golden brown. Slice and serve warm. **Yield:** 16 servings.

CRAB-STUFFED MUSHROOMS
(Pictured below)

Tonya Farmer, Iowa City, Iowa

Mushroom caps stuffed with plump crabmeat make a wonderful appetizer for entertaining. If you like, use the recipe as a light entree, served on salad greens or with pasta.

  1 medium tomato, seeded and diced
1/2 cup soft bread crumbs
  2 tablespoons mayonnaise
  1 tablespoon minced fresh parsley
  1 garlic clove, minced
1/4 teaspoon salt
Dash cayenne pepper
  1 can (6 ounces) crabmeat, drained,
     flaked and cartilage removed
30 medium fresh mushrooms
  1 tablespoon olive oil
1/4 cup shredded Parmesan cheese

In a large bowl, combine the first seven ingredients. Fold in crabmeat; set aside.

Remove and discard the mushroom stems. Brush inside of mushroom caps with oil. Spoon 1-2 teaspoons of crab mixture into each cap; sprinkle with Parmesan cheese.

Place in a 15-in. x 10-in. x 1-in. baking pan coated with cooking spray. Bake at 400° for 15-20 minutes or until the mushrooms are tender and filling is lightly browned. Serve warm. **Yield:** 2-1/2 dozen.

PARMESAN ONION WEDGES
(Pictured above)

Diane Hixon, Niceville, Florida

I like to substitute these soft, oniony wedges for Italian bread when I serve spaghetti. They're also the perfect accompaniment to soup or salad.

  2 cups biscuit/baking mix
2/3 cup milk
1/2 cup grated Parmesan cheese
  1 small onion, chopped
1/2 cup mayonnaise
  1 teaspoon Italian seasoning

In a small bowl, stir the biscuit mix and milk just until moistened. Turn onto a floured surface and gently knead 6-8 times. Roll out to an 11-in. circle; transfer to a greased 12-in. pizza pan. Build up edges slightly.

Combine the Parmesan cheese, onion and mayonnaise; spread over dough. Sprinkle with Italian seasoning.

Bake at 400° for 15-20 minutes or until golden brown. Cut into wedges; serve warm. Refrigerate leftovers. **Yield:** 8 servings.

ITALIAN SEASONING

To make your own Italian seasoning, try substituting 1/4 teaspoon each of basil, thyme, rosemary and oregano for each teaspoon called for in a recipe. If you don't have all of the herbs, you can blend just a few with good results.

■▲■▲■▲■▲■▲■▲■▲■

HOT ALMOND AND CREAM DRINK

(Pictured above)

Kaye Kirsch, Bailey, Colorado

Just a few sips of this drink, with its rich almond flavor, will warm you up in a hurry. It's a favorite each year at our Christmas party.

    1 cup butter, cubed
    1 cup sugar
    1 cup packed brown sugar
    2 cups vanilla ice cream, softened
    2 teaspoons almond extract
Ground nutmeg

In a small saucepan over low heat, cook and stir butter and sugars for 12-15 minutes or until butter is melted. Pour into a large bowl; add ice cream and extract. Beat on medium speed for 1-2 minutes or until smooth, scraping the bowl often.

    To make one serving: Spoon 1/4 cup mix into a mug; add 3/4 cup boiling water and stir well. Sprinkle with nutmeg. Serve immediately. **Yield:** 4 cups mix.

    Editor's Note: Mix can be stored in a covered container in the refrigerator up to 1 week.

■▲■▲■▲■▲■▲■▲■▲■

SPINACH & ARTICHOKE DIP

Naomi Judd, Nashville, Tennessee

This is the perfect dip to serve to guests at your next get-together. It tastes delicious on either tortilla chips or bread.

    2 packages (10 ounces *each*) frozen
        chopped spinach, thawed and
        squeezed dry
    1 can (14 ounces) water-packed artichoke
        hearts, rinsed, drained and chopped
    1 cup (8 ounces) sour cream
    1 cup mayonnaise
    1 package (1.7 ounces) vegetable soup
        mix
    1/2 cup plus 2 tablespoons grated Parmesan
        cheese, *divided*
    1/2 cup shredded cheddar cheese
Assorted crackers and sliced bread

In a large bowl, combine the spinach, artichokes, sour cream, mayonnaise, soup mix and 1/2 cup Parmesan cheese. Transfer to a 1-1/2-qt. baking dish. Sprinkle with the cheddar cheese and the remaining Parmesan.

Bake, uncovered, at 350° for 30-35 minutes or until the cheese is melted. Serve warm with the crackers and bread. **Yield: 4 cups.**

░░░░░░░░░░░░░

BLUE CHEESE HEART TARTS
(Pictured below)

Rita Cox, Round Rock, Texas

These tasty little snacks pack a punch of flavor. They look as if they come from a fancy restaurant, but it's easy to make them. They are rich, so guests only need a few to stave off hunger.

> 2 packages (3 ounces *each*) cream cheese, softened
> 1 cup (4 ounces) crumbled blue cheese
> 2 tablespoons butter, softened
> 1/4 cup heavy whipping cream
> 3 eggs
> 2 teaspoons minced chives
> 1/4 teaspoon salt
> 1/8 teaspoon cayenne pepper
> 1/8 teaspoon pepper
> 3 packages (15 ounces *each*) refrigerated pie pastry

In a small bowl, beat cheeses until well blended. Add butter, cream, eggs, chives and seasonings. Beat until light and fluffy; set aside.

Using a 2-1/2-in. heart-shaped cookie cutter, cut pastry into 102 hearts. Gently press cutouts onto the bottom and up the sides of greased miniature muffin cups or miniature heart-shaped muffin cups. Spoon 1 teaspoon filling into each.

Bake at 375° for 10-12 minutes or until golden brown. Cool tarts in pans for 5 minutes before removing. Serve warm. **Yield: 8-1/2 dozen.**

░░░░░░░░░░░░░

GARLIC-ONION APPETIZER ROUNDS
(Pictured above)

Kristine Snyder, Kihei, Hawaii

I think this recipe is the perfect way to showcase our famous, local Maui sweet onions. They thrive in our balmy tropical climate and rich, volcanic soils.

> 2 large sweet onions, chopped (about 4 cups)
> 2 tablespoons butter
> 2 garlic cloves, minced
> 1 sheet frozen puff pastry, thawed
> 1 egg
> 1 tablespoon water
> 1/3 cup shredded Swiss cheese
> 1/4 cup grated Parmesan cheese
> 2 tablespoons minced fresh basil

In a large skillet over medium-low heat, cook the onions in butter until golden brown, stirring frequently. Add the garlic; cook 1 minute longer. Remove from the heat; cool to room temperature.

Unfold puff pastry. In a small bowl, whisk the egg and water; brush over pastry. Spread onion mixture to within 1/2 in. of edges. Sprinkle with cheeses and basil; roll up jelly-roll style. Cut into 16 slices.

Place 2 in. apart on greased baking sheets. Bake at 425° for 12-14 minutes or until puffed and golden brown. Serve warm. **Yield: 16 appetizers.**

BRING DELIGHT to the table and enjoy a memorable meal with a warm bowl of soup, a satisfying sandwich and a savory salad!

FAMILY FAVORITE. Blue Cheese Orzo Salad (p. 19).

Soups, Salads & Sandwiches

BLUE CHEESE ORZO SALAD
(Pictured at left)
Helen Conwell, Fairhope, Alabama

The crunch of walnuts and bacon creates a pleasant contrast to the creamy rice-shaped pasta. The blue cheese and arugula lend a satisfying, savory quality. On a summer day, this salad really hits the spot.

   3/4 cup uncooked orzo pasta
   3 cups fresh arugula, torn
   5 bacon strips, cooked and crumbled
   3/4 cup crumbled blue cheese
   1/4 cup sliced green onions
   1/4 cup chopped walnuts, toasted
VINAIGRETTE:
   2 tablespoons red wine vinegar
   1 garlic clove, peeled
   1 teaspoon Creole *or* whole grain mustard
   1/2 teaspoon salt
   1/2 teaspoon brown sugar
   1/4 cup chopped walnuts, toasted
   1/4 cup olive oil

Cook orzo according to package directions; drain and place in a large bowl. Add the arugula, bacon, blue cheese, onions and walnuts.

In a blender, combine the first six vinaigrette ingredients; cover and process until smooth. While processing, gradually add oil in a steady stream. Pour over the salad; toss to coat. **Yield:** 5 servings.

PEPPERONI CHEESE SOUP
Debbie Reid, Clearwater, Florida

Children and adults will go for this creative soup that tastes just like pizza in a bowl. It's just as fresh and flavorful as a real pizza, but you don't have to fuss with making a crust. It's a great meal for a party or a kids' get-together.

   1 pint grape tomatoes
   2 tablespoons olive oil, *divided*
   1/2 teaspoon dried oregano
   1/2 teaspoon pepper, *divided*
   3/4 cup chopped sweet onion
   3/4 cup chopped carrots
   3/4 cup chopped green pepper
   1 carton (32 ounces) reduced-sodium chicken broth
   1-1/4 cups cubed peeled potatoes
   3 cups (12 ounces) shredded part-skim mozzarella cheese, *divided*
   2 cups (8 ounces) shredded white cheddar cheese
   1 package (8 ounces) cream cheese, cubed
   1 cup milk
   2 teaspoons pizza *or* Italian seasoning
   1/4 teaspoon crushed red pepper flakes
   2 packages (one 8 ounces, one 3-1/2 ounces) sliced pepperoni, chopped, *divided*

Place the grape tomatoes in a greased 15-in. x 10-in. x 1-in. baking pan; drizzle with 1 tablespoon olive oil, oregano and 1/4 teaspoon pepper; toss gently. Bake at 400° for 10-15 minutes or until tender; set aside.

In a Dutch oven, saute the onion in the remaining oil until tender. Add the carrots, green pepper and remaining pepper; saute 4 minutes longer. Add the chicken broth and potatoes. Bring to a boil. Reduce the heat; cover and cook for 10-15 minutes or until the potatoes are tender. Cool slightly.

In a blender, process soup in batches until smooth. Return all to the pan; heat through. Stir in 2 cups mozzarella cheese, cheddar cheese, cream cheese, milk, pizza seasoning and pepper flakes until cheeses are melted. Add 1-1/3 cups pepperoni and reserved tomatoes; heat through. Serve with remaining mozzarella and pepperoni. **Yield:** 10 servings (2-1/2 quarts).

CLEANING YOUR BLENDER

Because blenders can be so difficult to clean, here's an easy and excellent method of cleaning them. Fill the blender halfway with hot water and add a drop of dishwashing liquid. Cover it and blend on high for 10-15 seconds. Then rinse it with hot water and air-dry.

Add wine to the onion mixture; cook until reduced by half. Stir in the broth, Worcestershire sauce, bay leaf, cayenne and pepper. Bring to a boil. Reduce the heat; simmer, uncovered, for 15-20 minutes.

Place bread on a baking sheet. Bake at 425° for 3-5 minutes or until golden brown, turning once. Spread each slice with Brie and mashed garlic; sprinkle with prosciutto.

Discard bay leaf from soup; ladle 1 cup each into nine ovenproof bowls. Top with one slice of toast; sprinkle with Parmesan cheese. Place bowls on a baking sheet. Bake for 10 minutes or until cheese is melted. **Yield:** 9 servings.

◆▪◆▪◆▪◆▪◆▪◆▪◆

CABBAGE PICNIC SALAD
(Pictured below)

Catherine Berra Bleem, Sparta, Illinois

The sweet-and-sour blend enhances the ingredients in this salad. Slightly different than coleslaw, it's a good dish to bring to potlucks and picnics. It keeps well and the taste is refreshing.

    1/4 cup cider vinegar
      2 tablespoons honey
    1/4 teaspoon salt
      1 cup chopped cabbage
    1/2 cup chopped carrot
    1/2 cup chopped green pepper
    1/4 cup chopped onion
      1 teaspoon minced fennel fronds, optional

In a small saucepan, bring the vinegar, honey and salt to a boil. Stir in the cabbage, carrot, green pepper and onion. Return to a boil.

Remove from the heat; stir in the fennel if desired. Cool. Transfer to a small bowl; cover and refrigerate until chilled. **Yield:** 2 servings.

◆▪◆▪◆▪◆▪◆▪◆▪◆

SPECIAL FRENCH ONION SOUP
(Pictured above)

Laura McAllister, Morganton, North Carolina

Combined with a salad, this rich soup is a meal for my husband and me. I top it with Brie cheese, prosciutto and garlic on French bread to make it extra tasty.

    1/4 cup butter, cubed
    1/4 cup plus 1 tablespoon olive oil, *divided*
      6 large sweet onions, thinly sliced
          (about 12 cups)
      1 whole garlic bulb
    1/4 cup dry red wine *or* beef broth
      6 cups beef broth
  1-1/2 teaspoons Worcestershire sauce
      1 bay leaf
Dash cayenne pepper
Pepper to taste
      9 slices French bread (1 inch thick)
      1 round (8 ounces) Brie cheese, rind
          removed and softened
      6 thin slices prosciutto *or* deli ham,
          chopped
      2 cups grated Parmesan cheese

In Dutch oven over medium heat, melt butter with 1/4 cup oil; add the onions. Cook, without stirring, for 15 minutes. Reduce heat to low. Cook 45 minutes longer or until the onions are golden, stirring occasionally.

Meanwhile, remove papery outer skin from the garlic (do not peel or separate cloves). Cut top off garlic bulb; brush with remaining oil. Wrap in heavy-duty foil.

Bake at 425° for 30-35 minutes or until softened. Cool for 10-15 minutes. Squeeze softened garlic into a small bowl; mash and set aside.

WARM DILL POTATO SALAD

(Pictured above)

Betty Claycomb, Alverton, Pennsylvania

*Everyone who tries this warm potato salad is delight-
ed. It's simple to make, and a nice change of pace from
other potato salads. A friend gave me the recipe a long
time ago, and we've been enjoying it ever since.*

- 1-1/2 pounds potatoes, peeled and cut into 1/2-inch cubes
- 1 tablespoon butter
- 1 tablespoon all-purpose flour
- 3/4 to 1 teaspoon salt
- 1/2 teaspoon dill seed
- 1/8 teaspoon pepper
- 1 cup milk
- 1/2 cup mayonnaise
- 2 tablespoons finely chopped onion
- 1/4 teaspoon paprika

Place potatoes in a large saucepan and cover
with water. Bring to a boil. Reduce heat; cover
and simmer for 8-10 minutes or until tender.
Drain and set aside.

In a large skillet, melt butter; stir in the flour,
salt, dill and pepper until blended. Gradually add
milk. Bring to a boil; cook and stir for 2 minutes
or until thickened and bubbly.

Remove from the heat. Stir in mayonnaise and
onion. Add potatoes; toss gently to coat. Sprinkle
with paprika. **Yield:** 5 servings.

PEELING SPUDS

To save time when peeling potatoes, cut them
in half first. That way, if they're bad inside, you
know before going through the trouble of
peeling them.

SUPREME PIZZA TORTILLAS

(Pictured below)

Jill Flory, Covington, Ohio

*Hungry for scratch pizza, but too busy to fix one, I
put together these delicious tortillas. Canadian bacon
is a good substitute for ham—cheddar or Swiss cheese
work as well as mozzarella. Any extra sauce makes
a great sandwich dip.*

- 1/2 pound ground beef
- 1/2 pound bulk pork sausage
- 1/2 cup chopped onion
- 1/2 cup chopped green pepper
- 1 can (4 ounces) mushroom stems and pieces, drained and chopped
- 1 can (2-1/4 ounces) sliced ripe olives, drained
- 1/2 pound fully cooked ham, thinly sliced
- 8 flour tortillas (10 inches), room temperature
- 2 cups pizza sauce, *divided*
- 40 slices pepperoni
- 40 banana pepper rings
- 2 cups (8 ounces) shredded part-skim mozzarella cheese

In a large skillet, cook the beef, sausage, onion and
green pepper over medium heat until meat is no
longer pink; drain. Stir in mushrooms and olives;
set aside.

Place one slice of ham on each tortilla; top with
about 1/2 cup beef mixture. Drizzle each tortilla
with 3 tablespoons pizza sauce. Layer with the
pepperoni, banana pepper rings and cheese. Fold
sides of tortillas over filling; secure with toothpicks.

Place in two 13-in. x 9-in. baking dishes. Bake,
uncovered, at 400° for 10-15 minutes or until
cheese is melted. Warm the remaining pizza sauce;
serve with wraps. **Yield:** 8 servings.

SHREDDED BEEF SANDWICHES
(Pictured below)

Bunny Palmertree, Carrollton, Mississippi

I like to serve these mouthwatering sandwiches with a side of coleslaw. The homemade barbecue sauce is exceptional...and it's wonderful for dipping!

>   1 can (10-1/2 ounces) condensed beef
>   broth, undiluted
>   1 cup ketchup
>   1/2 cup packed brown sugar
>   1/2 cup lemon juice
>   3 tablespoons steak sauce
>   2 garlic cloves, minced
>   1 teaspoon pepper
>   1 teaspoon Worcestershire sauce
>   1 beef eye round roast (3-1/2 pounds),
>   cut in half
>   1 teaspoon salt
>   16 sandwich buns, split
> **Dill pickle slices, optional**

In a small bowl, whisk the first eight ingredients. Pour half of mixture into a 5-qt. slow cooker. Sprinkle beef with salt; add to slow cooker and top with remaining broth mixture.

Cover and cook on low for 10-12 hours or until meat is tender. Shred meat with two forks and return to slow cooker. Using a slotted spoon, place 1/2 cup beef mixture on each bun. Top with pickles if desired. **Yield:** 16 servings.

CURRY RICE SALAD

Stacy Disney, Upper Darby, Pennsylvania

This healthy salad is a great for potlucks and entertaining because it's easy and delicious. It's a good way to use up leftover rice, too. I sometimes use a 50/50 mix of brown and white rice for extra fiber and flavor.

>   3 cups cooked long grain rice, cooled
>   1/2 cup sliced pimiento-stuffed olives
>   1/2 cup dry roasted peanuts
>   2 green onions, chopped
>   1/4 cup mayonnaise
>   2 tablespoons lemon juice
>   1 to 1-1/2 teaspoons curry powder
>   1/2 teaspoon ground mustard
>   1/4 teaspoon salt
>   1/8 teaspoon garlic powder
>   1/8 teaspoon pepper

In a large bowl, combine the rice, olives, peanuts and onions. In a small bowl, combine mayonnaise, lemon juice and seasonings. Gently stir into rice mixture. Cover and refrigerate for at least 1 hour before serving. **Yield:** 4 servings.

SWEET PASTA SALAD

June Herke, Watertown, South Dakota

I'm a retired farmwife and one of 16 children. I learned lots about cooking from my mother. This recipe is my version of a much simpler one. It's a great dish to bring to picnics and one-dish suppers.

>   1 package (16 ounces) spiral pasta
>   1 medium cucumber, finely chopped
>   1 jar (8 ounces) whole baby corn, drained
>   and cut into 1/2-inch pieces
>   1 jar (7-1/2 ounces) marinated artichoke
>   hearts, drained
>   1 cup sliced pimiento-stuffed olives
>   1 cup sliced ripe olives
>   1/2 cup finely chopped sweet red pepper
>   1/4 cup finely chopped onion
> **DRESSING:**
>   1 cup canola oil
>   1 cup cider vinegar
>   1 cup sugar
>   1/2 teaspoon pepper
>   2 tablespoons minced fresh parsley

Cook pasta according to package directions. Meanwhile, in a large bowl, combine cucumber, corn, artichokes, olives, red pepper and onion. Drain pasta and rinse in cold water; stir into the vegetable mixture.

In a small bowl, whisk the dressing ingredients.

Pour over salad; toss to coat. Cover and refrigerate for at least 2 hours. Serve with a slotted spoon. **Yield:** 16 servings.

SAUSAGE CORN CHOWDER
(Pictured below)

Kay Nichols, Wellsburg, West Virginia

Warm your body and soul with this comforting chowder. I love sausage and sweet corn, so I combined them, and voila! This is a great soup to serve on a chilly day, along with piping hot homemade biscuits.

- 1/2 **pound bulk sage-flavored sausage** *or* **sausage of your choice**
- 1/4 **cup chopped onion**
- 1/4 **cup chopped celery**
- 3 **cups water**
- 2 **medium red potatoes, cut into 1/2-inch cubes**
- 2 **teaspoons chicken bouillon granules**
- 1 **cup frozen corn**
- 3 **tablespoons butter**
- 1/4 **cup all-purpose flour**
- 1/8 **teaspoon pepper**
- 1-1/2 **cups milk**

In a large saucepan, cook the sausage, onion and celery over medium heat until meat is no longer pink; drain.

Stir in the water, potatoes and bouillon. Bring to a boil. Reduce the heat; simmer, uncovered, for 20 minutes. Add corn; simmer 10 minutes longer or until potatoes are tender.

Meanwhile, in a small saucepan, melt butter; stir in flour and pepper until smooth. Gradually stir in milk. Bring to a boil; cook and stir for 1-2 minutes or until thickened. Stir into the sausage mixture. **Yield:** 4 servings.

STRAWBERRY SUMMER SALAD
(Pictured above)

Mrs. Randi Gross, Lethbridge, Alberta

My daughter wanted me to submit this family-favorite salad. We love it served with juicy steak and baked potatoes. It's perfect for warm summer days.

- 7 **cups torn romaine**
- 2 **cups sliced fresh strawberries**
- 2 **celery ribs, finely chopped**
- 2 **green onions, finely chopped**
- 1/4 **cup canola oil**
- 2 **tablespoons sugar**
- 2 **tablespoons cider vinegar**
- 1/4 **teaspoon salt**
- 1/4 **teaspoon pepper**
- 1/8 **teaspoon hot pepper sauce**
- 1/2 **cup slivered almonds, toasted**

In a large bowl, combine romaine, strawberries, celery and onions. In a small bowl, whisk the oil, sugar, vinegar, salt, pepper and pepper sauce. Pour over the salad and toss to coat. Sprinkle with the almonds. **Yield:** 8 servings.

SAVVY ABOUT STRAWBERRIES

Purchase strawberries that are shiny, firm and fragrant. A strawberry should be completely red, although some whiteness near the leafy cap is acceptable. Refrigerate strawberries and just before using, wash and hull.

ZUCCHINI PIZZA LOAVES
(Pictured above)
Trisha Kruse, Eagle, Idaho

Full of healthy veggies, these loaves taste like indulgent pizzas—even picky eaters go back for seconds. In the summer, I assemble and freeze several to serve at winter potlucks and parties.

  2 medium zucchini, thinly sliced
  1 medium onion, finely chopped
  1 cup sliced fresh mushrooms
  2 teaspoons olive oil
  2 garlic cloves, minced
  1 can (8 ounces) no-salt-added tomato sauce
  1 medium tomato, seeded and chopped
  1 can (2-1/4 ounces) sliced ripe olives, drained
  2 teaspoons Italian seasoning
  2 tubes (11 ounces *each*) refrigerated crusty French loaf
  3 slices provolone cheese, chopped
  1 ounce sliced turkey pepperoni, julienned
  1 cup (4 ounces) shredded part-skim mozzarella cheese

In a large skillet, saute zucchini, onion, mushrooms in oil until tender. Add garlic; cook 1 minute longer. Stir in the tomato sauce, tomato, olives and Italian seasoning; remove from the heat.

Unroll one loaf of dough, starting at the seam. Pat into a 14-in. x 12-in. rectangle. Sprinkle half of the provolone and pepperoni to within 1/2 in. of edges. Spread with half of the zucchini mixture; sprinkle with half of the mozzarella.

Roll up jelly-roll style, starting with a long side; pinch seams to seal. Place seam side down on a baking sheet coated with cooking spray. Repeat with remaining dough, pepperoni, cheeses and zucchini mixture.

Bake at 350° for 30-35 minutes or until golden brown. Slice and serve warm. **Yield:** 2 loaves (4 servings each).

CHICKEN FIESTA SALAD
(Pictured below)
Katie Rankin, Columbus, Ohio

This is a dish I can prepare in fifteen minutes! My husband gave me the secret of using the broiler to cook chicken faster, and I discovered the spice blend as I tried to find ways to use this quick cooking technique. It became a very tasty success.

1-1/2 teaspoons lemon-pepper seasoning
1-1/2 teaspoons chili powder
1-1/2 teaspoons dried basil
  3/4 pound boneless skinless chicken breasts, cut into 1-inch pieces
    4 cups torn mixed salad greens
  2/3 cup canned black beans, rinsed and drained
  1/4 cup thinly sliced red onion
    1 small tomato, sliced
  1/2 cup shredded cheddar cheese
Tortilla chips, salsa and ranch salad dressing

In a large resealable plastic bag, combine the seasonings. Add chicken, a few pieces at a time, and shake to coat.

Place the chicken on a greased broiler pan. Broil 3-4 in. from the heat for 3-4 minutes on each side or no longer pink.

On two plates, arrange the salad greens, black beans, onion and tomato. Top with chicken and cheese. Serve with tortilla chips, salsa and ranch dressing. **Yield:** 2 servings.

■■■■■■■■■■■■■■■

CREAM OF MUSSEL SOUP

(Pictured above)

Donna Noel, Gray, Maine

Every New England cook has a personal version of mussel soup, depending on the favored regional herbs and cooking customs. Feel free to start with my recipe, and develop your own luscious variation.

   3 **pounds fresh mussels (about 5 dozen),**
      scrubbed and beards removed
   2 **medium onions, finely chopped**
   2 **celery ribs, finely chopped**
   1 **cup water**
   1 **cup white wine *or* chicken broth**
   1 **bottle (8 ounces) clam juice**
1/4 **cup minced fresh parsley**

   2 **garlic cloves, minced**
1/4 **teaspoon salt**
1/4 **teaspoon pepper**
   1 **cup half-and-half cream**

Tap mussels; discard any that do not close. Set aside. In a stockpot, combine the onions, celery, water, wine or broth, clam juice, parsley, garlic, salt and pepper.

Bring to a boil. Reduce the heat; add mussels. Cover and simmer for 5-6 minutes or until mussels have opened. Remove mussels with a slotted spoon, discarding any unopened mussels; set aside opened mussels and keep warm.

Cool cooking liquid slightly. In a blender, cover and process cooking liquid in batches until blended. Return all to pan. Add the cream and reserved mussels; heat through (do not boil). **Yield:** 5 servings.

It's a Wrap

WRAPS ARE all the rage because they are quick and easy. Filled with wholesome ingredients, they offer an entire meal in a neat little bundle. The four recipes here offer a variety of lunch and dinner ideas for cooks on the go.

▰▰▰▰▰▰▰▰▰▰▰▰▰

AVOCADO TOMATO WRAPS

(Pictured below)

Megan Wisener, Milwaukee, Wisconsin

I eat these super-fast wrap sandwiches all summer long. The creamy avocado and sweet tomato are deliciously fresh tasting.

    1 medium ripe avocado, peeled and thinly
      sliced
    2 flavored tortillas of your choice
      (10 inches), room temperature
    2 lettuce leaves
    1 medium tomato, thinly sliced
    2 tablespoons shredded Parmesan cheese
  1/4 teaspoon garlic powder
  1/8 teaspoon salt
  1/8 teaspoon pepper

In a small bowl, mash a fourth of the avocado with a fork; spread over the tortillas. Layer with lettuce, tomato slices and remaining avocado slices. Sprinkle with cheese, garlic powder, salt and pepper; roll up. Serve immediately. **Yield:** 2 servings.

▰▰▰▰▰▰▰▰▰▰▰▰▰

BUFFALO CHICKEN WRAPS

(Pictured above)

Sarah Gottschalk, Richmond, Indiana

This fuss-free meal is a favorite in our house, with its tender chicken, tortillas, crunchy vegetables and spicy buffalo wing sauce. Feel free to change the veggies to suit your taste.

  1-1/2 pounds chicken tenderloins
      1 cup buffalo wing sauce, *divided*
      8 lettuce leaves
      8 flour tortillas (10 inches), warmed
     16 bacon strips, cooked
      1 small green pepper, cut into strips
    1/2 cup ranch salad dressing

In a large skillet, bring the chicken and 1/2 cup buffalo wing sauce to a boil. Reduce heat; cover and simmer for 10-12 minutes or until meat is no longer pink. Remove from the heat; cool slightly. Shred chicken with two forks.

Place a lettuce leaf on each tortilla; spoon about 1/2 cup chicken mixture down the center. Top with bacon and green pepper. Drizzle with ranch dressing and remaining buffalo wing sauce; roll up. **Yield:** 8 servings.

ASIAN TURKEY LETTUCE WRAPS

(Pictured below)

Susan Riley, Allen, Texas

Frozen chopped vegetables make these wraps a snap. Add just a touch of Asian chile sauce if you want to spice it up a bit.

- 1-1/4 pounds extra-lean ground turkey
- 1 package (16 ounces) frozen stir-fry vegetable blend, thawed
- 1/3 cup reduced-sodium teriyaki sauce
- 1/4 cup hoisin sauce
- 3 tablespoons reduced-fat creamy peanut butter
- 2 tablespoons minced fresh gingerroot
- 3 garlic cloves, minced
- 1 tablespoon rice vinegar
- 1 tablespoon sesame oil
- 4 green onions, chopped
- 10 Boston lettuce leaves
Additional hoisin sauce, optional

In a large nonstick skillet coated with cooking spray, cook and stir turkey over medium-high heat until no longer pink.

Coarsely chop mixed vegetables; add to the pan. Stir in the teriyaki sauce, hoisin sauce, peanut butter, ginger, vinegar and oil. Cook and stir over medium-high heat for 5 minutes. Add garlic; cook 1 minute longer.

Remove from the heat; stir in onions. Place a scant 1/2 cup turkey mixture on each lettuce leaf;

fold lettuce over filling. Serve with additional hoisin sauce if desired. **Yield:** 5 servings.

TUNA SALAD WRAPS

(Pictured above)

Ivy Abbadessa, Loxahatchee, Florida

Usually, I make my tuna salad the night before, so the flavors have more time to blend. Plus, the sandwiches go together quickly for a neat and compact meal.

- 1 large cucumber, seeded and finely chopped
- 1/4 cup finely chopped red onion
- 1 tablespoon minced fresh parsley
- 2 teaspoons grated lemon peel
- 1/4 teaspoon seasoned salt
- 1/4 cup reduced-fat Italian salad dressing
- 1 can (12 ounces) light water-packed tuna, drained and flaked
- 1/4 cup reduced-fat mayonnaise
- 1/4 cup chopped celery
- 1/4 cup chopped green onions
- 6 flour tortillas (8 inches), room temperature

In a small bowl, combine first six ingredients. In another bowl, combine the tuna, mayonnaise, celery and green onions.

Spread 1/4 cup tuna mixture over each tortilla; top with 1/3 cup cucumber mixture. Fold in sides of tortillas and roll up. **Yield:** 6 servings.

Divide the greens between two salad plates; top with tomato and onion. Sprinkle with celery and celery leaves.

In a small bowl, whisk the oil, vinegar, cream and basil; drizzle over salads. **Yield:** 2 servings.

COUNTRY ITALIAN SOUP
(Pictured below)

Kim L'Hote, Neillsville, Wisconsin

My mom gave me this recipe a few years back, and it soon became a family favorite. It's very flavorful and hearty enough to be a meal in and of itself.

  1 pound bulk Italian sausage
  1 large onion, sliced
  2 celery ribs, sliced
  2 garlic cloves, minced
  5 cups water
  2 medium potatoes, peeled and chopped
  1 can (14-1/2 ounces) diced tomatoes, undrained
  2 medium carrots, sliced
  2 teaspoons salt
  1 teaspoon dried basil
  1 teaspoon dried thyme
1/2 teaspoon dried oregano
1/2 teaspoon pepper
1/4 teaspoon cayenne pepper, optional
  1 bay leaf
  2 medium zucchini, sliced

In a Dutch oven over medium heat, cook the sausage, onion and celery until meat is no longer pink; drain. Add garlic; cook 1 minute longer.

YOGURT FRUIT SALAD
(Pictured above)

Sue Day, Yakima, Washington

This pretty dish is similar to an ambrosia salad. The mixture of fruits is very refreshing, and it's quick and easy to fix, too.

  2 large apples, chopped
  1 cup green grapes, halved
  1 cup sliced peeled peaches *or* pears
  1 cup dried cherries
1/4 cup flaked coconut
1/4 cup chopped walnuts
1/2 cup vanilla yogurt
  6 lettuce leaves

In a large bowl, combine the first six ingredients. Add yogurt; toss to coat. Serve on lettuce. **Yield:** 6 servings.

RED ONION AND TOMATO SALAD

Vicky Witte, Manchester, Iowa

This is a pretty salad to serve any time of the year. It's a simple salad that goes well with a variety of entrees. The celery leaves are a nice touch in color and enhances the taste.

  1 cup torn mixed salad greens
  1 medium tomato, sliced
  2 slices red onion, separated into rings
  1 celery rib, sliced
  1 tablespoon chopped celery leaves
  1 tablespoon olive oil
2-1/2 teaspoons balsamic vinegar
1-1/2 teaspoons half-and-half cream
Pinch dried basil

Soups, Salads & Sandwiches

Add the water, potatoes, tomatoes, carrots and seasonings. Bring to a boil. Reduce the heat; cover and simmer for 15 minutes. Stir in the zucchini; simmer 8-10 minutes longer or until the vegetables are tender. Discard the bay leaf. **Yield:** 10 servings (2-1/2 quarts).

GOLDEN GRILLS
(Pictured above)

*American Egg Board, Linda Braun
Park Ridge, Illinois*

This is a great way to serve up eggs. These sandwiches will delight your family.

      6 hard-cooked eggs, chopped
  1/2 cup diced fully cooked ham
  1/3 cup finely chopped onion
  1/4 cup shredded Swiss cheese
      2 tablespoons sweet pickle relish
      2 tablespoons Miracle Whip
  1/2 teaspoon salt
Butter, softened
    12 slices rye bread

In a large bowl, combine first seven ingredients. Butter one side of each slice of bread. Place six slices on a griddle or skillet, buttered side down.

Spread about 1/3 cup filling on each slice. Top with remaining bread, buttered side up. Toast each side until golden brown and cheese is melted. **Yield:** 6 servings.

RHUBARB CHILI CUBANO
(Pictured below)

Lanesboro Rhubarb Festival, Lanesboro, Minnesota

Unwilling to confine rhubarb to a pie crust, this winner of the 2005 Rhubarb Festival used it to stir up chili. Stalks of rhubarb are paired with beef, pork and raisins.

      1 pound ground beef
      1 pound ground pork
      1 medium onion, chopped
      3 garlic cloves, minced
      1 can (28 ounces) crushed tomatoes
      1 can (14-1/2 ounces) beef broth
  1/3 cup raisins
      2 tablespoons chili powder
      2 tablespoons balsamic vinegar
  1/2 teaspoon salt
  1/2 teaspoon ground allspice
  1/4 teaspoon ground cloves
      2 cups thinly sliced fresh rhubarb
      1 can (15 ounces) black beans, rinsed and
        drained
  1/4 cup slivered almonds, toasted, optional

In a Dutch oven, cook the beef, pork and onion over medium heat until meat is no longer pink. Add garlic; cook 1 minute longer. Drain.

Stir in tomatoes, broth, raisins, chili powder, vinegar, salt, allspice and cloves. Bring to a boil. Reduce heat; simmer, uncovered, for 30 minutes or until heated through.

Stir in rhubarb and beans; cook for 10 minutes or until rhubarb is tender. Garnish with almonds if desired. **Yield:** 8 servings (2 quarts).

ITALIAN SAUSAGE BEAN SOUP
(Pictured below)

Glenna Reimer, Gig Harbor, Washington

In the cold months, I like to put on a big pot of this comforting soup. It cooks away while I do other things like baking bread, crafting or even cleaning the house.

- 1 pound Italian sausage links, casings removed
- 1 medium onion, finely chopped
- 3 garlic cloves, sliced
- 4 cans (14-1/2 ounces *each*) reduced-sodium chicken broth
- 2 cans (15 ounces *each*) pinto beans, rinsed and drained
- 1 can (14-1/2 ounces) diced tomatoes, undrained
- 1 cup medium pearl barley
- 1 large carrot, sliced
- 1 celery rib, sliced
- 1 teaspoon minced fresh sage
- 1/2 teaspoon minced fresh rosemary *or* 1/8 teaspoon dried rosemary, crushed
- 6 cups chopped fresh kale

Crumble sausage into a Dutch oven; add onion and garlic. Cook over medium heat until meat is no longer pink; drain. Add broth, beans, tomatoes, barley, carrot, celery, sage and rosemary. Bring to a boil. Reduce heat; cover and simmer for 45 minutes.

Stir in the kale; return to a boil. Reduce heat; cover and simmer for 25-30 minutes or until the vegetables are tender and the kale is wilted. **Yield:** 8 servings (3 quarts).

STEAK SAUCE SLOPPY JOES
(Pictured above)

Patti Basten, DePere, Wisconsin

Everyone in our family loves these flavorful barbecued sandwiches. The recipe makes a big batch, and it freezes nicely, too.

- 3 pounds ground beef
- 4 medium onions, chopped
- 2 celery ribs, chopped
- 1 garlic clove, minced
- 1 can (28 ounces) diced tomatoes, undrained
- 1/4 cup Worcestershire sauce
- 1/4 cup A.1. steak sauce
- 2 tablespoons chili powder
- 2 tablespoons paprika
- 1/4 teaspoon pepper
- 15 hamburger buns, split

In a Dutch oven, cook the beef, onions and celery over medium heat until meat is no longer pink. Add garlic; cook 1 minute longer. Drain.

Stir in the tomatoes, Worcestershire sauce, steak sauce, chili powder, paprika and pepper. Bring to a boil. Reduce heat; simmer, uncovered, for 20 minutes or until thickened and heated through. Serve on buns. **Yield:** 15 servings.

GROUND BEEF LABELING

Ground beef is often labeled using the cut of meat that it is ground from, such as ground chuck. It is also labeled according to the percentage of lean meat to fat, such as 85%. The higher the percentage, the leaner the meat.

Summer Squash Soup

(Pictured below)

Heidi Wilcox, Lapeer, Michigan

Delicate and lemony, this squash soup would set the stage for a memorable ladies' luncheon. It's the best of late summer in a bowl.

- 2 large sweet onions, chopped
- 1 medium leek (white portion only), chopped
- 2 tablespoons olive oil
- 6 garlic cloves, minced
- 6 medium yellow summer squash, seeded and cubed
- 4 cups reduced-sodium chicken broth
- 4 fresh thyme sprigs
- 1/4 teaspoon salt
- 2 tablespoons lemon juice
- 1/8 teaspoon hot pepper sauce
- 1 tablespoon shredded Parmesan cheese
- 2 teaspoons grated lemon peel

In a large saucepan, saute onions and leek in oil until tender. Add garlic; cook 1 minute longer. Add squash; saute 5 minutes. Stir in the broth, thyme and salt. Bring to a boil. Reduce heat; cover and simmer for 15-20 minutes or until squash is tender.

Discard the thyme sprigs. Cool slightly. In a blender, process soup in batches until smooth. Return all to the pan. Stir in the lemon juice and hot pepper sauce; heat through. Sprinkle each serving with the cheese and lemon peel. **Yield:** 8 servings (2 quarts).

Tomato Cucumber Salad

(Pictured above)

Kay Howe, Panama City, Florida

Pretty color and great taste make this salad a favorite. I like to serve it when we have guests for dinner. It's easy to prepare, and the dressing can be made several days in advance.

- 3 tablespoons white vinegar
- 1 teaspoon Worcestershire sauce
- 1/4 to 1/2 teaspoon hot pepper sauce
- 1/4 cup mayonnaise
- 1 teaspoon sugar
- 1/2 teaspoon salt
- 1 green onion, cut into 1-inch pieces
- 1 garlic clove, peeled
- 1/2 cup canola oil
- 1 cup minced fresh parsley
- 4 cups torn leaf lettuce
- 4 medium tomatoes, sliced
- 2 large cucumbers, peeled and thinly sliced

For dressing, place the first eight ingredients in a blender; cover and process until smooth. While processing, gradually add oil in a steady stream. Stir in parsley. Cover and refrigerate until serving.

Arrange the lettuce, tomatoes and cucumbers on a serving platter or on salad plates; serve with dressing. **Yield:** 8 servings (1 cup dressing).

ROASTED VEGGIE AND MEATBALL SOUP

Sandy Lund, Brookings, South Dakota

I make this appetizing soup almost every Sunday during our South Dakota winters. Roasted root vegetables and turkey meatballs perk up the broth. What a wonderful way to warm up!

5 medium red potatoes, cubed
4 large carrots, cut into 1/2-inch slices
1 large red onion, halved and cut into wedges
4 tablespoons canola oil, *divided*
1-1/4 teaspoons salt, *divided*
3 tablespoons minced fresh basil
3 garlic cloves, crushed
1 egg, lightly beaten
1/2 cup seasoned bread crumbs
1/4 cup grated Parmesan cheese
1/4 cup minced fresh parsley
1/2 teaspoon pepper
1 pound ground turkey
1 carton (32 ounces) reduced-sodium chicken broth
2 cups water
1 can (14-1/2 ounces) diced tomatoes, undrained

In a large bowl, combine the potatoes, carrots, onion, 2 tablespoons oil and 1/2 teaspoon salt. Place in a single layer in two greased 15-in. x 10-in. x 1-in. baking pans.

Bake at 425° for 20 minutes. Add the basil and garlic; toss to coat. Bake 10-15 minutes longer or until vegetables are tender.

In a large bowl, combine the egg, bread crumbs, cheese, parsley, 1/2 teaspoon salt and pepper. Crumble turkey over mixture; mix well. Shape into 1-in. balls. Brown in a Dutch oven in the remaining oil in batches; drain and set aside.

In the same pan, combine the broth, water, tomatoes, roasted vegetables and remaining salt. Return meatballs to pan. Bring to a boil. Reduce the heat; cover and simmer for 45-55 minutes or until the meatballs are no longer pink. **Yield:** 8 servings (3 quarts).

COOL TOMATO SOUP

(Pictured above)

Wendy Nickel, Kiester, Minnesota

It's easy to crave soup, even on a hot day, when it's chilled and filled with the fresh tastes of summer. Serve a tomatoey batch as an appetizer or a side for a main-dish salad.

4 cups tomato juice, *divided*
5 medium tomatoes, peeled, seeded and chopped
2 medium cucumbers, peeled, seeded and cut into chunks
1 medium green pepper, quartered
1 medium sweet red pepper, quartered
1 medium onion, peeled and quartered
2 garlic cloves, peeled
1 tablespoon minced fresh thyme
1/4 cup white balsamic vinegar
4 cups cubed bread, crusts removed
2 tablespoons olive oil
1/4 teaspoon pepper
Fat-free sour cream, fat-free croutons and parsley, optional

In a blender, cover and process 1 cup tomato juice and half of the tomatoes, cucumbers, peppers, onion, garlic and thyme until chopped. Transfer to a large bowl. Repeat.

Place vinegar and remaining tomato juice in the blender. Add the bread; cover and process until smooth. Add to vegetable mixture; stir in oil and pepper.

Cover; refrigerate for 1-2 hours before serving. Garnish with sour cream, croutons and parsley if desired. **Yield:** 9 servings.

MAKING MEATBALLS

For meatballs to cook evenly, it's important for them to be the same size. The easiest way to do this is by using a 1- or 1-1/2-inch cookie scoop. Scoop the meat mixture and level off the top. Gently roll into a ball.

VEGGIE BURGERS
(Pictured above)

Mary James, Port Orchard, Washington

We created these quick vegetable patties to use up some of our garden bounty. To suit your family's tastes, include more of the vegetables you like and leave out the ones you don't for a specialty sandwich that's all your own.

        1 small zucchini, grated
        1 medium uncooked potato, peeled and
           grated
        1 medium carrot, grated
     1/4 cup grated onion
     3/4 cup egg substitute
    Pepper to taste
       12 slices whole wheat bread, toasted
    Sliced red onion and lettuce leaves, optional

In a large bowl, combine the first six ingredients. Pour about 1/2 cup batter onto a hot griddle lightly coated with cooking spray. Fry for 2-3 minutes on each side or until golden brown. Serve on toasted bread with onion and lettuce if desired. **Yield:** 6 burgers.

HERBED ASPARAGUS SALAD

Dawn Szalai, Edwardsburg, Michigan

This salad is a wonderful way to serve fresh-cut asparagus. The tarragon and oregano are a nice surprise in the lemon and oil dressing.

        2 pounds fresh asparagus, trimmed and
           cut into 1-inch pieces
     3/4 cup canola oil
     1/2 cup lemon juice
    1-1/2 teaspoons sugar
        1 teaspoon salt
     1/2 teaspoon dried oregano
     1/2 teaspoon dried tarragon
     1/2 teaspoon coarsely ground pepper
        1 garlic clove, minced
        8 cups torn mixed salad greens
        3 hard-cooked eggs, sliced

In a large saucepan, bring 1/2 in. of water to a boil. Add asparagus; cover and boil for 3 minutes. Drain and immediately place asparagus in ice water. Drain and pat dry. Place in a large bowl.

In a small bowl, whisk the oil, lemon juice, sugar, salt, oregano, tarragon, pepper and garlic. Pour over asparagus; cover and refrigerate for at least 2 hours.

Place salad greens on a serving platter. With a slotted spoon, arrange the asparagus over greens. Garnish with egg slices. **Yield:** 6-8 servings.

CREAMY WALDORF SALAD
(Pictured below)

Romaine Wetzel, Ronks, Pennsylvania

I found this recipe in a local cookbook. The whipping cream makes it different than the usual Waldorf salad, but it's always good with any meal.

        4 cups chopped apples (about 3 large)
        1 tablespoon plus 1 teaspoon lemon juice,
           divided
        4 celery ribs, chopped
        1 cup chopped walnuts
     1/2 cup mayonnaise
        2 tablespoons sugar
     1/4 teaspoon salt
        1 cup heavy whipping cream, whipped

In a large bowl, toss apples with 1 tablespoon lemon juice. Stir in celery and walnuts.

In a small bowl, whisk the mayonnaise, sugar, salt and remaining lemon juice until blended. Fold in whipped cream. Gently stir into fruit mixture. Refrigerate until serving. **Yield:** 12 servings.

FANCY FRUIT SALAD
(Pictured below)

Janice Malcolm, Grande Prairie, Alberta

This fruity salad is a great option for church potlucks, barbecues and family gatherings. It keeps well in the refrigerator, so you don't have to be rushing at the last minute.

1-1/2 cups uncooked acini di pepe pasta
    1 can (20 ounces) unsweetened pineapple tidbits
    1 can (8 ounces) unsweetened crushed pineapple
    1 cup sugar
    3 tablespoons all-purpose flour
  1/2 teaspoon salt
    1 can (6 ounces) unsweetened pineapple juice
    2 tablespoons orange juice concentrate
    3 egg yolks
    2 cans (11 ounces *each*) mandarin oranges, drained
    1 carton (12 ounces) frozen whipped topping, thawed
    2 cups sliced fresh strawberries

Cook pasta according to package directions. Meanwhile, drain pineapple tidbits and crushed pineapple, reserving juice. Set pineapple aside.

In a small saucepan, combine the sugar, flour and salt. Gradually stir in the can of pineapple juice, orange juice concentrate and reserved pineapple juice.

Cook and stir until mixture comes to a boil. Stir a small amount of hot mixture into egg yolks; return all to the pan, stirring constantly. Bring to a gentle boil; cook and stir 2 minutes longer. Transfer mixture to a large bowl and cool to room temperature.

Drain pasta and rinse in cold water; add to sugar mixture. Stir in oranges and reserved pineapple. Fold in whipped topping. Cover and refrigerate until chilled. Just before serving, fold in strawberries. **Yield:** 14 servings (3/4 cup each).

Editor's Note: Acini di pepe are tiny pellets of pasta. This recipe was tested with DaVinci brand pasta. You may substitute 10 ounces of macaroni or other pasta if desired.

CREAM OF LENTIL SOUP

Kim Russell
North Wales, Pennsylvania

Lentil lovers will want a second bowl of this nourishing soup with a subtle touch of curry. It looks particularly appealing thanks to the color the fresh spinach adds.

    6 cups reduced-sodium chicken broth *or* vegetable broth
    2 cups dried lentils, rinsed
    1 bay leaf
    1 whole clove
    1 medium red onion, chopped
    2 celery ribs, chopped
    2 tablespoons butter
    2 medium carrots, chopped
    1 teaspoon salt
    1 teaspoon sugar
  1/2 teaspoon curry powder
  1/8 teaspoon pepper
    2 garlic cloves, minced
    3 cups coarsely chopped fresh spinach
1-1/2 cups heavy whipping cream
    1 tablespoon lemon juice
  1/3 cup minced fresh parsley

In a large saucepan, combine the broth, lentils, bay leaf and clove. Bring to a boil. Reduce heat; cover and simmer for 25-30 minutes or until lentils are tender.

Meanwhile, in a Dutch oven, saute onion and celery in butter until crisp-tender. Add the carrots, salt, sugar, curry powder and pepper; saute 2-3 minutes longer or until vegetables are tender. Add garlic; cook for 1 minute.

Drain the lentils; discard bay leaf and clove. Add to vegetable mixture. Stir in the spinach, cream, lemon juice and parsley; cook over low heat until heated through and spinach is wilted. **Yield:** 9 servings (2-1/4 quarts).

PIGS IN A BLANKET

(Pictured above)

Linda Young, Longmont, Colorado

These baked hot dog sandwiches appeal to kids of all ages. Even my husband admits to enjoying every bite! We like to dip them in ketchup and mustard.

   1 tube (8 ounces) refrigerated
      crescent rolls
   8 hot dogs
   1 egg, lightly beaten
   1 tablespoon water
Caraway seeds
Carrots and celery sticks, optional

Separate crescent dough into triangles. Place hot dogs at wide end of triangles and roll up. Place on an ungreased baking sheet. Combine egg and water; brush over rolls. Sprinkle with caraway and press lightly into rolls.

   Bake at 375° for 12-15 minutes or until golden. Serve with the carrots and celery if desired. **Yield:** 4 servings.

MUSTARD FOR DIPPING

Pigs in a Blanket are especially delicious when served with Honey Mustard Sauce. It's easy to make! In a bowl, whisk together until smooth, 1/2 cup *each* of Dijon mustard and honey, 4 teaspoons soy sauce and 2 teaspoons sugar.

MARINATED ITALIAN SALAD

(Pictured below)

Muggs Nash, Bloomington, Minnesota

This is a perfect salad for potlucks and other occasions year-round. In winter, the ingredients are available when many other vegetables aren't in season...and in summer, it's a worry-free picnic food since it doesn't have a mayonnaise-based dressing.

   4 cups fresh broccoli florets
   3 cups fresh cauliflowerets
1/2 pound sliced fresh mushrooms
   2 celery ribs, chopped
   4 green onions, thinly sliced
   1 can (8 ounces) sliced water chestnuts,
      drained
   1 bottle (16 ounces) Italian salad dressing
   1 envelope Italian salad dressing mix
   1 pint cherry tomatoes, halved
   1 can (2-1/4 ounces) sliced ripe olives,
      drained

In a large bowl, combine the broccoli, cauliflower, mushrooms, celery, onions and water chestnuts. Combine salad dressing and dressing mix; drizzle over vegetables and toss to coat.

   Cover and refrigerate overnight. Just before serving, add tomatoes and olives; toss to coat. **Yield:** 12 servings.

CHICKEN SALAD SANDWICHES
(Pictured above)

Shannon Tucker, Land O' Lakes, Florida

I made these simple-yet-special sandwiches for a birthday party. Tangy cranberries and crunchy celery pep up the chicken. Leftover turkey works well, too.

- 1/2 cup mayonnaise
- 2 tablespoons honey Dijon mustard
- 1/4 teaspoon pepper
- 2 cups cubed rotisserie chicken
- 1 cup (4 ounces) shredded Swiss cheese
- 1/2 cup chopped celery
- 1/2 cup dried cranberries
- 1/4 cup chopped walnuts
- 1/2 teaspoon dried parsley flakes
- 8 lettuce leaves
- 16 slices pumpernickel bread

In a large bowl, combine the mayonnaise, mustard and pepper. Stir in the chicken, cheese, celery, cranberries, walnuts and parsley.

Place lettuce on eight slices of bread; top each with 1/2 cup chicken salad and remaining bread. **Yield:** 8 servings.

FESTIVE CABBAGE SALAD

Jeanette Krembas
Laguna Niguel, California

Our family doesn't care for traditional coleslaw, but this cabbage salad always has them begging for more. It's great for picnics and tailgate parties.

- 1 small head cabbage, shredded
- 2 celery ribs, chopped
- 2 green onions, thinly sliced
- 1 medium tomato, seeded and chopped
- 1/3 cup mayonnaise
- 3 tablespoons sugar
- 1 tablespoon lemon juice
- 1 tablespoon white wine vinegar
- 1 teaspoon celery seed
- 1/4 teaspoon seasoned salt
- 1/4 teaspoon pepper
- 1 medium ripe avocado, peeled and diced

In a large bowl, combine the cabbage, celery, onions and tomato. In a small bowl, combine the mayonnaise, sugar, lemon juice, vinegar, celery seed, seasoned salt and pepper. Pour over cabbage mixture and toss to coat.

Cover and refrigerate for at least 30 minutes. Add avocado just before serving; toss gently to combine. **Yield:** 6 servings.

GARDEN STATE SALAD
(Pictured below)

Weda Mosellie, Phillipsburg, New Jersey

New Jersey is the Garden State, so I enjoy preparing this vegetable salad using some of my state's best fresh produce.

    3 tablespoons cranberry juice
    3 tablespoons olive oil
    1 tablespoon lemon juice
    1 tablespoon honey
    2 green onions, finely chopped
    2 garlic cloves, minced
    1 teaspoon dried oregano
  1/4 teaspoon salt
  1/8 teaspoon pepper
SALAD:
    1 medium head iceberg lettuce, shredded
    2 medium carrots, shredded
    2 celery ribs, chopped
    2 green onions, thinly sliced
    2 medium tomatoes, seeded and diced
    1 small cucumber, sliced

In a small bowl, whisk the first nine ingredients. Refrigerate for at least 1 hour.

In a large salad bowl, combine the lettuce, carrots, celery, onions, tomatoes and cucumber. Just before serving, whisk dressing and pour over salad; toss to coat. **Yield:** 6 servings.

SWEET SURPRISE CHILI
(Pictured above)

Brooke Pekkala, Duluth, Minnesota

I've won three chili cook-offs with this recipe. Everyone loves it, and they're always amazed when I reveal the secret ingredient!

    3 pounds beef top sirloin steak, cubed
    1 tablespoon canola oil
  1/2 pound bulk Italian sausage
    1 large onion, chopped
    5 garlic cloves, minced
    2 cups water
    1 can (16 ounces) chili beans, undrained
    1 can (15 ounces) tomato sauce
    1 can (14-1/2 ounces) beef broth
    1 package (12 ounces) pitted dried plums, chopped
    3 teaspoons chili powder
    2 teaspoons ground cumin
    1 teaspoon dried oregano
    1 teaspoon paprika
  3/4 teaspoon salt
Dash cayenne pepper

In a Dutch oven, brown beef in oil in batches. Remove and keep warm. Add the sausage and onion to the pan; cook and stir over medium heat until meat is no longer pink. Add the garlic; cook 1 minute longer.

Return beef to the pan; stir in the remaining ingredients. Bring to a boil. Reduce heat; cover and simmer for 1-3/4 to 2 hours or until beef is tender. **Yield:** 8 servings (2-3/4 quarts).

DILLY TURKEY BURGERS
(Pictured below)

Andrea Ros, Moon Township, Pennsylvania

This recipe originally called for ground lamb, but my family prefers turkey instead. Dill is a great herb to enhance the flavor of turkey.

    1 egg, lightly beaten
    2 tablespoons lemon juice
    1 to 2 tablespoons snipped fresh dill *or*
      1 to 2 teaspoons dill weed
    1 garlic clove, minced
  1/2 teaspoon salt
  1/2 teaspoon dried oregano
  1/4 teaspoon pepper
  1/2 cup soft bread crumbs
    1 pound ground turkey
    4 hamburger buns, split
Lettuce leaves
    8 slices tomato, optional
    2 tablespoons mayonnaise, optional

In a large bowl, combine first eight ingredients. Crumble turkey over mixture and mix well. Shape into four patties.

Grill, covered, over medium heat or broil 4 in. from the heat for 8-10 minutes or until a meat thermometer reads 165°, turning once. Serve on buns with lettuce and tomato and mayonnaise if desired. **Yield:** 4 servings.

SCOTCH BROTH
(Pictured above)

Kelsey Hamilton, Highland Park, New Jersey

Add a side of bread to this luscious concoction of lamb, vegetables and barley, and you'll have all a hungry body needs.

    1 lamb shank (about 1 pound)
    2 teaspoons canola oil
    4 cups water
    2 cans (14-1/2 ounces *each*) reduced-
      sodium beef broth
    2 whole cloves
    1 medium onion, halved
    1 medium carrot, halved
    1 celery rib, halved
    1 bay leaf
  1/4 cup minced fresh parsley
  1/4 teaspoon dried rosemary, crushed
  1/4 teaspoon dried thyme
  1/4 teaspoon whole peppercorns
SOUP:
  1/3 cup medium pearl barley
1-1/2 cups julienned peeled turnips (1-inch
      pieces)
    1 cup coarsely chopped carrots
    1 medium leek (white portion only),
      thinly sliced
  1/4 teaspoon salt
  1/4 teaspoon pepper

In a Dutch oven, brown lamb in oil on all sides; drain. Stir in water and broth. Insert cloves into onion. Add the onion, carrot, celery and seasonings to the pan. Bring to a boil. (Skim off foam if necessary.) Reduce the heat; cover and simmer for 2 hours or until meat is very tender.

Remove lamb shank from the broth. When cool enough to handle, remove meat from bone and cut into small pieces. Strain broth, discarding vegetables and seasonings. Cover and refrigerate broth and lamb meat in separate containers overnight.

Skim and discard fat from broth. In a large saucepan, bring broth to a boil. Stir in barley. Reduce heat; cover and simmer for 40 minutes.

Stir in the turnips, carrots, leek, salt and pepper. Return to a boil. Reduce heat; cover and simmer for 15 minutes or until vegetables are tender. Add lamb meat; heat through. **Yield:** 4 servings.

GRILLED POTATO SALAD WITH BALSAMIC DRESSING

Elaine Sweet, Dallas, Texas

A Texas-size family reunion requires a substantial salad like this one on the buffet table. Made with red potatoes, real bacon, tangy dressing and more, it's guaranteed to be gobbled up quickly.

    6 medium red potatoes (about 1-1/2
        pounds), quartered
2-1/4 teaspoons canola oil
    3 cups fresh baby spinach
    1 cup fresh *or* frozen corn, thawed
  1/2 medium sweet red pepper, julienned
  1/2 poblano pepper, seeded and julienned
  1/2 medium red onion, thinly sliced
    3 green onions, chopped
    6 bacon strips, diced
    3 garlic cloves, minced
    2 shallots, minced
  1/2 cup balsamic vinegar
    2 tablespoons whole grain mustard
    1 teaspoon pepper
    2 hard-cooked eggs, coarsely chopped
  1/4 cup sunflower kernels

Place the potatoes in a large saucepan; cover with water. Bring to a boil. Reduce heat; cover and cook for 8-10 minutes or until crisp-tender. Drain; toss potatoes with oil.

Place potatoes in a grill wok or basket. Grill, covered, over medium heat for 8-12 minutes or golden brown, stirring frequently. Transfer to a large salad bowl; add the spinach, corn, peppers and onions. Set aside.

In a large skillet, cook the bacon over medium heat until partially cooked but not crisp. Add the garlic and shallots; cook for 1-2 minutes or until tender. Stir in vinegar, mustard and pepper. Bring to a gentle boil; cook and stir for 2-3 minutes or until slightly thickened.

Drizzle over potato mixture and gently toss to coat. Sprinkle with eggs and sunflower kernels. Serve immediately. **Yield:** 12 servings.

Editor's Note: When cutting hot peppers, disposable gloves are recommended. Avoid touching your face.

BROCCOLI & SWEET POTATO SALAD

(Pictured below)

Mary Ann Dell, Phoenixville, Pennsylvania

A symphony of flavor is yours the minute you bite into this refreshing, colorful salad. The veggies are lightly coated with a simple dressing and accented with thyme and feta cheese.

    4 cups cubed peeled sweet potatoes
        (about 2 large)
    2 medium sweet red peppers, sliced
    6 fresh thyme sprigs
    7 teaspoons olive oil, *divided*
    4 cups fresh broccoli florets
  1/2 cup crumbled feta cheese
    2 tablespoons sunflower kernels
    2 tablespoons cider vinegar
  1/2 teaspoon salt
  1/4 teaspoon pepper

Place the sweet potatoes, red peppers and thyme in a greased 15-in. x 10-in. x 1-in. baking pan. Drizzle with 3 teaspoons oil. Bake, uncovered, at 400° for 30-45 minutes or until the potatoes are tender, stirring once. Cool; discard thyme sprigs.

Fill a large saucepan half full of water; bring to a boil. Add broccoli; cover and boil for 2 minutes. Drain and immediately place in ice water. Drain and pat dry.

In a large bowl, combine roasted vegetables, broccoli, cheese and sunflower kernels. In a small bowl, whisk vinegar, salt, pepper and remaining oil. Pour over vegetable mixture and gently toss to coat. **Yield:** 8 servings.

MOROCCAN CHICKPEA STEW

(Pictured above)

Cindy Beberman, Orland Park, Illinois

This spicy stew was the main dish at our family's Christmas Eve dinner. The guests, including three vegetarians, were thrilled with the abundance of squash, potatoes, tomatoes and onion.

  1 large onion, finely chopped
  2 tablespoons olive oil
  1 tablespoon butter
  2 garlic cloves, minced
  2 teaspoons ground cumin
  1 cinnamon stick (3 inches)
1/2 teaspoon chili powder
  4 cups vegetable broth
  2 cups cubed peeled butternut squash
  1 can (15 ounces) chickpeas *or* garbanzo
    beans, rinsed and drained
  1 can (14-1/2 ounces) diced tomatoes,
    undrained
  1 medium red potato, cut into 1-inch
    cubes
  1 medium sweet potato, peeled and cut
    into 1-inch cubes
  1 medium lemon, thinly sliced
1/4 teaspoon salt
  2 small zucchini, cubed
  3 tablespoons minced fresh cilantro

In a Dutch oven, saute the onion in oil and butter until tender. Add the garlic, cumin, cinnamon stick and chili powder; saute 1 minute longer.

Stir in the broth, squash, chickpeas, tomatoes, potatoes, lemon and salt. Bring to a boil. Reduce the heat; cover and simmer for 15-20 minutes or until potatoes and squash are almost tender.

Add the zucchini; return to a boil. Reduce heat; cover and simmer for 5-8 minutes or until vegetables are tender. Discard cinnamon stick and lemon slices. Stir in cilantro. **Yield:** 9 servings (about 2 quarts).

BARBECUED PORK SANDWICHES

(Pictured below)

Thelma Waggoner, Hopkinsville, Kentucky

These delicious sandwiches taste even better if the pork is prepared a day ahead for the flavors to blend. We welcomed my mother's pork sandwiches for any occasion, but especially for our birthday celebration. We never wanted her to change that menu!

    1 pork shoulder roast (about 5 pounds),
      trimmed and cut into 1-inch cubes
    2 medium onions, coarsely chopped
    2 tablespoons chili powder
  1/2 teaspoon salt, optional
1-1/2 cups water
    1 cup ketchup
  1/4 cup white vinegar
   16 *each* hamburger buns, split

In a Dutch oven, combine the meat, onions, chili powder, salt if desired, water, ketchup and vinegar. Cover and simmer for 4 hours or until the meat falls apart easily.

Skim off the excess fat. With a slotted spoon, remove meat, reserving cooking liquid. Shred the meat with two forks. Return to the cooking liquid and heat through. Serve on rolls. **Yield:** 16 servings.

If Cooking for Two: Freeze in serving-size portions to have a quick and easy meal.

▪▪▪▪▪▪▪▪▪▪▪▪▪▪▪▪

LEMONY MUSHROOM LETTUCE SALAD

(Pictured above)

Marie Hattrup, The Dalles, Oregon

Looking for a way to use mushrooms? This crisp salad is topped with plenty of fresh mushrooms that have been marinated in a zesty lemon dressing.

    6 tablespoons lemon juice
    1/4 cup olive oil
    1/4 cup heavy whipping cream
    2 teaspoons sugar
    1 teaspoon salt
    1/4 teaspoon white pepper
    2 pounds whole fresh mushrooms, stems
        removed
    1 cup chopped celery with leaves
    1 cup thinly sliced green onions
    4 cups torn Bibb *or* Boston lettuce
    1/4 teaspoon paprika
Parsley sprigs

In a small bowl, whisk together the lemon juice, olive oil, heavy whipping cream, sugar, salt and pepper until blended.

Place the mushrooms, celery and onions in a large bowl; drizzle with dressing and toss to coat. Cover and refrigerate until chilled.

Divide lettuce among 12 salad plates or arrange on a platter; top with the mushroom mixture. Sprinkle with paprika and garnish with parsley. **Yield:** 12 servings.

SALAD DRESSINGS

The "shelf life" of salad dressings varies somewhat. Generally, vinaigrettes can be kept refrigerated for up to 2 weeks. Dairy-based dressings, like buttermilk, and dressings made with fresh ingredients, like chopped onion, fresh herbs, tomato sauce and chopped hard-cooked egg, will keep up to 1 week.

DIG IN *to the comforting goodness of a hot and hearty dinner that's sure to satisfy the whole family. In this chapter, you'll find plenty of main dish choices!*

MENU MAINSTAY: Pepperoni 'n' Tomato Pasta (p. 43).

Main Dishes

IRISH BEEF STEW

Carrie Karleen
St. Nicolas, Quebec

Rich and robust, this stew is my husband's top choice for dinner. The beef is incredibly tender. Served with crusty bread, it's an ideal cool-weather meal that is perfect for St. Patrick's Day.

8 bacon strips, diced
1/3 cup all-purpose flour
1 teaspoon salt
1/2 teaspoon pepper
3 pounds beef stew meat, cut into 1-inch cubes
1 pound whole fresh mushrooms, quartered
3 medium leeks (white portion only), chopped
2 medium carrots, chopped
1/4 cup chopped celery
1 tablespoon canola oil
4 garlic cloves, minced
1 tablespoon tomato paste
4 cups reduced-sodium beef broth
1 cup dark stout beer *or* additional reduced-sodium beef broth
2 bay leaves
1 teaspoon dried thyme
1 teaspoon dried parsley flakes
1 teaspoon dried rosemary, crushed
2 pounds Yukon Gold potatoes, cut into 1-inch cubes
2 tablespoons cornstarch
2 tablespoons cold water
1 cup frozen peas

In a stockpot, cook raw bacon over medium heat until crisp. Using a slotted spoon, remove to paper towels. In a large resealable plastic bag, combine the flour, salt and pepper. Add beef, a few pieces at a time, and shake to coat. Brown beef in the bacon drippings. Remove and set aside.

In the same pan, saute the mushrooms, leeks, carrots and celery in oil until tender. Add garlic; cook 1 minute longer. Stir in tomato paste until blended. Add the broth, beer, bay leaves, thyme, parsley and rosemary. Return beef and bacon to the pan. Bring to a boil. Reduce heat; cover and simmer for 2 hours or until beef is tender.

Add potatoes. Return to a boil. Reduce heat; cover and simmer 1 hour longer or until potatoes are tender. Combine the cornstarch and water until smooth; stir into stew. Bring to a boil; cook and stir for 2 minutes or until thickened. Add the peas; heat through. Discard bay leaves. **Yield:** 15 servings (3-3/4 quarts).

PEPPERONI 'N' TOMATO PASTA
(Pictured at left)

Dawn Onuffer, Crestview, Florida

A casual dinner turns into a bow-tie affair when I toss pasta, mushrooms, pepperoni and tomato sauce together. This recipe is my own version of a favorite restaurant dish.

1 medium onion, chopped
1 large green pepper, chopped
1 cup sliced fresh mushrooms
1 tablespoon olive oil
2 cans (15 ounces *each*) tomato sauce
2 cans (14-1/2 ounces *each*) stewed tomatoes, chopped
2 bay leaves
1 tablespoon sugar
1/2 teaspoon dried basil
1/2 teaspoon dried oregano
1/2 teaspoon fennel seed, crushed
1/2 teaspoon crushed red pepper flakes
1/4 teaspoon pepper
1 package (8 ounces) sliced pepperoni, quartered
4 cups uncooked ziti *or* bow tie pasta
1/2 cup grated Parmesan cheese
1-1/2 cups (6 ounces) shredded part-skim mozzarella cheese

In a large saucepan, saute the onion, green pepper and mushrooms in oil until tender.

Stir in tomato sauce, tomatoes, bay leaves, sugar and seasonings. Bring to a boil. Stir in pepperoni. Reduce heat; simmer, uncovered, for 15 minutes.

Meanwhile, cook pasta according to package directions. Drain and place in a large serving bowl. Discard bay leaves from the sauce; stir in Parmesan cheese. Pour over pasta; toss to coat. Sprinkle with mozzarella cheese. **Yield:** 8 servings.

minutes or until slightly thickened, stirring constantly. Return chicken to pan.

Drain the pasta; toss with chicken mixture. Garnish with cheese. **Yield:** 6 servings.

.·.·.·.·.·.·.·.·.·.·.·.

PORK TENDERLOIN WITH GLAZED ONIONS
(Pictured below)

Janice Christofferson, Eagle River, Wisconsin

My husband and I love pork, especially when it's dressed up like this. Sweet apricots and glazed onions go beautifully with the juicy meat.

     4 large sweet onions, sliced (about
       8 cups)
   1/4 cup butter, cubed
     1 cup chopped dried apricots *or* golden
       raisins
   1/4 cup packed brown sugar
   1/4 cup balsamic vinegar
   1/2 teaspoon salt
   1/2 teaspoon pepper
     2 pork tenderloins (1 pound *each*)

In large skillet, saute the onions in butter for 2 minutes. Stir in the apricots, brown sugar, vinegar, salt and pepper; cook until the onions are tender.

Place pork tenderloins on a rack coated with cooking spray in a shallow roasting pan; top with onion mixture.

Bake, uncovered, at 375° for 40-45 minutes or until a meat thermometer reads 160°. Let stand for 5-10 minutes before slicing. Serve with onion mixture. **Yield:** 8 servings.

.·.·.·.·.·.·.·.·.·.·.·.

CREAMY CHICKEN ANGEL HAIR
(Pictured above)

Vanessa Sorenson, Isanti, Minnesota

Our pasta-loving family often requests this recipe featuring chicken and vegetables. Lemon juice adds a light touch to the sauce, which is well seasoned with garlic and herbs.

     1 package (16 ounces) angel hair pasta
 1-1/4 pounds boneless skinless chicken
       breasts, cut into 1-inch cubes
   1/2 teaspoon salt
   1/4 teaspoon pepper
     3 tablespoons olive oil, *divided*
     1 large carrot, diced
     2 tablespoons butter
     1 medium onion, chopped
     1 celery rib, diced
     3 large garlic cloves, minced
     2 cups heavy whipping cream
     5 bacon strips, cooked and crumbled
     3 tablespoons lemon juice
     1 teaspoon Italian seasoning
     1 cup shredded Parmesan cheese

Cook pasta according to package directions. Meanwhile, in a large skillet, saute the chicken, salt and pepper in 2 tablespoons oil until no longer pink. Remove and keep warm.

In the same skillet, saute the carrot in butter and remaining oil for 1 minute. Add the onion and celery; saute 3-4 minutes longer or until tender. Add garlic; cook for 1 minute.

Stir in the heavy cream, bacon, lemon juice and the Italian seasoning. Bring to a boil. Reduce the heat and simmer, uncovered, for 2-3

Main Dishes

CRUNCHY BAKED CHICKEN

(Pictured below)

Elva Jean Criswell, Charleston, Mississippi

I've fixed this dish many times for company, and I've never had anyone fail to ask for the recipe. The leftovers—if there are any—are very good heated up in the microwave.

> 1 egg
> 1 tablespoon milk
> 1 can (2.8 ounces) french-fried onions, crushed
> 3/4 cup grated Parmesan cheese
> 1/4 cup dry bread crumbs
> 1 teaspoon paprika
> 1/2 teaspoon salt
> Dash pepper
> 1 broiler/fryer chicken (3 to 4 pounds), cut up
> 1/4 cup butter, melted

In a shallow bowl, whisk the egg and milk. In another shallow bowl, combine the onions, cheese, bread crumbs, paprika, salt and pepper. Dip the chicken in egg mixture, then roll in the onion mixture.

Place in a greased 13-in. x 9-in. baking dish. Drizzle with butter. Bake, uncovered, at 350° for 50-60 minutes or until juices run clear. **Yield:** 4-6 servings.

BLUE CHEESE-TOPPED STEAKS

(Pictured above)

Tiffany Vancil, San Diego, California

These juicy tenderloin steaks, lightly crusted with blue cheese and bread crumbs, are special enough for holiday dining. When drizzled with wine sauce, the beef melts in your mouth.

> 2 tablespoons crumbled blue cheese
> 4-1/2 teaspoons dry bread crumbs
> 4-1/2 teaspoons minced fresh parsley
> 4-1/2 teaspoons minced chives
> Dash pepper
> 4 beef tenderloin steaks (4 ounces *each*)
> 1-1/2 teaspoons butter
> 1 tablespoon all-purpose flour
> 1/2 cup reduced-sodium beef broth
> 1 tablespoon Madeira wine
> 1/8 teaspoon browning sauce, optional

In a small bowl, combine the blue cheese, bread crumbs, parsley, chives and pepper. Press onto one side of each steak.

In a large nonstick skillet coated with cooking spray, cook the steaks over medium-high heat for 2 minutes on each side. Transfer to a 15-in. x 10-in. x 1-in. baking pan coated with cooking spray.

Bake at 350° for 6-8 minutes or until meat reaches desired doneness (for medium-rare, a meat thermometer should read 145°; medium, 160°; well-done, 170°).

Meanwhile, in a small saucepan, melt butter. Whisk in flour until smooth. Gradually whisk in broth and wine. Bring to a boil; cook and stir for 2 minutes or until thickened. Stir in browning sauce if desired. Serve with steaks. **Yield:** 4 servings.

chicken and keep warm. Drain the drippings and reserve 1 tablespoon.

In the drippings, saute garlic for 1 minute. Add the broth, sherry or additional broth and thyme. Bring to a boil; cook until liquid is reduced to 1 cup. Discard thyme. Stir in the butter, lemon juice and remaining pepper. Serve with chicken. **Yield:** 4 servings.

VENISON MEAT LOAF
(Pictured below)

Gretchen Schade, Pine Grove, Pennsylvania

I caught my fiance eating this meat loaf cold, right out of the fridge! He encouraged me to send in the recipe. If you have a deer hunter in the family, be sure to give this a try.

- 2 eggs
- 2 cups soft bread crumbs
- 1/2 cup chopped sweet onion
- 1/4 cup packed brown sugar
- 1/4 cup ketchup
- 1 tablespoon cider vinegar
- 1 teaspoon garlic powder
- 1/2 teaspoon Worcestershire sauce
- 1 pound ground venison
- 1/2 pound bulk pork sausage
- 4 bacon strips

In a large bowl, combine first eight ingredients. Crumble the venison and sausage over mixture and mix well. Shape into a loaf in a greased 11-in. x 7-in. baking dish. Top with bacon strips.

Bake, uncovered, at 400° for 40-45 minutes or until the meat is no longer pink and a meat thermometer reads 160°. Let stand for 5-10 minutes before slicing. **Yield:** 6 servings.

ROASTED CHICKEN WITH GARLIC-SHERRY SAUCE
(Pictured above)

Sheri Sidwell, Alton, Illinois

This garlic-kissed chicken is delicious, plain or fancy. It's an elegant entree for guests—and my husband and I love its leftovers in rice casseroles and hot, open-face sandwiches.

- 2 quarts water
- 1/2 cup salt
- 4 bone-in chicken breast halves (12 ounces *each*)
- 3/4 teaspoon pepper, *divided*
- 2 teaspoons canola oil
- 8 garlic cloves, peeled and thinly sliced
- 1 cup reduced-sodium chicken broth
- 1/2 cup sherry *or* additional reduced-sodium chicken broth
- 3 fresh thyme sprigs
- 1/4 cup butter, cubed
- 1 teaspoon lemon juice

For brine, in a large saucepan, bring the water and salt to a boil. Cook and stir until salt is dissolved. Remove from the heat; cool to room temperature.

Place a large heavy-duty resealable plastic bag inside a second large resealable plastic bag; add chicken. Carefully pour cooled brine into bag. Squeeze out as much air as possible; seal bags and turn to coat. Refrigerate for 1-2 hours, turning several times.

Drain and discard brine. Rinse chicken with cold water; pat dry. Sprinkle with 1/2 teaspoon pepper. In a large ovenproof skillet, brown the chicken in oil over medium heat.

Bake, uncovered, at 400° for 20-25 minutes or until a meat thermometer reads 170°. Remove

Main Dishes

▪▪▪▪▪▪▪▪▪▪▪▪▪

VEGETABLE SHRIMP STIR-FRY

(Pictured above)

Athena Russell, Florence, South Carolina

Tossed in a wok or sizzled in a skillet, this stir-fry couldn't be simpler. Sesame oil and seeds add a delicate, nutty flavor to vegetables and tender shrimp.

- 2 teaspoons cornstarch
- 2 tablespoons water
- 2 tablespoons soy sauce
- 2 tablespoons hoisin sauce
- 1 tablespoon honey
- 1 teaspoon sesame oil
- 1-1/2 pounds uncooked medium shrimp, peeled and deveined
- 4 teaspoons canola oil, *divided*
- 2 green onions, sliced
- 1 garlic clove, minced
- 1 tablespoon minced fresh gingerroot
- 1/2 pound fresh snow peas, trimmed
- 1 can (8-3/4 ounces) whole baby corn, drained
- 2 teaspoons sesame seeds, toasted
- Asian rice noodles, optional

In a small bowl, combine the first six ingredients until smooth; set aside.

In a large skillet or wok, stir-fry the shrimp in 2 teaspoons oil for 2-3 minutes or until shrimp turn pink. Remove shrimp with a slotted spoon and keep warm.

Stir-fry onions, garlic and ginger in remaining oil for 3 minutes. Add the peas and corn; stir-fry 2-3 minutes longer or until the vegetables are crisp-tender.

Stir cornstarch mixture and add to the pan. Bring to a boil; cook and stir for 2 minutes or until thickened. Add the shrimp; heat through. Sprinkle with the sesame seeds. Serve with rice noodles if desired. **Yield:** 6 servings.

CRYSTALLIZED HONEY

Crystallization is the natural process by which liquid honey becomes solid. To dissolve the crystals, place the jar in warm water and stir. Or, in a microwave-safe container, microwave the honey on high, stirring every 30 seconds.

Rise and Shine

A SATISFYING meal at the top of the morning is a great way to start the day. And we've made it easy with four one-dish breakfast meals that are a cinch to prepare and super delicious!

BACON QUICHE TARTS

(Pictured below)

Kendra Schertz, Nappanee, Indiana

Flavored with vegetables, cheese and bacon, these memorable morsels are bound to be requested at your house. The tarts are an impressive addition to brunch, but they're quite easy to make.

- 2 packages (3 ounces *each*) cream cheese, softened
- 5 teaspoons milk
- 2 eggs
- 1/2 cup shredded Colby cheese
- 2 tablespoons chopped green pepper
- 1 tablespoon finely chopped onion
- 1 tube (8 ounces) refrigerated crescent rolls
- 5 bacon strips, cooked and crumbled

In a small bowl, beat cream cheese and milk until smooth. Add the eggs, cheese, green pepper and onion; mix well.

Separate dough into eight triangles; press onto the bottom and up the sides of greased muffin cups. Sprinkle half of the bacon into cups. Pour egg mixture over bacon; top with remaining bacon. Bake, uncovered, at 375° for 18-22 minutes or until a knife comes out clean. Serve warm. **Yield:** 8 servings.

SAUSAGE JOHNNYCAKE

(Pictured above)

Lorraine Guyn, Calgary, Alberta

This robust morning entree has tons of old-fashioned flair. My bed and breakfast customers love it.

- 1 cup cornmeal
- 2 cups buttermilk
- 12 uncooked breakfast sausage links
- 1-1/3 cups all-purpose flour
- 1/4 cup sugar
- 1-1/2 teaspoons baking powder
- 1/2 teaspoon baking soda
- 1/2 teaspoon salt
- 1/3 cup shortening
- 1 egg, lightly beaten
- 1/2 teaspoon vanilla extract

Maple syrup

In a small bowl, combine cornmeal and buttermilk; let stand for 10 minutes.

Meanwhile, in a large skillet over medium heat, cook sausage until no longer pink; drain on paper towels. Arrange eight links in a spoke-like pattern in a greased 9-in. deep-dish pie plate. Cut the remaining links in half; place between whole sausages.

In a large bowl, combine the flour, sugar, baking powder, baking soda and salt. Cut in shortening until mixture resembles coarse crumbs.

Stir egg and vanilla into cornmeal mixture; add to dry ingredients and stir just until blended. Pour batter over sausages.

Bake at 400° for 35-40 minutes or until a toothpick inserted near the center comes out clean. Serve warm with syrup. **Yield:** 6 servings.

HEARTY BREAKFAST CASSEROLE

Ruth Rigoni, Hurley, Wisconsin

I make this dish for breakfast and sometimes for a main meal. You can substitute finely diced lean ham or crumbled turkey bacon for the sausage.

- 1/2 **pound bulk pork sausage**
- 3 **large potatoes, peeled and thinly sliced**
- 1/2 **teaspoon salt**
- 1/4 **teaspoon pepper**
- 1 **jar (2 ounces) diced pimientos, drained**
- 3 **eggs**
- 1 **cup 2% milk**
- 2 **tablespoons minced chives**
- 3/4 **teaspoon dried thyme *or* oregano**

Additional minced chives, optional

In a large skillet, cook sausage over medium heat until no longer pink; drain.

Arrange half of the potatoes in a greased 8-in. square baking dish; sprinkle with salt, pepper and half of the sausage. Top with the remaining potatoes and sausage; sprinkle with pimientos. In a small bowl, whisk the eggs, milk, chives and thyme; pour over the top.

Cover and bake at 375° for 45-50 minutes or until a knife inserted near the center comes out clean. Uncover; bake 10 minutes longer or until lightly browned. Let stand for 10 minutes before cutting. Sprinkle with additional chives if desired. **Yield:** 6 servings.

DELICIOUS TOMATO PIE

(Pictured below)

Edie DeSpain, Logan, Utah

This savory staple is a wonderful way to use summer's abundance of tomatoes from the garden or farm stand.

- 1-1/4 **pounds plum tomatoes (about 5 large), cut into 1/2-inch slices**
- 1 **pastry shell (9 inches), baked**
- 1/2 **cup thinly sliced green onions**
- 2 **tablespoons minced fresh basil**
- 1/4 **teaspoon salt**
- 1/4 **teaspoon pepper**
- 1/2 **cup reduced-fat mayonnaise**
- 1/2 **cup shredded cheddar cheese**
- 2 **bacon strips, cooked and crumbled**
- 2 **tablespoons shredded Parmesan cheese**

Place half of the tomatoes in pastry shell. Top with onions and remaining tomatoes. Sprinkle with the basil, salt and pepper. Combine mayonnaise and cheddar cheese; spread over the tomatoes, leaving 1-1/2 in. around the edge. Sprinkle with bacon and Parmesan cheese.

Bake at 350° for 30-35 minutes or until the tomatoes are tender. **Yield:** 8 servings.

CHIPOTLE-RUBBED BEEF TENDERLOIN

(Pictured above)

Taste of Home Test Kitchen

Go ahead, rub it in! Coating traditional tenderloin with lively, peppery flavors gives it a south-of-the-border twist. Your family or dinner guests will be more than impressed.

  1 beef tenderloin roast (2 pounds)
  2 teaspoons canola oil
  3 teaspoons coarsely ground pepper
  3 garlic cloves, minced
2-1/2 teaspoons brown sugar
  1 teaspoon salt
  1 teaspoon ground coriander
1/2 teaspoon ground chipotle pepper
1/4 teaspoon cayenne pepper

Brush the beef with oil. Combine the remaining ingredients; rub over meat. Cover and refrigerate for 2 hours.

    Place on a rack coated with cooking spray in a shallow roasting pan. Bake, uncovered, at 400° for 45-55 minutes or until the meat reaches desired doneness (for medium-rare, a meat thermometer should read 145°; medium, 160°; well-done, 170°). Let stand for 10 minutes before slicing. **Yield:** 8 servings.

GARLIC

When a recipe calls for cloves of garlic and you have no fresh bulbs, substitute 1/4 teaspoon of garlic powder for each clove. Or, use garlic from jars of fresh minced garlic. Use 1/2 teaspoon of minced garlic for each clove.

TANGY PORK KABOBS

(Pictured above)

Horseradish Festival, Collinsville, Illinois

Tasters at a recent Horseradish Festival rooted for this recipe. They got a culinary kick out of the grilled kabobs made sweetly sassy with an easy-to-prepare horseradish-raspberry glaze.

    1 cup canola oil
    3 tablespoons honey
    2 tablespoons onion powder
    2 tablespoons soy sauce
    2 pork tenderloins (1 pound *each*), cut
      into 1-inch cubes
1-1/2 teaspoons seasoned salt
  1/2 teaspoon pepper

HORSERADISH RASPBERRY SAUCE:

    1 jar (18 ounces) seedless raspberry
      preserves, warmed
  1/4 cup red wine vinegar
    3 tablespoons prepared horseradish
    2 tablespoons soy sauce
    3 teaspoons garlic powder
1-1/2 teaspoons ketchup

In a large resealable plastic bag, combine the oil, honey, onion powder and soy sauce; add pork. Seal bag and turn to coat; refrigerate overnight.

Coat the grill rack with cooking spray before starting the grill. Prepare grill for indirect heat. Drain and discard marinade. Sprinkle pork with seasoned salt and pepper; thread onto six metal or soaked wooden skewers. In a small bowl, combine the sauce ingredients.

Grill the kabobs, covered, over medium heat for 8-10 minutes or until juices run clear, turning occasionally and brushing with some of the sauce during the last minute. Serve remaining sauce with kabobs. **Yield:** 6 servings (1-1/2 cups sauce).

FOUR-CHEESE BAKED ZITI

(Pictured below)

Lisa Varner, Charleston, South Carolina

This pasta dish is deliciously different because it's made with Alfredo sauce rather than a typical tomato-based sauce. Extra cheesy, it goes together quickly and is always popular at potlucks.

    1 package (16 ounces) ziti *or* small tube
      pasta
    2 cartons (10 ounces *each*) refrigerated
      Alfredo sauce
    1 cup (8 ounces) sour cream
    2 eggs, lightly beaten
    1 carton (15 ounces) ricotta cheese
  1/2 cup grated Parmesan cheese, *divided*
  1/4 cup grated Romano cheese
  1/4 cup minced fresh parsley
1-3/4 cups shredded part-skim mozzarella
      cheese

Cook pasta according to package directions; drain and return to the pan. Stir in Alfredo sauce and sour cream. Spoon half into a lightly greased 3-qt. baking dish.

Combine the eggs, ricotta cheese, 1/4 cup Parmesan cheese, Romano cheese and parsley; spread over pasta. Top with remaining pasta mixture; sprinkle with mozzarella and remaining Parmesan.

Cover and bake at 350° for 25 minutes or until a thermometer reads 160°. Uncover; bake 5-10 minutes longer or until bubbly. **Yield:** 12 servings.

SAVORY GRILLED TURKEY
(Pictured below)

Karen Buenting, Livermore, Iowa

My family likes this recipe so much that we tried grilling it in a sheltered spot during the winter. It worked! Now we can enjoy this juicy grilled bird all year long.

        1 turkey (12 pounds)
        1 cup butter, cubed
    1/2 cup cider vinegar
    1/2 cup lemon juice
        1 tablespoon Worcestershire sauce
        1 tablespoon A.1. steak sauce
        1 teaspoon salt
        1 teaspoon pepper
        1 teaspoon Louisiana-style hot sauce

Remove giblets from turkey (discard or save for another use). Coat grill rack with cooking spray before starting the grill. Prepare grill for indirect heat, using a drip pan. Skewer turkey openings; tie drumsticks together.

Place turkey over drip pan; grill, covered, over indirect medium heat for 1 hour.

Meanwhile, in a small saucepan, combine the remaining ingredients. Bring to a boil. Reduce heat; simmer for 10 minutes, stirring occasionally. Remove from heat. Set aside 2/3 cup for serving.

Grill turkey 1-2 hours longer or until a meat thermometer reads 180°, basting frequently with remaining sauce. Cover; let stand for 15 minutes before carving. Serve with reserved sauce. **Yield:** 12 servings.

CHICKEN PATTIES WITH ROASTED TOMATO SALSA
(Pictured above)

Mary Relyea, Canastota, New York

Bold and zesty tomato salsa perks up these moist and tender chicken patties. Great for lunch or dinner, this recipe ranks high among my southwestern specialties.

        6 plum tomatoes
        3 teaspoons olive oil, *divided*
    3/4 teaspoon salt, *divided*
    1-1/2 cups fresh cilantro leaves, *divided*
        1 teaspoon adobo sauce
        2 cups cubed cooked chicken breast, *divided*
        1 small zucchini, cut into 3/4-inch chunks
    1/3 cup dry bread crumbs
    1/3 cup reduced-fat mayonnaise
    1/4 teaspoon pepper

Core tomatoes and cut in half lengthwise. Place cut side up on a broiler pan coated with cooking spray; brush with 2 teaspoons oil and sprinkle with 1/4 teaspoon salt. Turn tomatoes cut side down. Bake at 425° for 30-40 minutes or until edges are well browned. Cool slightly. Remove and discard tomato peels.

Place cilantro in a food processor; cover and process until coarsely chopped. Set aside 1/4 cup cilantro for chicken patties. Add the roasted tomatoes, adobo sauce and 1/4 teaspoon salt to the food processor; cover and process just until chunky. Place salsa in a small bowl; set aside.

For chicken patties, in same food processor, combine 1-1/2 cups chicken and zucchini. Cover and process just until chicken is coarsely chopped. Add bread crumbs, mayonnaise, pepper, reserved cilantro and remaining chicken and salt. Cover and process just until mixture is chunky.

Shape into eight 3-in. patties. In a large nonstick skillet coated with cooking spray, cook patties in remaining oil for 4 minutes on each side or until golden brown. Serve with salsa. **Yield:** 8 servings.

░░░░░░░░░░░░

SOUTHWESTERN SCALLOPS

(Pictured below)

Maggie Fontenot, The Woodlands, Texas

These saucy sea scallops are popular at dinner parties—plus, they're in my repertoire of easy weekday meals. The seasoning gives the shellfish a pleasant kick.

> 2 teaspoons chili powder
> 1/2 teaspoon ground cumin
> 1/4 teaspoon salt
> 1/8 teaspoon pepper
> 1 pound sea scallops (about 12)
> 2 tablespoons butter, *divided*
> 1/2 cup white wine *or* chicken broth

In a small bowl, combine the chili powder, cumin, salt and pepper. Pat the scallops dry with paper towels. Rub seasoning mixture over scallops.

In a large heavy skillet over medium heat, melt 1 tablespoon butter. Cook scallops for 2 minutes on each side or until opaque and golden brown. Remove from the skillet; keep warm.

Add wine to the skillet, stirring to loosen any browned bits from pan. Bring to a boil; cook until liquid is reduced by half. Stir in the remaining butter until melted. Serve with the scallops. **Yield:** 4 servings.

░░░░░░░░░░░░

SWEET 'N' SASSY MEATBALLS

(Pictured above)

Dawn Onuffer, Crestview, Florida

I often serve these tasty meatballs at potlucks and family gatherings. When I declare, "The buffet is open," guests make a beeline for this dish. The combination of lean turkey, sausage, chili sauce and preserves is scrumptious!

> 2 eggs, lightly beaten
> 2 tablespoons Worcestershire sauce
> 2 tablespoons plus 1 cup chili sauce, *divided*
> 1 cup soft whole wheat bread crumbs
> 2 tablespoons dried minced onion
> 1 teaspoon dried oregano
> 3/4 teaspoon garlic powder
> 1/2 teaspoon salt
> 1/2 teaspoon pepper
> 1 pound lean ground turkey
> 1 pound Italian turkey sausage links, casings removed
> 1/2 cup reduced-sugar apricot preserves

In a large bowl, combine the eggs, Worcestershire sauce and 2 tablespoons chili sauce. Stir in the bread crumbs, onion, oregano, garlic powder, salt and pepper. Crumble the turkey and sausage over mixture and mix well. Shape into 1-in. balls.

Place on a rack coated with cooking spray in a shallow baking pan. Bake at 375° for 15-20 minutes or until meat is no longer pink.

In a large bowl, combine apricot preserves and remaining chili sauce. Add meatballs and toss gently. Place in a 15-in. x 10-in. x 1-in. baking pan coated with cooking spray. Bake 5-10 minutes longer or until glazed, stirring every 3 minutes. **Yield:** about 4 dozen.

BURGUNDY BEEF

(Pictured above)

Lora Snyder, Columbus, Massachusetts

On chilly days, it's a pleasure coming home to this savory pot roast bubbling in the slow cooker. The tender beef, vegetables and tasty gravy are mouth-watering over a bed of noodles.

  1/2 **pound sliced fresh mushrooms**
  1/2 **pound fresh baby carrots**
    1 **medium green pepper, julienned**
    1 **boneless beef chuck roast (2-1/2 pounds)**
    1 **can (10-3/4 ounces) condensed golden mushroom soup, undiluted**
  1/4 **cup Burgundy wine *or* beef broth**
    1 **tablespoon Worcestershire sauce**
    1 **envelope onion soup mix**
  1/4 **teaspoon pepper**
    2 **to 3 tablespoons cornstarch**
    2 **tablespoons cold water**
Hot cooked wide egg noodles

In a 5-qt. slow cooker, combine the mushrooms, carrots and green pepper; place roast on top. In a large bowl, combine soup, wine, Worcestershire sauce, soup mix and pepper; pour over the roast. Cover; cook on low for 8-9 hours or until the meat is tender.

Transfer the roast and vegetables to a serving platter; keep warm. Strain cooking juices and skim fat; place in a large saucepan. Combine the cornstarch and cold water until smooth; gradually stir into cooking juices. Bring to a boil; cook and stir for 2 minutes or until thickened. Serve with the beef, vegetables and noodles. **Yield:** 6-8 servings.

EXTRA MUSHROOMS

Fresh mushrooms should be used within a few days of purchase. If that's not possible, you can blanch them with a bit of lemon juice or saute them in a jiffy, then freeze for up to 1 month for use in soups, sauces and casseroles.

SICILIAN SUPPER

Gloria Warczak
Cedarburg, Wisconsin

Ground beef, tomato and a tasty cream cheese sauce come together in this hot, hearty casserole. I recently took it to a banquet, and recipe requests came from every table. It's okay to adjust the seasonings to your tastes—increasing them will give this recipe a much more robust flavor.

        2 cups uncooked egg noodles
        1 pound ground beef
    1/2 cup chopped onion
    1/4 cup chopped green pepper
        1 can (6 ounces) tomato paste
    3/4 cup water
  1-1/2 teaspoons sugar, *divided*
    1/2 teaspoon salt
    1/2 teaspoon dried basil
    1/4 teaspoon garlic powder
    1/4 teaspoon chili powder
    1/4 teaspoon pepper, *divided*
        1 tablespoon finely chopped green onion
        1 tablespoon olive oil
        1 package (8 ounces) cream cheese, cubed
    3/4 cup milk
    1/3 cup plus 2 tablespoons grated Parmesan
        cheese, *divided*

Cook noodles according to package directions. Meanwhile, in a large skillet, cook the beef, onion and green pepper over medium heat until meat is no longer pink; drain. Stir in the tomato paste, water, 1 teaspoon sugar, salt, basil, garlic powder, chili powder and 1/8 teaspoon pepper.

In a large saucepan, saute the green onion in oil until tender. Add the cream cheese and milk; stir until blended. Stir in 1/3 cup cheese, and the remaining sugar and pepper. Drain noodles; stir into cheese mixture.

In a greased 8-in. square baking dish, arrange alternate rows of the beef and noodle mixtures. Sprinkle with the remaining cheese. Cover and bake at 350° for 20-25 minutes or until bubbly.
Yield: 4 servings.

GRILLED CHICKEN WITH CHUTNEY

(Pictured at right)

Gilda Lester, Wilmington, North Carolina

My husband didn't like plums until he tasted them cooked with peaches, dried cranberries and spices in this tasty chutney. It wakes up just about any kind of meat, from chicken breasts to pork tenderloin.

        3 medium plums, chopped
    2/3 cup sugar
    1/2 cup white wine vinegar
        3 tablespoons balsamic vinegar
        2 tablespoons dried cranberries
        1 garlic clove, minced
        1 teaspoon minced fresh gingerroot
    1/4 teaspoon ground allspice
    1/4 teaspoon crushed red pepper flakes
        2 cups chopped peeled peaches
    1/4 cup finely chopped red onion
        1 teaspoon Dijon mustard
    1/2 teaspoon minced seeded jalapeno pepper
        6 boneless skinless chicken breast halves
        (5 ounces *each*)
        2 tablespoons olive oil
        1 tablespoon Tex-Mex chili seasoning mix
Red leaf lettuce
Additional chopped jalapenos, optional

For chutney, in a large saucepan, combine the first nine ingredients. Bring to a boil; cook and stir for 6-8 minutes or until thickened. Stir in the peaches, onion, mustard and jalapeno. Cool to room temperature.

Brush the chicken with oil; sprinkle with the chili seasoning mix. Grill the chicken, covered, over medium heat for 5-6 minutes on each side or until a meat thermometer reads 170°. Slice chicken; serve on lettuce leaves with chutney. Sprinkle with additional jalapenos if desired.
Yield: 6 servings.

Editor's Note: When cutting hot peppers, disposable gloves are recommended. Avoid touching your face.

In a Dutch oven, saute the garlic in oil for 1 minute. Stir in the tomatoes, 2 cups water, tomato sauce and paste, parsley, cheese, basil and sugar; bring to a boil. Reduce the heat; carefully add meatballs.

Cover and simmer for 3 hours, adding more water if needed to achieve desired consistency. Season with salt and pepper. **Yield:** 6 servings.

🔲🔲🔲🔲🔲🔲🔲🔲🔲🔲🔲

CHEESE-TOPPED SLOPPY JOES
(Pictured below)

Mary Dempsey, Overland Park, Kansas

I got this recipe for quick-to-fix sandwiches from my Aunt Nellie—a busy farm wife who used to serve these to the harvest crew. Microwaved leftovers taste delicious the next day.

    1 pound ground beef
    2 celery ribs, chopped
    1 tablespoon chopped onion
    1 tablespoon all-purpose flour
    1 tablespoon brown sugar
  1/2 teaspoon ground mustard
  3/4 cup ketchup
    6 hamburger buns, split
    6 slices Swiss cheese

In a large skillet, cook the beef, celery and onion over medium heat until the meat is no longer pink; drain. Stir in the flour, brown sugar, mustard and ketchup.

Bring to a boil. Reduce heat; simmer, uncovered, for 10 minutes, stirring occasionally. Serve on buns with cheese. **Yield:** 6 servings.

GARLIC LOVER'S MEATBALLS AND SAUCE
(Pictured above)

Toni Holcomb, Rogersville, Missouri

This dish is a staple in our part of the country. My daughter Amber and I invented our version after eating at an Italian restaurant in St. Louis. We came pretty close to copying that dish, but added our own little twist.

    2 eggs, lightly beaten
  1/2 cup dry bread crumbs
  1/4 cup grated Parmesan *or* Romano cheese
    2 tablespoons minced fresh parsley
    2 garlic cloves, minced
  1/8 teaspoon pepper
    1 pound ground beef
    2 tablespoons olive oil
SAUCE:
    2 to 3 garlic cloves, minced
    1 tablespoon olive oil
    2 cans (28 ounces *each*) crushed
      tomatoes in puree
    2 to 3 cups water, *divided*
    1 can (8 ounces) tomato sauce
    1 can (6 ounces) tomato paste
  1/2 cup minced fresh parsley
  1/4 cup grated Parmesan *or* Romano cheese
    1 tablespoon dried basil
    2 teaspoons sugar
  1/2 teaspoon salt
  1/4 teaspoon pepper

In a large bowl, combine the first six ingredients. Crumble beef over mixture and mix well. Shape into 12 meatballs. In a large skillet, brown the meatballs in oil on all sides; drain.

▰▰▰▰▰▰▰▰▰▰▰▰▰

HICKORY BARBECUED SALMON WITH TARTAR SAUCE

(Pictured above)

Linda Chevalier, Battle Ground, Washington

Guests of all ages fall for this succulent seafood entree. The idea to use hickory chips came from my dad. He always prepared his salmon this way.

    1/2 cup butter, cubed
      2 garlic cloves, minced
      1 salmon fillet (3 pounds)
      2 medium lemons, thinly sliced
      2 cups soaked hickory chips
TARTAR SAUCE:
      1 cup mayonnaise
    1/4 cup chopped sweet pickles
      1 teaspoon finely chopped onion
    3/4 teaspoon ground mustard
    1/4 teaspoon Worcestershire sauce

In a small saucepan, combine butter and garlic; cook and stir over medium heat until butter is melted. Drizzle 2 tablespoons butter mixture over salmon; top with lemon slices. Set aside remaining butter mixture for basting.

Coat the grill rack with cooking spray before starting the grill. Add wood chips to grill according to manufacturer's directions. Place the salmon, skin side down, on grill rack. Grill, covered, over medium heat for 5 minutes.

Carefully spoon some reserved butter mixture over the salmon. Cover and grill 15-20 minutes longer or until the fish flakes easily with a fork, basting occasionally with remaining butter mixture.

Meanwhile, in a small bowl, combine the tartar sauce ingredients. Serve with salmon. **Yield:** 8 servings (1 cup sauce).

▰▰▰▰▰▰▰▰▰▰▰▰▰

SEAFOOD-STUFFED SHELLS

(Pictured below)

Mrs. Ezra Weaver, Wolcott, New York

These stuffed shells are really good, and we have them often. Even if you don't like fish, you'll love this dish.

     30 uncooked jumbo pasta shells
    1/2 pound bay scallops
      2 teaspoons butter
      2 eggs
      2 cups (16 ounces) cream-style cottage cheese
      1 carton (15 ounces) ricotta cheese
    1/2 teaspoon ground nutmeg
    1/4 teaspoon pepper
      1 can (6 ounces) lump crabmeat, drained
    3/4 pound frozen cooked small shrimp, thawed
      1 jar (15 ounces) Alfredo sauce

Cook pasta shells according to package directions. Meanwhile, in a small skillet over medium heat, cook scallops in butter for 1-2 minutes or until opaque. Transfer to a large bowl.

Place one egg and half of the cottage cheese, ricotta, nutmeg and pepper in a blender; cover and process until smooth. Add to scallops. Repeat with the remaining egg, cottage cheese, ricotta, nutmeg and pepper. Add to scallops. Stir in crab and shrimp.

Drain shells and rinse in cold water. Stuff with seafood mixture. Place in a greased 13-in. x 9-in. baking dish. Top with cheese sauce. Cover and bake at 350° for 30-35 minutes or until bubbly. **Yield:** 10 servings.

CREAMED CHICKEN OVER CORN BREAD

(Pictured below)

Nancy Lange, Hindsboro, Illinois

This comforting dish was a favorite with our kids, and now our 11 grandkids request it. The recipe is easily doubled or tripled for our Sunday family dinners.

1 package (8-1/2 ounces) corn bread/muffin mix
1 tablespoon chopped onion
1/8 teaspoon minced garlic
1/4 cup butter, cubed
2 cups cubed rotisserie chicken
1 package (16 ounces) frozen chopped broccoli, thawed
2 tablespoons all-purpose flour
1-1/2 teaspoons salt
2 egg yolks, lightly beaten
1 cup (8 ounces) sour cream
3/4 cup milk
Shredded cheddar cheese

Prepare the corn bread batter and bake according to the package directions, using a 9-in. round baking pan.

Meanwhile, in a large skillet, saute onion and garlic in butter for 2-3 minutes; stir in chicken and broccoli. Cook and stir for 5-7 minutes or until heated through.

In a small bowl, combine flour and salt; stir in the egg yolks, sour cream and milk until smooth. Add to the chicken mixture; cook and stir for 3-5 minutes or until thickened.

Cut the warm corn bread into wedges; top with the chicken mixture. Sprinkle with the cheddar cheese. **Yield:** 6 servings.

TOMATO BAGUETTE PIZZA

(Pictured at right)

Lorraine Caland, Thunder Bay, Ontario

When my tomatoes conspire to ripen all at once, I use them up in simple recipes like this one. Cheesy baguette pizzas, served with a salad, make an ideal lunch.

3 cups sliced fresh mushrooms
2 medium onions, sliced
2 teaspoons olive oil
2 garlic cloves, minced
1/2 teaspoon Italian seasoning
1/4 teaspoon salt
Dash pepper
1 French bread baguette (10-1/2 ounces), halved lengthwise
1-1/2 cups (6 ounces) shredded part-skim mozzarella cheese, *divided*
3/4 cup thinly sliced fresh basil leaves, *divided*
3 medium tomatoes, sliced

In a large skillet, saute the mushrooms and onions in oil until tender. Add garlic, Italian seasoning, salt and pepper; cook 1 minute longer.

Place the baguette halves on a baking sheet; sprinkle with 3/4 cup cheese. Top with 1/2 cup basil, mushroom mixture, tomatoes and the remaining cheese.

Bake at 400° for 10-15 minutes or until cheese is melted. Sprinkle with remaining basil. Cut each portion into three slices. **Yield:** 6 servings.

SLICING FRESH BASIL

Chopping one basil leaf at a time can be a bit tedious. To quickly chop a lot of basil and end up with attractive results, create basil chiffonade, which is just a fancy term for thin strips. Stack several basil leaves and roll them into a tight tube. Then, slice the stacked leaves widthwise into narrow pieces to create long thin strips.

to tomato mixture; cook for 4-5 minutes or until shrimp turn pink and scallops are opaque. Stir in the parsley.

Drain the linguine. Serve the seafood mixture over linguine; garnish with cheese if desired. **Yield:** 8 servings.

THAI PORK BURRITOS
(Pictured below)

Jennifer Gardner, Castle Rock, Colorado

This main dish has a flavorful filling of seasoned ground pork and coleslaw. One of the great things about the tasty recipe is how fast it goes together. To make more than one burrito, simply multiply the recipe ingredients according to how many burritos you would like to serve.

- 1/4 pound ground pork
- 2 thin onion slices
- 2 tablespoons stir-fry sauce
- 1 teaspoon minced fresh cilantro
- 1/8 teaspoon crushed red pepper flakes
- 3/4 cup coleslaw mix
- 1 to 2 flour tortillas (7 inches)

In a large skillet, cook the pork over medium heat until no longer pink; drain. Add onion; saute for 1 minute or until crisp-tender. Add stir-fry sauce, cilantro and red pepper flakes; cook for 1 minute. Add coleslaw mix; cook 2 minutes longer or until crisp-tender. Spoon filling down the center of tortilla. Fold end and sides over filling. **Yield:** 1 serving.

SEAFOOD MEDLEY WITH LINGUINE
(Pictured above)

Charlene Chambers, Ormond Beach, Florida

Who can resist a savory blend of seafood and pasta? This dish—featuring scallops, shrimp, tomatoes and linguine—is nutritious and rich in flavor.

- 1 large onion, chopped
- 2 tablespoons butter
- 1 tablespoon olive oil
- 3 garlic cloves, minced
- 1 cup white wine *or* chicken broth
- 1 can (28 ounces) diced fire-roasted tomatoes
- 1 tablespoon minced fresh rosemary *or* 1 teaspoon dried rosemary, crushed
- 1 teaspoon sugar
- 1 teaspoon minced fresh oregano *or* 1/4 teaspoon dried oregano
- 1/4 teaspoon salt
- 1/4 teaspoon pepper
- 1 package (16 ounces) linguine
- 1 pound sea scallops
- 9 ounces uncooked large shrimp, peeled and deveined
- 2 tablespoons minced fresh parsley

Shredded Parmesan cheese, optional

In a large skillet, saute onion in butter and oil until tender. Add garlic; cook 1 minute longer. Add the wine. Bring to a boil; cook until liquid is reduced to 1/2 cup. Add the tomatoes, rosemary, sugar, oregano, salt and pepper. Bring to a boil over medium heat. Reduce the heat and simmer, uncovered, for 15 minutes.

Meanwhile, cook the linguine according to package directions. Add the scallops and shrimp

Main Dishes

out remaining pastry to fit top of pie; place over filling. Trim, seal and flute edges. Cut slits in pastry. Cover edges loosely with foil.

Bake at 400° for 15 minutes. Remove the foil. Reduce the heat to 375°; bake 30-35 minutes longer or until the crust is golden brown and a meat thermometer reads 160°. **Yield:** 6-8 servings.

◆◆◆◆◆◆◆◆◆◆◆◆◆

PRESTO PAPRIKA CHICKEN
(Pictured below)

Gloria Warczak, Cedarburg, Wisconsin

On busy evenings, I have to wing it for dinner, and this meal hits the spot. The mild, paprika-spiced sauce nicely coats the rotisserie chicken and noodles.

  1 medium onion, chopped
  3 tablespoons butter
  4 teaspoons all-purpose flour
  2 cups chicken broth
  2 tablespoons plus 1-1/2 teaspoons
    paprika
  1 bay leaf
1-1/2 cups (12 ounces) sour cream
  1 rotisserie chicken, cut into serving-size
    pieces
Hot cooked noodles

In a large skillet, saute the onion in butter. Stir in flour until blended; gradually add the broth, paprika and bay leaf. Bring to a boil; cook and stir for 2 minutes or until thickened.

Reduce heat to low. Stir in sour cream. Add chicken; heat through. Discard bay leaf. Serve with noodles. **Yield:** 6 servings.

◆◆◆◆◆◆◆◆◆◆◆◆◆

FRENCH CANADIAN MEAT PIE
(Pictured above)

Angie Moline, Calgary, Alberta

I'm a seventh-generation French Canadian, and my ancestors started the tradition of serving this meat pie on Christmas Eve. One year I didn't make it, and my daughter and I felt something was missing. The savory pie goes well with salad and fresh rolls for a lighter meal, and it's good served in small portions with turkey and all the trimmings, too.

1-1/4 pounds ground pork
  1/2 pound ground beef
  1/4 pound ground veal
    1 cup grated peeled potatoes
  1/2 cup grated onion
    3 garlic cloves, minced
1-1/2 teaspoons salt
  1/2 teaspoon pepper
  1/4 teaspoon dried savory
  1/4 teaspoon rubbed sage
  1/8 teaspoon ground cloves
  1/4 cup plus 2 tablespoons water, *divided*
  1/4 cup dry bread crumbs
    1 egg
Pastry for double-crust pie (9 inches)

In a large skillet over medium heat, cook the pork, beef, veal, potatoes and onion until meat is no longer pink; drain. Stir in garlic, seasonings and 1/4 cup water. Bring to a boil. Reduce heat; cover and simmer for 15 minutes, stirring frequently.

Remove from heat; cool to room temperature. Stir in bread crumbs. Combine egg and remaining water; stir into meat mixture.

Line a 9-in. pie plate with bottom pastry; trim even with edge. Fill with the meat mixture. Roll

HERBED ORANGE ROUGHY

(Pictured above)

Sue Kroening, Mattoon, Illinois

The simple seasonings in this quick-and-easy recipe enhance the pleasant, mild flavor of orange roughy. You can also use red snapper, catfish or trout.

  2 tablespoons lemon juice
  1 tablespoon butter, melted
1/2 teaspoon dried thyme
1/2 teaspoon grated lemon peel
1/4 teaspoon salt
1/4 teaspoon paprika
1/8 teaspoon garlic powder
  4 orange roughy, red snapper, catfish *or* trout fillets (6 ounces *each*)

In a small shallow bowl, combine the first seven ingredients; dip fillets on both sides in the lemon mixture. Grill, covered, over medium-hot heat for 10 minutes or until fish flakes easily with a fork. **Yield:** 4 servings.

STUFFED PORK CHOPS

Taste of Home Test Kitchen

Tart apple adds a delicious hint of autumn to the moist stuffing that fills these savory chops. The dish is elegant and looks like you fussed, but it takes just an hour or less to prepare.

  1 bacon strip, diced
1/4 cup chopped onion
1/2 cup corn bread stuffing mix
1/2 cup chopped peeled tart apple
  2 tablespoons chopped pecans
  2 tablespoons raisins
  2 tablespoons plus 1 cup chicken broth, *divided*

1/4 teaspoon rubbed sage
Dash ground allspice
  2 bone-in pork loin chops (1 inch thick and 7 ounces *each*)
  1 tablespoon butter

In a 6-qt. pressure cooker, cook the bacon and onion over medium heat until the bacon is crisp. In a small bowl, combine bacon mixture, stuffing mix, apple, pecans, raisins, 2 tablespoons broth, sage and allspice. Cut a pocket in each pork chop by slicing almost to bone; fill with stuffing.

In pressure cooker, brown chops in butter on both sides; add remaining broth. Close cover securely; place pressure regulator on vent pipe. Bring cooker to full pressure over high heat. Reduce heat to medium-high and cook for 15 minutes. (Pressure regulator should maintain a slow, steady rocking motion; adjust heat if needed.)

Remove from the heat; immediately cool according to manufacturer's directions until pressure is completely reduced. Sprinkle with parsley. **Yield:** 2 servings.

Editor's Note: This recipe was tested at 13 pounds of pressure (psi).

STUFFED CABBAGE ROLLS

Shirley Felts, Jackson, Mississippi

We have been making this dish in my family since I was a little girl. Mother served it with corn bread fritters—I like to serve it with corn bread muffins.

  1 medium head cabbage
  1 to 1-1/4 pounds ground beef
  1 cup cooked rice
  1 small onion, chopped
  1 egg, lightly beaten
  2 teaspoons salt-free seasoning
1/2 teaspoon pepper
1/2 teaspoon dried thyme
  1 can (16 ounces) tomato sauce
  4 teaspoons brown sugar
1/4 cup water
  1 tablespoon lemon juice *or* vinegar

Remove core from cabbage. Steam 12 large outer leaves until limp. Drain well. In a bowl, combine ground beef, rice, onion, egg and seasonings; mix well. Put about 1/3 cup meat mixture on each cabbage leaf. Fold in sides, starting at an unfolded edge, and roll up leaf completely to enclose filling.

Repeat with remaining leaves and filling. Place rolls in a large skillet or Dutch oven. Combine tomato sauce, brown sugar, water and lemon juice or vinegar; pour over cabbage rolls. Cover and simmer for 1 hour, spooning sauce over rolls occasionally during cooking. **Yield:** 4-6 servings.

CRAWFISH ETOUFFEE
(Pictured above)

Crawdad Days Festival, Harrison, Arkansas

Folks stand in line at Crawdad Days for this Cajun favorite made with aromatic vegetables and crawfish smothered in savory sauce. One bite takes you down on the Bayou.

1 medium onion, finely chopped
1 medium green pepper, finely chopped
1 celery rib, finely chopped
1/2 cup butter, cubed
4 garlic cloves, minced
1 can (10-3/4 ounces) condensed cream of celery soup, undiluted
3 teaspoons paprika
1 teaspoon Creole seasoning
1 pound frozen cooked crawfish tail meat, thawed
2 cups hot cooked rice

In a large saucepan, saute the onion, green pepper and celery in butter for 3 minutes. Add the garlic; cook 1 minute longer. Reduce the heat to medium and cook 5-7 minutes longer or until the vegetables are tender.

Stir in the condensed soup, paprika and Creole seasoning. Bring to a boil. Reduce the heat and simmer, uncovered, for 5 minutes. Stir in the crawfish and heat through. Serve with cooked rice. **Yield:** 4 servings.

CREOLE SEASONING

Don't have any Creole seasoning? It's easy to make your own. For every teaspoon that is called for in a recipe, combine 1/4 teaspoon *each* of salt, garlic powder and paprika, then add to this a pinch *each* of dried thyme, ground cumin and cayenne pepper.

Around the World

IT'S ALWAYS FUN to spice up the dinner table once in awhile with a tantalizing entree that uses flavors from around the globe.

★★★★★★★★★★★★★

WASABI BEEF FAJITAS

(Pictured below)

Taste of Home Test Kitchen

Beef fajitas take on an Asian flavor by using Japanese horseradish, also known as wasabi. You can find it in the Asian food section of your local supermarket.

- 1 large sweet red pepper, julienned
- 12 green onions with tops, cut in half lengthwise
- 2 tablespoons sesame oil, *divided*
- 1 pound uncooked beef stir-fry strips
- 2 teaspoons cornstarch
- 3 tablespoons reduced-sodium soy sauce
- 2 teaspoons prepared wasabi
- 2 teaspoons minced fresh gingerroot
- 1 teaspoon minced garlic
- 8 flour tortillas (8 inches), warmed
- 1 cup coleslaw mix

In a large skillet, stir-fry red pepper and onions in 1 tablespoon oil for 3 minutes or until tender; remove and set aside. In the same skillet, stir-fry beef in remaining oil for 5 minutes or until no longer pink.

In a small bowl, combine the cornstarch, soy sauce, wasabi, ginger and garlic until blended; pour over beef. Bring to a boil; cook and stir for 2 minutes or until thickened. Return red pepper mixture to the pan; heat through.

Spoon 1/2 cup beef mixture down the center of each tortilla; top with 2 tablespoons coleslaw mix. Fold one side of tortilla over filling and roll up. Serve immediately. **Yield:** 8 servings.

★★★★★★★★★★★★★

MOROCCAN SALMON

Taste of Home Test Kitchen

If you're trying to add more fish to your diet, here's a deliciously simple recipe for baked salmon. Salmon is topped with sauteed onion, tomatoes, golden raisins and spices, transforming an ordinary weeknight meal into a culinary adventure. You and your guests won't be disappointed.

- 2 cups sliced onions, separated into rings
- 1 tablespoon canola oil
- 4 garlic cloves, minced
- 2 cups sliced plum tomatoes
- 1/4 cup golden raisins
- 1/2 teaspoon salt
- 1/2 teaspoon ground cumin
- 1/2 teaspoon ground turmeric
- 1/8 teaspoon ground cinnamon
- 4 salmon fillets (4 ounces *each*)

Hot cooked couscous, optional

In a large nonstick skillet, saute onions in oil for 5 minutes or until tender. Add garlic; cook 1 minute longer. Add the tomatoes, raisins and seasonings; cook and stir for 5 minutes.

Place salmon in a 13-in. x 9-in. baking dish coated with cooking spray. Top with the onion mixture.

Cover and bake at 375° for 25-30 minutes or until fish flakes easily with a fork. Serve with the couscous if desired. **Yield:** 4 servings.

PEANUT CHICKEN CURRY

Eilley Brandlin, Arcadia, California

To make this delectable chicken dish even quicker, use canned diced tomatoes and bottled minced garlic. I serve it with jasmine rice.

  1 cup sliced fresh baby carrots
  1 large onion, chopped
  1 tablespoon canola oil
  2 garlic cloves, minced
  1 cup chicken broth
  2 plum tomatoes, seeded and chopped
  4 cups thinly sliced rotisserie chicken
  1 can (14 ounces) coconut milk
1/3 cup creamy peanut butter
  3 teaspoons curry powder
Hot cooked rice

In a large skillet, saute the carrots and onion in oil until tender. Add garlic; saute 1 minute longer. Stir in broth and tomatoes. Bring to a boil. Reduce heat; simmer, uncovered, for 10 minutes.

  Stir in chicken, coconut milk, peanut butter and curry powder; heat through. Serve with rice. **Yield:** 6 servings.

SPICY PORK TENDERLOIN SKEWERS

(Pictured above right)

Dawn Bryant, Thedford, Nebraska

My prep-ahead skewers are easy to grill at the last minute, making them handy for time-pressed days.

  1 large onion, chopped
1/3 cup reduced-sodium soy sauce
1/4 cup water
  2 tablespoons brown sugar
  1 tablespoon ground coriander
  1 tablespoon ground cumin
  1 tablespoon minced fresh gingerroot
  1 tablespoon lemon juice
  1 tablespoon canola oil
  2 teaspoons crushed red pepper flakes
1/2 teaspoon pepper
  2 pork tenderloins (3/4 pound *each*),
    cut into 1-inch cubes
Cooked rice and green beans, optional

In a blender, combine first 11 ingredients; cover and process until smooth. Pour into a large resealable plastic bag; add pork. Seal bag and turn to coat pork; refrigerate for 6 hours or overnight.

  Drain and discard the marinade. Thread the pork cubes onto six metal or soaked wooden skewers. Grill, covered, over medium heat for 8-10 minutes or until the juices run clear, turning the skewers occasionally. Serve with rice and green beans if desired. **Yield:** 6 servings.

GINGERROOT

Look for fresh gingerroot that has smooth, wrinkle-free skin. Fresh, unpeeled gingerroot should be wrapped in a paper towel and plastic wrap and refrigerated for up to 3 weeks. It can also be frozen for up to 2 months.

mild enchilada sauce into each of two greased 13-in. x 9-in. baking dishes. Sprinkle each with 1 cup cheese.

Place a heaping 1/3 cup halibut mixture down the center of each tortilla. Roll up each tortilla and place seam side down over cheese. Pour the remaining sauce over top.

Cover and bake at 350° for 30 minutes. Sprinkle with the green onions, olives and remaining cheese. Bake, uncovered, for 10-15 minutes longer or until cheese is melted. **Yield:** 12 servings.

HALIBUT ENCHILADAS
(Pictured above)

Carole Lynn Derifield, Valdez, Alaska

The Northwest meets south-of-the-border in this dish where local Alaskan halibut is rolled into tortillas. It's one of my most requested recipes and a mainstay for potlucks and wedding buffets.

 3 pounds halibut fillets
1/2 teaspoon salt
1/8 teaspoon pepper
1/8 teaspoon cayenne pepper
 1 medium onion, finely chopped
 1 medium green pepper, finely chopped
 1 tablespoon canola oil
 2 garlic cloves, minced
 1 can (10 ounces) hot enchilada sauce
 1 can (10 ounces) green enchilada sauce
 1 cup (8 ounces) sour cream
 1 cup mayonnaise
 2 cans (4 ounces *each*) chopped green chilies
 2 cans (10 ounces *each*) mild enchilada sauce
 4 cups (16 ounces) shredded Colby-Monterey Jack cheese
24 flour tortillas (6 inches), warmed
 1 bunch green onions, thinly sliced
 2 tablespoons chopped ripe olives

Place fillets on a greased baking sheet. Sprinkle with salt, pepper and cayenne. Bake, uncovered, at 350° for 15-20 minutes or until fish flakes easily with a fork.

Meanwhile, in a large skillet, saute onion and green pepper in oil until tender. Add garlic; cook 1 minute longer.

Flake the fish with two forks; set aside. In a large bowl, combine the hot enchilada sauce, green enchilada sauce, sour cream, mayonnaise, chilies, onion mixture and fish. Spread 1/2 cup

SPICY BARBECUED CHICKEN
(Pictured below)

Patricia Parker, Connelly Springs, North Carolina

My grown children still beg for my chicken. They like the savory barbecue sauce so much, they've been known to hover over me as I cook, trying to snitch a spoonful behind my back.

1-1/2 cups sugar
1-1/2 cups ketchup
 1/2 cup water
 1/4 cup lemon juice
 1/4 cup cider vinegar
 1/4 cup Worcestershire sauce
 2 tablespoons plus 2 teaspoons chili powder
 2 tablespoons plus 2 teaspoons prepared mustard
 1 teaspoon salt
 1/2 teaspoon crushed red pepper flakes
 2 broiler/fryer chickens (3-1/2 to 4 pounds *each*), cut up

In a large saucepan, combine first 10 ingredients; bring to a boil. Reduce heat; simmer, uncovered, for 15 minutes.

Grill chicken, covered, over medium heat for 40 minutes, turning several times. Set half of the

barbecue sauce aside. Baste the chicken with the remaining sauce; grill 5-10 minutes longer or until juices run clear. Serve with reserved sauce. **Yield:** 8 servings.

HOMEMADE PASTA SAUCE
(Pictured above)

Jennifer Stephens, Pearland, Texas

This hearty sauce satisfies my pasta-loving husband much more than the store-bought kind. For a change of pace, I add ground beef or Italian sausage. It's also good with black olives, fresh mushrooms and green peppers.

  1 medium onion, chopped
 10 fresh baby carrots, diced
  1 tablespoon olive oil
  3 garlic cloves, minced
  2 cans (14-1/2 ounces *each*) diced
     tomatoes, undrained
  1 can (14-1/2 ounces) chicken broth
  1 can (6 ounces) tomato paste
  1 teaspoon dried oregano
  1 teaspoon dried basil
1/2 teaspoon salt
Hot cooked pasta

In a large saucepan, saute onion and carrots in oil until tender. Add garlic; cook 1 minute longer.

Add the tomatoes, broth, tomato paste and the seasonings. Bring to a boil. Reduce heat; simmer, uncovered, for 45-50 minutes or until carrots are tender, stirring occasionally. Serve with pasta. **Yield:** 5 servings.

CRAB CAKE-STUFFED PORTOBELLOS
(Pictured below)

Jennifer Coduto, Kent, Ohio

Served as a light main dish or an hors d'oeuvre, these stuffed mushrooms are pretty and delicious. Canned crabmeat becomes absolutely elegant.

  6 large portobello mushrooms
3/4 cup finely chopped sweet onion
  2 tablespoons olive oil, *divided*
  1 package (8 ounces) cream cheese,
     softened
  1 egg
1/2 cup seasoned bread crumbs
1/2 cup plus 1 teaspoon grated Parmesan
     cheese, *divided*
  1 teaspoon seafood seasoning
  2 cans (6-1/2 ounces *each*) lump
     crabmeat, drained
1/4 teaspoon paprika

Remove stems from mushrooms (discard or save for another use); set caps aside. In a small skillet, saute onion in 1 tablespoon oil until tender. In a small bowl, combine the cream cheese, egg, bread crumbs, 1/2 cup cheese and seafood seasoning. Gently stir in crab and onion.

Spoon 1/2 cup crab mixture into each mushroom cap; drizzle with remaining oil. Sprinkle with paprika and remaining cheese. Place in a greased 15-in. x 10-in. x 1-in. baking pan.

Bake, uncovered, at 400° for 15-20 minutes or until mushrooms are tender. **Yield:** 6 servings.

sesame oil, white pepper and remaining soy sauce until smooth; set aside.

In a large skillet or wok, stir-fry the pork in 1 teaspoon canola oil for 4-5 minutes or until no longer pink. Remove with a slotted spoon and keep warm.

Stir-fry the onion, carrots and ginger in the remaining oil for 3-4 minutes. Add the garlic; cook 1 minute longer. Add the pineapple, red pepper and green onions; stir-fry for 3-4 minutes or until vegetables are crisp-tender.

Stir the cornstarch mixture and add to the pan. Bring to a boil; cook and stir for 2 minutes or until thickened. Return pork to the pan; heat through. Serve with rice if desired. **Yield:** 6 servings.

PORK 'N' PINEAPPLE STIR-FRY
(Pictured above)

Rebecca Baird, Salt Lake City, Utah

A light sweet-and-sour sauce gently coats lean pork and mixed vegetables in this colorful stir-fry. Ginger and garlic give it zip, and pineapple adds a touch of the tropics.

4-1/2 teaspoons all-purpose flour
   5 tablespoons reduced-sodium soy sauce, *divided*
   1 pork tenderloin (1 pound), cut into 1/2-inch cubes
   2 tablespoons plus 1 teaspoon cornstarch
   1 cup reduced-sodium chicken broth
 1/4 cup packed brown sugar
 1/4 cup rice vinegar
 1/4 cup sherry *or additional reduced-sodium chicken broth*
   1 teaspoon sesame oil
 1/4 teaspoon white pepper
   2 teaspoons canola oil, *divided*
   1 large onion, chopped
   2 medium carrots, thinly sliced
   1 tablespoon minced fresh gingerroot
   2 garlic cloves, minced
   1 cup cubed fresh pineapple
   1 large sweet red pepper, cut into 3/4-inch pieces
 1/2 cup thinly sliced green onions
Hot cooked rice, optional

Place flour and 1 tablespoon soy sauce in a large resealable plastic bag; add pork. Seal bag and turn to coat; refrigerate for 30 minutes.

In a small bowl, combine the cornstarch, broth, brown sugar, vinegar, sherry or additional broth,

---

CHICKEN STEW WITH GNOCCHI
(Pictured below)

Marge Drake, Juniata, Nebraska

My chicken stew makes the house smell wonderful as it gently bubbles in the slow cooker. One whiff of it and my family heads to the kitchen to see if it's ready.

   3 medium parsnips, peeled and cut into 1/2-inch pieces
   2 large carrots, cut into 1/2-inch slices
   2 celery ribs, chopped
   1 large sweet potato, peeled and cut into 1-inch cubes
   4 green onions, chopped
   3 pounds bone-in chicken thighs, skin removed
 1/2 teaspoon dried sage leaves

1/4 teaspoon salt
1/4 teaspoon pepper
4 cups chicken broth
1 cup water
3 tablespoons cornstarch
1/4 cup cold water
1 package (16 ounces) potato gnocchi
Hot pepper sauce, optional

Place the parsnips, carrots, celery, sweet potato and onions in a 5-qt. slow cooker. Top with the chicken; sprinkle with the sage, salt and pepper. Add broth and water. Cover and cook on low for 6 hours or until a meat thermometer reads 180°.

Remove chicken; when cool enough to handle, remove the meat from bones and discard bones. Cut meat into bite-size pieces and return to the slow cooker.

Mix cornstarch and cold water until smooth; stir into stew. Add the gnocchi. Cover and cook on high for 30 minutes or until thickened. Season with the hot pepper sauce if desired. **Yield:** 8 servings (3 quarts).

CREOLE BLACK BEANS 'N' SAUSAGE

Cheryl Landers, LaTour, Missouri

When I make this flavorful stew, I brown the meat, cut up veggies and measure spices the night before, and then assemble and start it cooking the next morning. When I get home, I make the rice…and before you know it, dinner is served!

2 pounds smoked sausage, cut into 1-inch slices
3 cans (15 ounces *each*) black beans, rinsed and drained
1-1/2 cups *each* chopped onion, celery and green pepper
1 cup water
1 can (8 ounces) tomato sauce
4 garlic cloves, minced
2 teaspoons dried thyme
1 teaspoon chicken bouillon granules
1 teaspoon white pepper
1/4 teaspoon cayenne pepper
2 bay leaves
Hot cooked rice

In a large skillet, brown the sausage over medium heat; drain. Transfer to a 5-qt. slow cooker.

In a large bowl, combine beans, onion, celery, green pepper, water, tomato sauce, garlic, thyme, bouillon, white pepper, cayenne and bay leaves; pour over the sausage. Cover and cook on low for 6 hours or until the vegetables are tender. Discard the bay leaves. Serve with the rice. **Yield:** 10 servings.

SALMON WITH ORANGE VINAIGRETTE

(Pictured below)

Lorie Rice, Liverpool, New York

Here's my favorite way to add zip to classic salmon. The tangy vinaigrette complements the naturally sweet fish, and the golden orange color is so appealing on the plate.

1 cup orange juice
4-1/2 teaspoons finely chopped red onion
4-1/2 teaspoons lime juice
1 teaspoon chili powder
1 teaspoon honey Dijon mustard
1/2 cup fat-free Italian salad dressing
4 salmon fillets (6 ounces *each*)
Salt and pepper to taste
1 tablespoon olive oil
4 teaspoons minced fresh cilantro

Place the orange juice in a small saucepan. Bring to a boil; cook until liquid is reduced to 1/4 cup. Cool slightly. Transfer to a blender. Add the onion, lime juice, chili powder and mustard; cover and process until blended. While processing, gradually add the salad dressing in a steady stream; process until blended.

Season fillets with salt and pepper. In a large skillet, cook fillets in oil over medium-high heat for 2 minutes on each side or until golden brown.

Transfer to a greased 15-in. x 10-in. x 1-in. baking pan. Bake at 400° for 5-10 minutes or until the fish flakes easily with a fork. Serve with orange vinaigrette. Garnish with cilantro. **Yield:** 4 servings.

Delicious Orange Chicken

(Pictured below)

Lorri Cleveland, Kingsville, Ohio

Orange slices add a refreshing twist to tender, juicy baked chicken—a wonderful meal for company. The appealing glaze coats the poultry with tangy sweetness.

    6 bone-in chicken breast halves (7 ounces
        each), skin removed
    1 tablespoon butter, melted
    1 garlic clove, minced
    1 teaspoon dried basil
  1/2 teaspoon salt
  1/8 teaspoon pepper
    1 medium onion, thinly sliced
    1 medium navel orange, thinly sliced
    3 tablespoons brown sugar
    2 teaspoons cornstarch
  1/2 cup orange juice
    3 tablespoons soy sauce

Place the chicken in a 13-in. x 9-in. baking dish coated with cooking spray. Combine the butter, garlic, basil, salt and pepper; drizzle over chicken. Arrange the onion and orange slices on top. Bake, uncovered, at 350° for 50 minutes.

In a small saucepan, combine the brown sugar, cornstarch, orange juice and soy sauce until smooth. Bring to a boil; cook and stir for 1-2 minutes or until thickened.

Drain the chicken; brush with orange juice mixture. Bake 15-20 minutes longer or until a meat thermometer reads 170°. **Yield:** 6 servings.

Roasted Vegetable Lasagna

(Pictured above)

Susanne Ebersol, Bird-in-Hand, Pennsylvania

Bursting with garden favorites, this lasagna is a vegetable lover's dream. The pasta layers are generously stuffed with roasted zucchini, mushrooms, peppers and onion in homemade tomato sauce.

    1 large onion, chopped
    1 tablespoon olive oil
    6 garlic cloves, minced
    1 can (28 ounces) tomato puree
    1 can (8 ounces) tomato sauce
    3 tablespoons minced fresh basil
    3 tablespoons minced fresh oregano
    1 teaspoon sugar
  1/2 teaspoon crushed red pepper flakes
ROASTED VEGETABLES:
    4 cups sliced zucchini
    3 cups sliced fresh mushrooms
    2 medium green peppers, cut into 1-inch
        pieces
    1 medium onion, cut into 1-inch pieces
  1/2 teaspoon salt
  1/4 teaspoon pepper
    6 lasagna noodles, cooked, rinsed and
        drained
    4 cups (16 ounces) shredded part-skim
        mozzarella cheese
    1 cup (4 ounces) shredded Parmesan
        cheese

In a large saucepan, saute the onion in oil until tender; add garlic and cook 1 minute longer. Stir in the tomato puree, sauce and seasonings. Bring to a boil. Reduce the heat; simmer, uncovered, for 20-25 minutes or until slightly thickened.

Meanwhile, in a large bowl, combine vegetables, salt and pepper. Transfer to two 15-in. x 10-in. x 1-in. baking pans coated with cooking spray. Bake at 450° for 15-18 minutes or until golden brown.

Spread 1/2 cup of the sauce into a 13-in. x 9-in. baking dish coated with cooking spray. Layer with three noodles, 1-3/4 cups sauce, and half of the roasted vegetables and cheeses. Repeat layers.

Cover and bake at 400° for 10 minutes. Uncover; bake 10-15 minutes longer or until bubbly and golden brown. Let stand for 10 minutes before serving. **Yield:** 12 servings.

SUNDAY PORK ROAST

Brandy Schaefer, Glen Carbon, Illinois

This recipe proves you don't have to slave over a hot stove to prepare a delicious down-home meal like Grandma used to make. Slices of the roast turn out tender and savory every time, making this a real crowd-pleaser for any occasion.

    1 boneless whole pork loin roast
        (3-1/2 to 4 pounds), trimmed
    1 teaspoon dried oregano
    1/2 teaspoon onion salt
    1/2 teaspoon pepper
    1/2 teaspoon caraway seeds
    1/4 teaspoon garlic salt
    6 medium carrots, peeled and cut into
        1-1/2-inch pieces
    3 large potatoes, peeled and quartered
    3 small onions, quartered
    1-1/2 cups beef broth
    1/3 cup all-purpose flour
    1/3 cup cold water
    1/4 teaspoon browning sauce, optional

Cut roast in half. In a small bowl, combine the seasonings; rub over roast. Wrap in plastic wrap and refrigerate overnight.

Place carrots, potatoes and onions in a 6-qt. slow cooker; add the broth. Unwrap roast and place in the slow cooker. Cover and cook on high for 2 hours. Reduce the heat to low and cook 6 hours longer.

Transfer the roast and vegetables to a serving platter; keep warm. Pour broth into a saucepan. Combine flour and water until smooth; stir into broth. Bring to a boil; cook and stir for 2 minutes or until thickened. Add browning sauce if desired. Serve with roast. **Yield:** 12-14 servings.

MUSHROOM POT ROAST

(Pictured below)

Colleen Fausett, Pahrump, Nevada

Mushroom lovers will tingle with excitement when they see this tender, slow-cooked roast. My recipe calls for a half pound of fresh sliced mushrooms along with onion, garlic and other seasonings and ingredients.

    1 boneless beef chuck roast (3 to 4
        pounds)
    1 teaspoon garlic powder
    1/2 teaspoon pepper
    2 tablespoons olive oil
    4 cups water
    1 large onion, chopped
    1 celery rib, sliced
    4 garlic cloves, peeled and sliced
    4 teaspoons beef bouillon granules
    2 bay leaves
    1/2 pound sliced fresh mushrooms

Sprinkle the beef with garlic powder and pepper. In a Dutch oven over medium-high heat, brown the meat in oil on all sides. Add the water, onion, celery, garlic, bouillon and bay leaves; bring to a boil. Reduce heat; cover and simmer for 1 hour.

Add the mushrooms. Cover and simmer 30 minutes longer or until meat is tender. Discard bay leaves. Thicken cooking liquid if desired; serve with beef. **Yield:** 8-10 servings.

THE DELICIOUS vegetable, rice and potato side dishes in this chapter will easily round out any meal. You'll be pleased with these tasty accompaniments!

A FABULOUS ADDITION. Maple-Glazed Acorn Squash (p. 73).

Side Dishes & Condiments

MAPLE-GLAZED ACORN SQUASH
(Pictured at left)

Nancy Mueller, Menomonee Falls, Wisconsin

With the glaze of maple syrup, brown sugar and spices, the squash becomes pleasantly sweet.

    1 medium acorn squash, halved
1-1/2 cups water
  1/4 cup maple syrup
    2 tablespoons brown sugar
  1/2 teaspoon ground cinnamon
  1/4 teaspoon ground ginger
  1/4 teaspoon salt

Scoop out and discard seeds from squash. Place cut side down in a 13-in. x 9-in. baking dish; add water. Bake, uncovered, at 350° for 45 minutes.

Drain the water from pan; turn squash cut side up. Combine the syrup, brown sugar, cinnamon, ginger and salt; pour into squash halves. Bake, uncovered, for 10 minutes or until the glaze is heated through. **Yield:** 2 servings.

GLAZED GREEN BEANS

Karen Scola, Worcester, Massachusetts

These simply seasoned green beans are a reliable addition to all of my menus.

1-1/4 pounds fresh green beans, trimmed
    2 garlic cloves, peeled
1-1/4 cups chicken broth
    1 teaspoon cornstarch
    1 tablespoon cold water
4-1/2 teaspoons lemon juice
    3 teaspoons minced fresh oregano
    2 teaspoons olive oil
  1/2 teaspoon honey mustard
  1/8 teaspoon pepper
  1/4 cup crumbled feta cheese

Place beans and garlic in a large saucepan; add broth. Bring to a boil. Reduce the heat; cover and simmer for 8-10 minutes or until the beans are crisp-tender.

Meanwhile, in a small bowl, combine the cornstarch and water until smooth. Stir in lemon juice, oregano, oil, mustard and pepper; set aside.

Drain beans, reserving 1 garlic clove and 1/4 cup broth. Place beans in a serving bowl and keep warm. In the same saucepan, mash reserved garlic clove; stir in reserved broth.

Stir cornstarch mixture and gradually stir into broth. Bring to a boil; cook and stir for 1 minute or until thickened. Pour over beans and toss to coat. Sprinkle with feta cheese. **Yield:** 6 servings.

CAESAR ASPARAGUS

Patsy Phillips, Sanford, North Carolina

This delicious dish is an easy way to get my daughter to eat asparagus.

    1 pound fresh asparagus, trimmed
    1 cup cubed French bread
    1 tablespoon olive oil
Dash salt and pepper
VINAIGRETTE:
  1/4 cup rice vinegar
    2 tablespoons grated Parmesan cheese
    1 teaspoon sugar
    1 teaspoon Dijon mustard
    1 garlic clove, minced
  1/2 teaspoon Worcestershire sauce
  1/4 cup olive oil

In a large bowl, toss asparagus, bread, oil, salt and pepper. Transfer to a greased 15-in. x 10-in. x 1-in. baking pan. Bake at 425° for 10-12 minutes or until asparagus is tender and bread is golden brown.

Meanwhile, for vinaigrette, whisk the vinegar, cheese, sugar, mustard, garlic and Worcestershire sauce. Whisk in the oil. Drizzle 1/4 cup over the asparagus mixture and toss to coat. Serve immediately with remaining vinaigrette. **Yield:** 4 servings.

PREPARING ASPARAGUS

Rinse asparagus stalks well and snap off the stalk ends as far down as they will easily break when gently bent, or cut off the tough white portion. If stalks are large, gently peel off the tough area of the stalk to just below the tip.

In a large saucepan, saute chopped apple in butter until tender. Add squash; bring to a boil. Reduce the heat; cover and simmer for 5 minutes, stirring often. Stir in salt, 1/4 teaspoon nutmeg and remaining brown sugar. Spoon into the baked apples; sprinkle with remaining nutmeg.

Bake 30-35 minutes longer or until heated through, basting occasionally. Drizzle with pan juices before serving. **Yield:** 8 servings.

VIDALIA ONION BAKE
(Pictured below)

Katrina Stitt, Zephyrhills, Florida

The mild taste of Vidalias makes this dish appealing to onion lovers and non-fans alike. It's an excellent addition to beef, pork or chicken.

> 6 large sweet onions, sliced (about 12 cups)
> 1/2 cup butter, cubed
> 2 cups crushed butter-flavored crackers
> 1 cup shredded Parmesan cheese
> 1/2 cup shredded cheddar cheese
> 1/4 cup shredded Romano cheese

In a large skillet, saute the onions in butter until tender and liquid has evaporated. Place half of the onions in a greased 2-qt. baking dish; sprinkle with half of the cracker crumbs and cheeses. Repeat layers.

Bake, uncovered, at 325° for 20-25 minutes or until golden brown. **Yield:** 8 servings.

SQUASH-STUFFED BAKED APPLES
(Pictured above)

Carolyn Buschkamp, Emmetsburg, Iowa

My husband and our four children enjoy my baked creations, including these apples filled with squash and festive spices. They make a healthful and delicious accompaniment to a holiday meal.

> 8 medium tart apples
> 1/2 cup plus 1 tablespoon packed brown sugar, *divided*
> 1/2 cup orange juice
> 1/2 cup water
> 2 tablespoons butter
> 2-1/2 cups mashed cooked butternut squash
> 1/4 teaspoon salt
> 1/2 teaspoon ground nutmeg, *divided*

Core apples, leaving bottoms intact. Peel the top third of each apple. Remove apple pulp, leaving a 1/2-in. shell. Chop the removed apple; set aside.

Place the cored apples in an ungreased 13-in. x 9-in. baking dish. Combine 1/2 cup brown sugar, orange juice and water; pour over the apples. Bake, uncovered, at 325° for 1 hour or until tender, basting occasionally.

Side Dishes & Condiments

⬛⬛⬛⬛⬛⬛⬛⬛⬛⬛⬛⬛

COLORFUL VEGGIE SAUTE

(Pictured above)

Pamela Stewart, Belcher, Kentucky

A low-fat meal won't skimp on flavor with this tasty saute on its side. The medley of squash and other garden-fresh ingredients is brightened by the hearty steak seasoning.

- 1 small zucchini, sliced
- 1 yellow summer squash, sliced
- 1 small onion, halved and sliced
- 1 cup sliced fresh mushrooms
- 1 small green pepper, julienned
- 1/2 cup thinly sliced fresh carrots
- 1 tablespoon butter
- 3 cups coarsely chopped fresh spinach
- 1/2 teaspoon steak seasoning
- 1/4 teaspoon garlic salt

In a large skillet, saute the zucchini, yellow squash, onion, mushrooms, green pepper and carrots in butter until crisp-tender.

Add the spinach, steak seasoning and garlic salt; saute 3-4 minutes longer or just until spinach is wilted. **Yield:** 5 servings.

Editor's Note: This recipe was tested with McCormick's Montreal Steak Seasoning. Look for it in the spice aisle.

FRESH SPINACH

A 1-pound head of fresh spinach will yield 10-12 cups of torn leaves. To wash, submerge the trimmed leaves in a large bowl of cold water, swish around and let sit for 10 minutes. Then, use tongs to transfer the leaves to a strainer, leaving the sandy water in the bowl.

⬛⬛⬛⬛⬛⬛⬛⬛⬛⬛⬛⬛

CHERRY CRANBERRY CHUTNEY

(Pictured below)

Joann Ciboch, St. Joseph, Michigan

I found this recipe in a cookbook compiled by a friend's quilting group. Try it with chicken—but don't stop there. It's good with a variety of meats, such as turkey, ham, pork and venison, too.

- 1 cup dried cherries
- 1/2 cup fresh or frozen cranberries
- 1/2 cup raisins
- 1/4 cup sugar
- 1/4 cup cider vinegar
- 1/4 cup unsweetened apple juice
- 1/4 cup chopped celery
- 1-1/2 teaspoons grated lemon peel
- 1/4 to 3/4 teaspoon crushed red pepper flakes
- 1/2 cup chopped walnuts, toasted

In a small saucepan, combine the first nine ingredients. Bring to a boil. Reduce the heat to medium; cover and cook for 15-20 minutes or until celery is tender, stirring occasionally.

Remove from the heat; stir in walnuts. Serve warm or at room temperature. Refrigerate the leftovers. **Yield:** 2 cups.

Cut the squash in half; discard seeds. Place the cut side down in a microwave-safe dish; add 1/2 in. of water. Microwave, uncovered, on high for 10-12 minutes or until almost tender.

Meanwhile, in a small bowl, combine butter, brown sugar, chili powder, cilantro, salt, pepper and cinnamon; set aside. When squash is cool enough to handle, peel and discard rind. Cut pulp into 1/2-in. pieces.

In a large skillet, saute peppers and onion in oil until tender. Add tomatoes and squash; heat through. Transfer to a large bowl; add butter mixture and toss to coat. **Yield:** 9 servings.

Editor's Note: This recipe was tested with Land O'Lakes light stick butter.

GRANDMA'S SCALLOPED CORN

Connie Hoffa, Okatie, South Carolina

This colorful, comforting dish is near and dear to my heart. Even today, it's a favorite with our grown children. It has all the goodness of a down-home recipe, but you'd be surprised at how easy it is to prepare. Plus, cleanup is a breeze.

   1 celery rib, chopped
1/2 small onion, chopped
   2 tablespoons butter
   1 can (14-3/4 ounces) cream-style corn
   1 cup milk
   1 cup crushed saltines (about 20 crackers)
2/3 cup cubed process cheese (Velveeta)
   2 eggs, lightly beaten
   1 teaspoon salt
1/4 teaspoon paprika

In a small skillet, saute the celery and onion in butter until tender. Transfer to a large bowl; cool to room temperature. Stir in the corn, milk, saltines, cheese, eggs and salt.

Transfer to a greased 1-1/2-qt. baking dish. Sprinkle with the paprika. Cover and bake at 350° for 45-55 minutes or until golden brown. **Yield:** 6 servings.

RAINBOW VEGETABLE SKILLET
(Pictured above)

Jennifer Schmidt, Dickens, Texas

Even my kids eat their vegetables when I serve this nicely spiced skillet. It's attractive and absolutely scrumptious. Sometimes, I turn it into a main dish by stirring in cubes of cooked chicken.

   1 medium butternut squash (about 2 pounds)
1/4 cup reduced-fat butter, melted
   2 tablespoons brown sugar
   1 tablespoon chili powder
   1 tablespoon minced fresh cilantro
   1 teaspoon salt
1/2 teaspoon pepper
1/4 teaspoon ground cinnamon
   1 medium green pepper, cut into 1-inch pieces
   1 medium sweet yellow pepper, cut into 1-inch pieces
   1 medium red onion, cut into wedges
   1 tablespoon olive oil
   2 cups grape tomatoes

TRANSPORTING A CASSEROLE

To easily transport a hot dish when carrying it to a potluck or get-together, place the dish inside a clear plastic oven bag. The bag traps any spills, doesn't melt and people can see what's inside. It's so easy to slide the dish in and seal it with a twist tie.

Side Dishes & Condiments

ARTICHOKES WITH TARRAGON BUTTER

(Pictured above)

Marie Hattrup, The Dalles, Oregon

Artichokes are fun to prepare and to eat as an appetizer or side dish. Serve each person a small bowl of herby butter to dip the leaves in.

- 2 medium artichokes
- 4 teaspoons lemon juice, *divided*
- 1/4 cup butter, melted
- 1/4 teaspoon dill weed
- 1/4 teaspoon dried oregano
- 1/4 teaspoon dried tarragon

Using a sharp knife, level the bottom of each artichoke and cut 1 in. from the top. Using kitchen scissors, snip off tips of outer leaves. Brush cut edges with 1 teaspoon lemon juice.

Place artichokes in a deep 8-in. microwave-safe dish; add 1 in. of water. Cover and microwave on high for 10-12 minutes or until leaves near the center pull out easily. Let stand for 5 minutes.

Meanwhile, in a small bowl, combine butter, dill, oregano, tarragon and remaining lemon juice. Serve with artichokes. **Yield:** 2 servings.

HASH BROWN BROCCOLI BAKE

(Pictured at right)

Jeanette Volker, Walton, Nebraska

Here's a perfect dish for a potluck or holiday buffet. It goes well with fish, poultry, pork or beef. Cheddar cheese can be substituted for Swiss. Often, I double the recipe to serve a crowd.

- 4 tablespoons butter, *divided*
- 2 tablespoons all-purpose flour
- 1 teaspoon salt
- 1/8 teaspoon ground nutmeg
- 1/8 teaspoon pepper
- 2 cups milk
- 1 package (8 ounces) cream cheese, cubed
- 2 cups (8 ounces) shredded Swiss cheese
- 6 cups frozen shredded hash brown potatoes, thawed
- 1 package (16 ounces) frozen chopped broccoli, thawed
- 1/2 cup dry bread crumbs

In a large saucepan, melt 2 tablespoons butter. Stir in the flour, salt, nutmeg and pepper until smooth; gradually add milk. Bring to a boil; cook and stir for 2 minutes or until thickened. Remove from the heat. Add cheeses; stir until melted. Stir in the potatoes.

Spoon half of the potato mixture into a greased 2-qt. baking dish. Top with the broccoli and the remaining potato mixture. Cover and bake at 350° for 35 minutes.

Melt the remaining butter; toss with bread crumbs. Sprinkle over casserole. Bake, uncovered, for 15-20 minutes or until heated through and topping is golden. **Yield:** 12-14 servings.

APRICOT SWEET POTATO BAKE

(Pictured below)

Jessie Sarrazin, Livingston, Montana

I fancy up convenient canned sweet potatoes and apricots with brown sugar, cinnamon and raisins. This speedy side dish is delicious for holiday dinners.

        2 cans (15 ounces *each*) cut sweet
          potatoes
        1 can (15-1/4 ounces) apricot halves
        3 tablespoons brown sugar
        1 tablespoon cornstarch
    1/4 teaspoon salt
    1/8 teaspoon ground cinnamon
        3 tablespoons dry sherry *or* chicken broth
    1/3 cup raisins
    1/8 teaspoon grated orange peel

Drain sweet potatoes and apricots, reserving 1/2 cup juice from each; set aside. Cut apricots in half. Place sweet potatoes and apricots in a greased shallow 1-qt. baking dish; set aside.

In a small saucepan, combine brown sugar, cornstarch, salt and cinnamon; stir in reserved juices until smooth. Bring to a boil, stirring constantly. Cook and stir for 2 minutes or until thickened. Remove from the heat; stir in the sherry, raisins and orange peel.

Pour over the sweet potato mixture. Bake, uncovered, at 375° for 12-15 minutes or until bubbly. **Yield:** 6 servings.

STEAMED VEGGIE BUNDLES

(Pictured above)

Terri Mule, Angola, New York

In late summer, when we have an abundance of garden produce, we enjoy this medley of fresh veggies. Usually, we pop the packets on the grill, alongside our main dish meat, fish or poultry.

        1 medium yellow summer squash, halved
          and cut into 3/4-inch slices
        1 medium zucchini, cut into 3/4-inch
          slices
        6 large fresh mushrooms, quartered
        2 large tomatoes, cut into wedges
        1 medium sweet red pepper, julienned
        1 medium green pepper, julienned
    1/2 cup fresh baby carrots, quartered
          lengthwise
    1/4 cup prepared ranch salad dressing
    1/4 cup prepared Italian salad dressing

Divide vegetables between two pieces of double thickness heavy-duty foil (about 18 in. square). Fold foil around vegetables and seal tightly. Grill, covered, over medium heat for 10-13 minutes on each side or until vegetables are tender.

Open foil carefully to allow steam to escape. With a slotted spoon, remove the vegetables to a serving dish. Combine the salad dressings; drizzle over vegetables and toss to coat. **Yield:** 6 servings.

Side Dishes & Condiments

COMFORTING CARROT CASSEROLE

Caroline Hoyt, Scranton, Iowa

Creamy cheese and crunchy chips add unusual taste to this rich, easy-to-prepare dish.

- 4 cups sliced fresh carrots
- 1 cup cubed process cheese (Velveeta)
- 2 tablespoons dried minced onion
- 1/4 cup butter, melted
- 1 cup crushed potato chips

Place 1 in. of water in a large saucepan; add carrots. Bring to a boil. Reduce heat; cover and simmer for 7-9 minutes or until crisp-tender. Drain.

Place carrots in a greased shallow 2-qt. baking dish. Top with the cheese and onion. Drizzle with butter; sprinkle with potato chips.

Cover and bake at 350° for 20-25 minutes or until bubbly. **Yield:** 8 servings.

SALSA BEAN DIP

(Pictured below)

Beverly Smith, Ferndale, Washington

Here's an easy dip perfect for your nutrition-conscious guests. The pineapple in the salsa makes for a nice, smooth flavor profile. I serve this with low-fat chips or fresh veggies.

- 1/2 cup pineapple salsa
- 1 tablespoon lemon juice
- 1 can (15 ounces) garbanzo beans *or* chickpeas, rinsed and drained
- 1/4 cup minced fresh parsley
- 1/4 teaspoon pepper

Tortilla chips

In a food processor, combine the salsa, lemon juice, beans, parsley and pepper; cover and process until smooth. Transfer to a serving dish. Serve with the tortilla chips. Refrigerate the leftovers. **Yield:** 1-1/2 cups.

SWEET POTATO BANANA BAKE

(Pictured above)

Susan McCartney, Onalaska, Wisconsin

This yummy casserole makes what's good for you taste good, too. Pairing bananas with sweet potatoes unites two power foods into a change-of-pace side dish. Try it with roasted poultry.

- 2 cups mashed sweet potatoes
- 1 cup mashed ripe bananas (2 to 3 medium)
- 1/2 cup reduced-fat sour cream
- 1 egg, lightly beaten
- 3/4 teaspoon curry powder
- 1/2 teaspoon salt

In a large bowl, combine all ingredients until smooth. Transfer to a 1-qt. baking dish coated with cooking spray.

Cover and bake at 350° for 30-35 minutes or until a thermometer inserted near the center reads 160°. **Yield:** 6 servings.

3 medium potatoes, peeled
Oil for deep-fat frying
1/2 cup grated Parmesan cheese

Cut the potatoes into very thin slices; soak in cold water for 30 minutes. Drain; pat dry with paper towels.

In an electric skillet or deep-fat fryer, heat oil to 375°. Fry potatoes in batches for 3-4 minutes or until golden brown, stirring frequently. Remove with a slotted spoon; drain on paper towels. Sprinkle with cheese. Serve warm. **Yield:** 4 servings.

▬▬▬▬▬▬▬▬▬

BACON POTATO BAKE
(Pictured below)

Helen Haro, Yucaipa, California

This cheesy potato casserole is always popular. It's a nice change from mashed potatoes, and with a bread crumb and crumbled bacon topping, it looks as good as it tastes.

    8 cups thinly sliced peeled red potatoes
    2 tablespoons all-purpose flour
    2 eggs, lightly beaten
    1 cup (8 ounces) sour cream
    2 tablespoons butter, melted, *divided*
1-1/2 teaspoons salt
1-1/2 cups (6 ounces) shredded Monterey
      Jack cheese
  1/4 cup dry bread crumbs
    8 bacon strips, cooked and crumbled

▬▬▬▬▬▬▬▬▬

ZIPPY CRANBERRY MUSTARD
(Pictured above)

Margaret McCarthy, Hiles, Wisconsin

Whether you enjoy this mustard with poultry, beef or pork, its zesty taste will become your favorite flavor enhancer. A little bit packs a punch.

    2 cups chopped fresh *or* frozen
      cranberries
1-1/2 cups sugar
    1 cup ground mustard
    1 cup cider vinegar
  1/4 cup packed brown sugar
    2 tablespoons unsweetened apple juice
    3 eggs

In a large saucepan, whisk all ingredients. Cook and stir over low heat until mixture is thickened and reaches 160°. Pour into small jars. Cool slightly. Cover and refrigerate for up to 3 weeks. **Yield:** 3-1/3 cups.

▬▬▬▬▬▬▬▬▬

PARMESAN POTATO CHIPS

Charlie Quarry, Valparaiso, Indiana

I created this recipe to make the most of my love for freshly grated Parmesan cheese. When I serve my "special fries" with burgers or ribs, people usually can't stop eating them.

Side Dishes & Condiments

Place the potatoes in a Dutch oven; cover with water. Bring to a boil. Reduce the heat; cover and simmer for 10-15 minutes or until tender. Drain; cool for 10 minutes.

In a small bowl, combine the flour, eggs, sour cream, 1 tablespoon butter and salt. Spoon over potatoes and toss to coat. Place half of the potato mixture in a greased 2-qt. baking dish; top with half of the cheese. Repeat layers.

Toss bread crumbs with remaining butter; sprinkle over the top. Bake, uncovered, at 350° for 1 hour or until a thermometer reads 160° and potatoes are tender. Sprinkle with bacon. **Yield:** 12 servings.

ONION TOPPING FOR SAUSAGES
(Pictured above)

Betty Claycomb, Alverton, Pennsylvania

Here's a great onion recipe I've been making for many years. It's a hit served over hot dogs or any kind of sausage. My mouth is watering just thinking about it!

      2 cups thinly sliced onions
      1 tablespoon butter
      1 tablespoon canola oil
  4-1/2 teaspoons ketchup
  1-1/2 teaspoons sugar
      1 teaspoon white vinegar
    1/2 teaspoon salt
    1/4 teaspoon ground turmeric

In a large skillet over medium heat, cook the onions in butter and oil until tender. Stir in the remaining ingredients. Cook until liquid is absorbed, stirring occasionally. Serve warm. **Yield:** 2/3 cup.

EASY REFRIGERATOR PICKLES
(Pictured below)

Catherine Seibold, Elma, New York

If you don't have nine days to spend on pickling your cucumbers, or just want a smaller batch, try this incredibly simple recipe.

      6 cups thinly sliced cucumbers
      2 cups thinly sliced onions
  1-1/2 cups sugar
  1-1/2 cups cider vinegar
    1/2 teaspoon salt
    1/2 teaspoon mustard seed
    1/2 teaspoon celery seed
    1/2 teaspoon ground turmeric
    1/2 teaspoon ground cloves

Place cucumbers and onions in a large bowl; set aside. Combine remaining ingredients in a saucepan; bring to a boil. Cook and stir just until the sugar is dissolved. Pour over the cucumber mixture; cool. Cover tightly and refrigerate for at least 24 hours before serving. **Yield:** 6 cups.

PEAR-ADISE BUTTER
(Pictured below)

Kristina Pontier, Hillsboro, Oregon

Vanilla and rosemary accent this thick, smooth butter that positively shouts "pears" throughout.

>   4 cups pear juice
>   4 pounds pears, peeled and cut into
>   1-inch pieces
> 1/4 teaspoon salt
>   1 vanilla bean (3 inches), split in half
>   lengthwise
>   3 fresh rosemary sprigs (4 inches)
>   1 teaspoon white balsamic vinegar

In a large saucepan, bring pear juice to a boil; cook for 30 minutes or until reduced to 1 cup. Stir in pears and salt; return to a boil. Reduce the heat; cover and cook for 15-20 minutes or until pears are tender. Cool slightly.

Transfer pear mixture to a food processor; cover and process until smooth. Return to the pan; add the vanilla bean. Bring to a boil over medium heat, stirring constantly. Reduce heat; simmer, uncovered, for 65-75 minutes or until thickened, stirring occasionally.

Remove from the heat. Discard vanilla bean. Stir in rosemary and vinegar; cover and let stand for 30 minutes.

Discard rosemary. Cool to room temperature. Cover and refrigerate for at least 4 hours before serving. **Yield:** 2 cups.

VEGGIE BEAN CASSEROLE
(Pictured above)

LaRue Ritchie, Bellevue, Alberta

I serve this as a meatless main dish, but it also makes a nice side dish. It freezes and reheats well, so I'll sometimes double the recipe. It has a colorful mix of carrots, corn, beans and tomatoes.

>   2 medium carrots, diced
>   2 celery ribs, chopped
>   1 large onion, chopped
>   1 medium green pepper, chopped
>   2 tablespoons canola oil
>   3 garlic cloves, minced
>   2 tablespoons chili powder
> 1/2 teaspoon ground cumin
>   1 can (28 ounces) diced tomatoes,
>   undrained
>   2 cups frozen corn
>   1 can (16 ounces) kidney beans, rinsed
>   and drained
>   1 can (15 ounces) garbanzo beans *or*
>   chickpeas, rinsed and drained
>   1 can (15 ounces) tomato sauce
>   2 tablespoons picante sauce

In a large Dutch oven, saute the carrots, celery, onion, green pepper in oil for 5 minutes. Add the garlic, chili powder and cumin; cook 1 minute longer. Stir in the remaining ingredients; bring to a boil.

Cover and bake at 350° for 45-50 minutes or until thickened and the vegetables are tender. **Yield:** 8 servings.

BROCCOLI RICE CASSEROLE
(Pictured below)

Jennifer Fuller, Ballston Spa, New York

When I was little, serving this dish was the only way my mother could get me to eat broccoli. It is an excellent recipe to serve anytime, and is especially good with poultry.

1-1/2 cups water
1/2 cup butter, cubed
1 tablespoon dried minced onion
2 cups uncooked instant rice
1 package (16 ounces) frozen chopped broccoli, thawed
1 can (10-3/4 ounces) condensed cream of mushroom soup, undiluted
1 jar (8 ounces) process cheese sauce

In a large saucepan, bring the water, butter and onion to a boil. Stir in rice. Remove from the heat; cover and let stand for 5 minutes or until the water is absorbed.

Stir in the broccoli, soup and cheese sauce. Transfer to a greased 2-qt. baking dish. Bake, uncovered, at 350° for 30-35 minutes or until bubbly. **Yield:** 8 servings.

BLUE CHEESE ONIONS
(Pictured above)

Norma Reynolds, York, Pennsylvania

When the tangy cheese softens and melds with baked onions and butter, you have a delicious side dish fit for company. It's wonderful, straight from the oven, served with any meat.

1-1/2 cups (6 ounces) crumbled blue cheese
2 tablespoons Worcestershire sauce
1/2 teaspoon dill weed
1/4 teaspoon pepper
2 large onions, thinly sliced
6 tablespoons butter, melted

In a food processor, combine the blue cheese, Worcestershire sauce, dill and pepper; cover and process until blended.

Place the onions in an ungreased 13-in. x 9-in. baking dish. Drizzle with the butter; top with tablespoonfuls of blue cheese mixture.

Bake, uncovered, at 425° for 20-25 minutes or until the onions are golden brown. Serve immediately. **Yield:** 2 cups.

MELTED BUTTER

When melted butter is called for in a recipe, the butter is measured first, then melted. The convenient markings on the wrappers of the butter make it easy to slice off the amount you need before you melt it.

A BASKETFUL *of goodness is what you'll find with the home-baked recipes in this chapter. Fill your home with the enticing aroma of fresh-from-the-oven biscuits, muffins, breads, sweet rolls and more!*

BAKE UP SMILES. Cherry Yeast Coffee Cake (p. 85).

Breads, Rolls & More

▗▖▘▝▗▖▘▝▗▖▘▝▗▖▘

CHERRY YEAST COFFEE CAKE
(Pictured at left)

Ginnie Patterson, Taft, Tennessee

My mother taught me how to bake, and this delightful recipe is from her. Whoever tries it says it's the best coffee cake ever invented! It requires no kneading, and you can tint the icing any color you want.

2-1/2 to 3 cups all-purpose flour
  1/4 cup sugar
    1 package (1/4 ounce) active dry yeast
    1 teaspoon salt
  1/2 cup water
  1/2 cup 2% milk
  1/2 cup butter, cubed
    2 eggs
    1 can (21 ounces) cherry pie filling
GLAZE:
  1/2 cup confectioners' sugar
  1/4 teaspoon almond extract
    3 to 4 teaspoons 2% milk

In a large bowl, combine 1-1/2 cups flour, sugar, yeast and salt. In a small saucepan, heat the water, milk and butter to 120°-130°. Add to the dry ingredients; beat just until moistened. Beat in the eggs until smooth. Stir in enough remaining flour to form a soft dough (dough will be sticky). Cover and let rise in a warm place until doubled, about 40 minutes.

Stir dough down and spoon two-thirds into a greased 13-in. x 9-in. baking pan. Top with pie filling. Drop remaining dough by tablespoonfuls over pie filling. Cover and let rise in a warm place until doubled, about 30 minutes.

Bake at 350° for 35-40 minutes or until golden brown. Place pan on a wire rack. Combine the confectioners' sugar, extract and enough milk to achieve a drizzling consistency; drizzle over warm coffee cake. **Yield:** 12 servings.

QUICK GLAZE

Place store-bought vanilla frosting from its can in a microwave-safe cup; microwave, stirring frequently, until it's the right consistency.

▗▖▘▝▗▖▘▝▗▖▘▝▗▖▘

FROSTED CINNAMON ROLLS

Shenai Fisher, Topeka, Kansas

This roll recipe, from my husband's family, is one I always prepare for our church conferences. Serve them with scrambled eggs, and you have a filling breakfast. As a variation, you can replace the cinnamon filling with a mixture of raisins and pecans.

    1 package (1/4 ounce) active dry yeast
    1 cup warm milk (110° to 115°)
  1/2 cup sugar
  1/3 cup butter, melted
    2 eggs
    1 teaspoon salt
    4 to 4-1/2 cups all-purpose flour
FILLING:
  1/4 cup butter, melted
  3/4 cup packed brown sugar
    2 tablespoons ground cinnamon
FROSTING:
  1/2 cup butter, softened
1-1/2 cups confectioners' sugar
  1/4 cup cream cheese, softened
  1/2 teaspoon vanilla extract
  1/8 teaspoon salt

In a large bowl, dissolve yeast in warm milk. Add the sugar, butter, eggs, salt and 2 cups flour; beat until smooth. Stir in enough remaining flour to form a soft dough (dough will be sticky).

Turn onto a floured surface; knead until smooth and elastic, about 6-8 minutes. Place in a greased bowl, turning once to grease top. Cover and let rise in a warm place until doubled, about 1 hour.

Punch the dough down. Turn onto a floured surface; divide in half. Roll each portion into an 11-in. x 8-in. rectangle; brush with the butter. Combine brown sugar and cinnamon; sprinkle over the dough to within 1/2 in. of edges. Roll up jelly-roll style, starting from a long side; pinch seam to seal.

Cut each into eight slices. Place cut side down in two greased 13-in. x 9-in. baking pans. Cover and let rise until nearly doubled, about 1 hour.

Bake at 350° for 20-25 minutes or until golden brown. Cool in pans on wire racks. In a small bowl, combine frosting ingredients until smooth. Frost rolls. Store in the refrigerator. **Yield:** 16 rolls.

GARLIC HOAGIE ROLLS
(Pictured below)

Patty Ryan, Merrill, Wisconsin

These homemade yeast rolls feature a crunchy, golden crust and a soft texture inside. The garlic and chives add a little pizzazz.

- 1/2 cup water (70° to 80°)
- 1/2 cup warm milk (70° to 80°)
- 1 egg, lightly beaten
- 2 tablespoons sugar
- 1 tablespoon butter, softened
- 1 tablespoon minced chives
- 1/2 teaspoon salt
- 1/2 teaspoon garlic salt
- 3-1/4 cups bread flour
- 3 teaspoons active dry yeast

In bread machine pan, place all the ingredients in order suggested by manufacturer. Select the dough setting (check dough after 5 minutes of mixing; add 1-2 tablespoons of water or flour if needed).

When cycle is completed, turn dough onto a lightly floured surface; divide into nine pieces. Shape each into a 4-1/2-in. x 1-1/2-in. roll. Place 4 in. apart on greased baking sheets.

Cover; let rise in a warm place until doubled, 20-30 minutes. Bake at 375° for 12-15 minutes or until golden brown. Remove from pans to wire racks to cool. **Yield:** 9 rolls.

Editor's Note: We recommend you do not use a bread machine's time-delay feature for this recipe.

SWEET POTATO CORN BREAD

Judy Roland, Mount Holly, North Carolina

This corn bread bakes to a deep golden color with flecks of sweet potato visible. It looks as good as it tastes.

- 2 cups all-purpose flour
- 2 cups cornmeal
- 1/2 cup sugar
- 7 teaspoons baking powder
- 2 teaspoons salt
- 4 eggs, lightly beaten
- 3/4 cup milk
- 1/3 cup canola oil
- 2-2/3 cups mashed cooked sweet potatoes

In a large bowl, combine the first five ingredients. In a small bowl, combine the eggs, milk, oil and sweet potatoes. Stir into the dry ingredients just until moistened. Pour into a greased 13-in. x 9-in. baking pan.

Bake at 425° for 30-35 minutes or until a toothpick inserted near the center comes out clean. Cut into squares. Serve warm. **Yield:** 12-16 servings.

CRANBERRY OAT MUFFINS

Ursula Maurer, Wauwatosa, Wisconsin

Have a healthy appetite for a snack? Try these muffins with the zest of tart cranberries. The streusel topping sweetens them up just a bit, adding a nice balance.

- 1-1/2 cups old-fashioned oats
- 1 cup all-purpose flour
- 1 cup whole wheat flour
- 1/2 cup packed brown sugar
- 1 teaspoon baking soda
- 1 teaspoon baking powder
- 1 teaspoon ground cinnamon
- 1/2 teaspoon salt
- 2 eggs
- 1-1/2 cups (12 ounces) plain yogurt
- 1/2 cup canola oil
- 1/4 cup honey
- 1 teaspoon vanilla extract
- 2 cups fresh *or* frozen cranberries, thawed
- 1/2 cup chopped walnuts *or* pecans, optional

STREUSEL:
- 1/3 cup packed brown sugar
- 1/4 cup all-purpose flour
- 2 teaspoons ground cinnamon
- 2 tablespoons cold butter

In a large bowl, combine first eight ingredients. In a small bowl, whisk the eggs, yogurt, oil, honey

and vanilla. Stir into dry ingredients just until moistened. Fold in cranberries and nuts if desired.

Fill greased or paper-lined muffin cups three-fourths full. For streusel, in a small bowl, combine the brown sugar, flour and cinnamon. Cut in butter until crumbly. Sprinkle over the tops. Bake at 375° for 15-20 minutes or until a toothpick inserted near the center comes out clean. Cool for 5 minutes before removing from pans to wire racks. Serve warm. **Yield:** 2 dozen.

▲▼▲▼▲▼▲▼▲▼▲▼▲▼

BUTTERY CRANBERRY SCONES
(Pictured above)

Joanna Caldwell, Paso Robles, California

Package up the dry ingredients for these yummy scones, add a recipe card and some tea bags, and you'll have a charming, easy-budget gift sure to make anyone smile!

2 cups all-purpose flour
1/4 cup sugar
2 teaspoons baking powder
1/2 teaspoon baking soda
1/2 teaspoon salt
1/2 cup cold butter, cubed
3/4 cup buttermilk
1/2 cup white baking chips
1/2 cup dried cranberries

In a large bowl, combine the flour, sugar, baking powder, baking soda and salt. Cut in the butter until mixture resembles coarse crumbs. Stir in the buttermilk just until moistened. Turn onto a floured surface. Add the chips and cranberries, kneading about 10 times.

Pat dough into a greased 9-in. springform pan. Cut into eight wedges, but do not separate.

Bake at 400° for 15-20 minutes or until golden brown. Cool for 5 minutes. Remove sides of pan; cut into wedges. Serve warm. **Yield:** 8 servings.

The Best of Country Cooking 2010

CHOCOLATE CHIP CHERRY BREAD

(Pictured below)

Terri Colgrove, Ashland, Wisconsin

Chips, cherries, bananas, pecans…Mom's quick bread is packed full of goodies. We baked a triple batch for my wedding reception.

> 2 cups all-purpose flour
> 1 cup sugar
> 2-1/2 teaspoons baking powder
> 1/2 teaspoon salt
> 2 eggs
> 1 cup mashed ripe bananas
> 1/2 cup butter, melted
> 1/2 cup 60% cacao bittersweet chocolate baking chips
> 1/4 cup chopped pecans
> 1/4 cup chopped maraschino cherries

In a large bowl, combine the flour, sugar, baking powder and salt. Combine the eggs, bananas and butter; stir into dry ingredients just until moistened. Fold in the chocolate chips, pecans and cherries.

Transfer to a greased 9-in. x 5-in. loaf pan. Bake at 350° for 45-50 minutes or until a toothpick inserted near the center comes out clean. Cool for 10 minutes before removing from pan to a wire rack. **Yield:** 1 loaf.

CHEESE CRESCENTS

(Pictured above)

Rosie Flanagan, Buchanan, Michigan

I've had this delicious crescent roll recipe for more than 20 years. It's a family favorite and a nice addition to any meal. My son won a championship ribbon with these rolls at our county fair.

> 4-1/4 cups all-purpose flour
> 1 cup (4 ounces) finely shredded cheddar cheese
> 2 tablespoons plus 1-1/2 teaspoons sugar
> 1 package (1/4 ounce) active dry yeast
> 1-1/2 teaspoons salt
> 1-1/2 teaspoons Italian seasoning
> 1-1/2 cups milk
> 2 tablespoons butter
> 1 egg yolk
> 1 tablespoon water

In a large bowl, combine 3 cups flour, cheese, sugar, yeast, salt and Italian seasoning. In a small saucepan, heat milk and butter to 120°-130°. Add to dry ingredients; beat until smooth. Stir in enough remaining flour to form a stiff dough.

Turn onto a floured surface; knead until smooth and elastic, about 6-8 minutes. Place in a greased bowl, turning once to grease top. Cover and let rise in a warm place until doubled, about 1 hour.

Punch dough down. Turn onto a lightly floured surface; divide into thirds. Roll each portion into a 12-in. circle; cut each circle into 12 wedges. Roll up wedges from the wide end and place point side down 2 in. apart on greased baking sheets. Curve ends to form a crescent shape. Cover and let rise for 45 minutes.

Beat the egg yolk and water; brush over the crescents. Bake at 375° for 16-18 minutes or until golden brown. Remove from pans to wire racks. **Yield:** 3 dozen.

Onion Swiss Loaf

(Pictured below)

Pat Bremson, Kansas City, Missouri

This is one of our favorite bread recipes. I hope you enjoy it just as much as our family and friends do.

> 1/2 cup butter, cubed
> 1 large sweet or yellow onion, halved and thinly sliced
> 1/2 teaspoon prepared mustard
> 1/4 teaspoon lemon juice
> 1 loaf (1 pound) French bread, halved lengthwise
> 12 slices Swiss cheese

Melt butter in a large skillet over medium heat. Add the onion, mustard and lemon juice; cook and stir for 10-12 minutes or until tender. Remove from the heat.

Brush cut sides of bread with some of the butter from the pan. Spoon onion mixture onto bread bottom; top with cheese. Replace bread top.

Wrap loaf in foil; place on a baking sheet. Bake at 350° for 15 minutes or until cheese is melted. Slice and serve warm. **Yield:** 10-12 servings.

Irish Bread

(Pictured above)

Sadie Rotondo, Rockland, Massachusetts

My friend Mary was born in Ireland and so was her easy-to-make bread recipe. Folks stand in line to get a slice. Serve it with butter, jam and a hot cup of tea any time of day.

> 3 cups all-purpose flour
> 1 cup sugar
> 3 teaspoons baking powder
> 1/4 teaspoon salt
> 1 egg
> 2 cups 2% milk
> 1/2 cup butter, melted
> 1-1/2 cups raisins
> 2 tablespoons caraway seeds, optional

In a large bowl, combine the flour, sugar, baking powder and salt. In a small bowl, whisk the egg, milk and butter. Stir into the dry ingredients just until moistened. Fold in raisins and caraway seeds if desired.

Transfer to a 9-in. square baking pan coated with cooking spray. Bake at 350° for 40-45 minutes or until a toothpick inserted near the center comes out clean. Cool bread on a wire rack. **Yield:** 12 servings.

Down-Home Biscuits

THERE'S NOTHING quite like warm biscuits fresh from the oven. Whether your preference is savory or sweet, you'll be able to satisfy your cravings with these easy-to-follow recipes.

PARKERHOUSE CORNMEAL BISCUITS

(Pictured below)

Katrina Rivera, Pittsfield, Massachusetts

There's just enough cornmeal in these tender little rolls to give them a lovely golden color, a delicate, buttery flavor and a subtle crunch.

1-1/3 cups all-purpose flour
  1/2 cup yellow cornmeal
    2 tablespoons sugar
1-3/4 teaspoons baking powder
1-1/2 teaspoons salt
    1 egg, lightly beaten
  3/4 cup sour cream
Melted butter

In a large bowl, combine the flour, cornmeal, sugar, baking powder and salt. Combine the egg and sour cream; stir into the dry ingredients just until moistened.

Turn onto a lightly floured surface; knead 6-8 times. Roll out to 1/2-in. thickness; cut with a floured 2-1/2-in. biscuit cutter.

Place 1 in. apart on a greased baking sheet. Brush with butter; fold dough over and seal edges with a fork.

Bake at 400° for 12-15 minutes or until golden brown. Serve warm. **Yield:** 1 dozen.

SMOKY ONION BISCUIT SQUARES

Donna-Marie Ryan, Topsfield, Massachusetts

Whip up a batch of my savory, biscuit-like squares to complement dinner or whenever you need a yummy bit of comfort.

    1 small onion, chopped
    2 tablespoons butter
  1/4 teaspoon sugar
    1 garlic clove, minced
1-1/2 cups biscuit/baking mix
  1/2 cup milk
    1 egg
  1/4 pound smoked mozzarella cheese, shredded, *divided*
    1 teaspoon salt-free Southwest chipotle seasoning blend

In a small skillet, cook the onion in butter over medium heat until tender. Add the sugar; cook 10-15 minutes longer or until golden brown. Add garlic; cook for 1 minute. Cool slightly.

BAKING BISCUITS

For biscuits to bake properly, arrange your oven rack so that the baking sheet is in the center of the oven. Use a hot oven (425°- 450°) and a baking time of 10-12 minutes.

In a large bowl, combine the flour, 2 tablespoons cinnamon-sugar, baking powder, baking soda and salt. Cut in butter until mixture resembles coarse crumbs. Stir in buttermilk and syrup just until moistened. Fold in pecans.

Turn onto a floured surface; knead 8-10 times. Roll out to 1/2-in. thickness; cut with a floured 2-1/2-in. biscuit cutter.

Place 2 in. apart on an ungreased baking sheet. Brush with the milk; sprinkle with the remaining cinnamon-sugar.

Bake at 400° for 12-15 minutes or until golden brown. Serve warm. **Yield:** 1 dozen.

BLUE CHEESE BISCUITS
(Pictured below)

Louise McConnell, Reno, Nevada

This simple addition to prepared biscuits is impressive. I have served them often for luncheons and they disappear fast.

> 2 individually frozen biscuits
> 1 tablespoon butter
> 1 tablespoon crumbled blue cheese
> 2 teaspoons minced fresh parsley

Place biscuits in an ungreased 9-in. round baking pan. In a small microwave-safe dish, combine butter and blue cheese. Microwave, uncovered, on high until butter is melted; spoon mixture over biscuits.

Bake according to package directions. Sprinkle with parsley. **Yield:** 2 servings.

In a small bowl, combine the biscuit mix, milk and egg. Fold in 1/2 cup cheese, seasoning blend and onion mixture. Transfer to an 8-in. square baking dish coated with cooking spray. Sprinkle with remaining cheese.

Bake at 400° for 18-22 minutes or until a toothpick inserted near the center comes out clean. Cut into squares; serve warm. **Yield:** 16 servings.

MAPLE CINNAMON BISCUITS
(Pictured above)

Mary Relyea, Canastota, New York

Pass around a basket of these oven-fresh biscuits for a memorable breakfast or brunch. Full of maple and cinnamon flavors, they're enhanced by a scattering of chopped pecans.

> 2-1/2 cups all-purpose flour
> 3 tablespoons cinnamon-sugar, *divided*
> 3 teaspoons baking powder
> 1/2 teaspoon baking soda
> 1/2 teaspoon salt
> 1/2 cup cold butter, cubed
> 1/2 cup buttermilk
> 1/2 cup maple syrup
> 1/2 cup finely chopped pecans
> 2 tablespoons milk

▚▚▚▚▚▚▚▚▚▚▚

TURTLE BREAD
(Pictured above)

Elizabeth Ingargiola, Galloway, New Jersey

When my son Nicholas' friends visit, they always want to make this yummy, turtle-shaped bread.

2-1/4 to 2-3/4 cups all-purpose flour
  1 tablespoon sugar
  1 package (1/4 ounce) quick-rise yeast
  1 teaspoon salt
1/2 cup water
1/3 cup milk
  1 tablespoon butter
  2 eggs
  2 raisins

In a large bowl, combine 2 cups flour, sugar, yeast and salt. In a small saucepan, heat the water, milk and butter to 120°-130°. Add to dry ingredients; beat just until moistened. Add 1 egg; beat until smooth. Stir in enough remaining flour to form a soft dough.

Turn onto a floured surface; knead until smooth and elastic, about 6-8 minutes. Cover and let rest for 10 minutes. Shape dough into one 2-in. ball, four 1-1/2-in. balls, one 1-in. ball and one large round ball.

For the turtle shell, place the large dough ball in the center of a greased baking sheet. Place the 2-in. ball at the top for head; position 1-1/2-in. balls on either side for feet. Shape the 1-in. ball into a triangle for tail; place on opposite side of large ball from head.

Press all the edges together to seal. Add raisins for eyes. Cover and let rise in a warm place until doubled, about 25 minutes.

Beat the remaining egg; brush over dough. With a sharp knife, make shallow diamond-shaped slashes across top of turtle shell.

Bake at 350° for 35-40 minutes or until golden brown. Remove bread to a wire rack to cool. **Yield:** 1 loaf.

▚▚▚▚▚▚▚▚▚▚▚

SQUASH MUFFINS

Salem Cross Inn, West Brookfield, Massachusetts

This is a great recipe for a delicious muffin. The nutmeg and cinnamon are delicious and add a lot of flavor!

  3 cups all-purpose flour
1-1/2 cups sugar
1-1/2 teaspoons ground cinnamon
  1 teaspoon baking powder
  1 teaspoon ground nutmeg
1/2 teaspoon baking soda
  4 eggs, lightly beaten
1-1/2 cups mashed cooked butternut squash
  1 cup canola oil

In a large bowl, combine flour, sugar, cinnamon, baking powder, nutmeg and baking soda. In another bowl, combine the eggs, squash and oil. Stir into dry ingredients just until moistened.

Fill greased or paper-lined muffin cups two-thirds full. Bake at 350° for 25-30 minutes or until a toothpick inserted near the center comes out clean. Cool for 5 minutes before removing from the pans to wire racks. Serve warm. **Yield:** 1-1/2 dozen.

▚▚▚▚▚▚▚▚▚▚▚

MOIST BANANA BREAD
(Pictured at right)

Emily Gedenberg, Battle Ground, Washington

I found this recipe in a family cookbook, and it's been a favorite ever since. Everyone seems to like it, even those who don't normally care for banana bread.

2-1/2 cups all-purpose flour
1-1/4 cups sugar
  2 packages (3.4 ounces *each*) instant vanilla pudding mix
1-1/4 teaspoons baking soda
  1 teaspoon salt
  1 teaspoon ground cinnamon
  5 eggs
  2 cups mashed ripe bananas (4 to 5 medium)
  1 cup canola oil
  1 teaspoon vanilla extract
  1 cup chopped nuts, optional

In a large bowl, combine the first six ingredients. In a large bowl, whisk the eggs, bananas, oil and vanilla. Stir into the dry ingredients just until moistened. Stir in nuts if desired.

Transfer to two greased 8-in. x 4-in. loaf pans. Bake at 350° for 55-65 minutes or until a toothpick inserted near the center comes out clean. Cool for 10 minutes before removing from pans to wire racks. **Yield:** 2 loaves (12 slices each).

COFFEE TIME ROLLS

(Pictured below)

Karen Gapp, Walhalla, North Dakota

I received this recipe from my mother and use it whenever I want to make rolls in a hurry. They're similar to the big rolls you get in restaurants.

    2 packages (1/4 ounce *each*) active dry
       yeast
    1/2 cup warm water (110° to 115°)
    2 cups warm milk (110° to 115°)
    1/2 cup sugar
    1/2 cup butter, softened, *divided*
    1 teaspoon salt
    5-3/4 to 6-1/4 cups all-purpose flour
    2/3 cup packed brown sugar
    1 teaspoon ground cinnamon
TOPPING:
    2 cups packed brown sugar
    1/4 cup cornstarch
    1 cup (8 ounces) sour cream
    3 teaspoons vanilla extract

In a large bowl, dissolve yeast in warm water. Add the milk, sugar, 1/4 cup butter, salt and 4 cups flour; beat until smooth. Stir in enough of the remaining flour to form a soft dough.

Turn onto a floured surface; knead until smooth and elastic, about 6-8 minutes. Place in a greased bowl, turning once to grease the top. Cover and let rise in a warm place until doubled, about 1 hour.

Punch dough down. Turn onto a lightly floured surface; divide in half. Roll each portion into a 12-in. x 10-in. rectangle; spread with remaining butter. Combine brown sugar and cinnamon; sprinkle over dough to within 1/2 in. of edges. Roll up jelly-roll style, starting with a long side; pinch seams to seal.

Cut each roll into 12 slices. Place cut side down in two greased 13-in. x 9-in. baking pans. Cover and let rise until doubled, about 30 minutes.

For topping, combine the brown sugar and cornstarch; stir in sour cream and vanilla. Spoon over rolls.

Bake at 400° for 20-25 minutes or until golden brown. Immediately invert onto serving platters. Serve warm. **Yield:** 2 dozen.

NUT ROLL COFFEE CAKE

Patricia Mele, Lower Burrell, Pennsylvania

This walnut-swirled coffee cake is a great taste to wake up to. As a finishing touch, drizzle with glaze or add a dusting of confectioners' sugar.

    2 packages (1/4 ounce *each*) active dry
       yeast
    1/4 cup warm water (110° to 115°)
    1 cup butter, melted
    4 egg yolks
    1/2 cup milk
    2 tablespoons sugar
    1 teaspoon salt
2-1/2 cups all-purpose flour
FILLING:
    4 egg whites
    1 cup plus 6 tablespoons sugar, *divided*
    2 cups ground walnuts
    1/4 cup milk
    2 teaspoons ground cinnamon

In a large bowl, dissolve the yeast in warm water. Add the butter, egg yolks, milk, sugar, salt and flour. Beat until smooth. Cover and refrigerate overnight.

For filling, in a small bowl, beat egg whites on medium speed until soft peaks form. Gradually beat in 1 cup sugar, about 2 tablespoons at a time, on high until sugar is dissolved. In a large bowl, combine the walnuts, milk, cinnamon and remaining sugar; fold in egg whites.

Divide dough in half. Roll each portion into an 18-in. x 12-in. rectangle. Spread filling evenly over each rectangle to within 1/2 in. of edges. Roll up jelly-roll style, starting with a long side; pinch seam to seal.

Place one filled roll seam side down in a greased 10-in. tube pan. Top with second roll. Bake at 350° for 35-40 minutes or until golden brown. Cool for 10 minutes before removing from pan to a wire rack. **Yield:** 12-16 servings.

AUNT LILLIAN'S CRUMB CAKE
(Pictured above)

Rose Gearheard, Phoenix, Oregon

My Aunt Lillian made her fabulous crumb cake every weekend when we came to visit. She created this recipe back in the '40s. Knowing my father loved it, she shared the recipe with my mother, who passed it on to me. I serve it as a coffee cake for Sunday brunch or for dessert.

    1/2 cup butter, softened
      1 cup sugar
      2 eggs
      1 cup (8 ounces) sour cream
      1 teaspoon vanilla extract
  1-1/2 cups all-purpose flour
      1 teaspoon baking soda
    1/4 teaspoon salt
  TOPPING:
    1/2 cup sugar
    1/4 cup chopped walnuts
      2 tablespoons flaked coconut
      2 teaspoons ground cinnamon

In a large bowl, cream the butter and sugar until light and fluffy. Add eggs, one at a time, beating well after each addition. Beat in sour cream and vanilla. Combine the flour, baking soda and salt; add to the creamed mixture and mix well. Spread half into a greased 9-in. square baking pan.

Combine topping ingredients; sprinkle half over batter. Carefully spread remaining batter on top; sprinkle with remaining topping. Gently swirl topping through batter with a knife.

Bake at 350° for 35-40 minutes or until a toothpick inserted near the center comes out clean. Cool for 15 minutes on a wire rack. Serve warm. **Yield:** 9 servings.

VIRGINIA BOX BREAD
(Pictured below)

Thelma Richardson, La Crosse, Wisconsin

This recipe for "melt in your mouth" rolls was given to me over 40 years ago when we lived in the South. My family has been known to devour them as soon as they come out of the oven! Dividing the dough into rolls in the pan is a time-saver.

        1 package (1/4 ounce) active dry yeast
      2/3 cup warm water (110° to 115°)
        2 eggs, lightly beaten
        5 tablespoons butter, melted and cooled
        2 tablespoons sugar
        1 teaspoon salt
  3-1/4 to 3-3/4 cups all-purpose flour

In a large bowl, dissolve yeast in warm water. Add the eggs, butter, sugar, salt and 2 cups flour; beat until smooth. Add enough remaining flour to form a soft dough.

Turn onto a floured surface; knead until smooth and elastic, about 6-8 minutes. Place in a greased bowl, turning once to grease top. Cover and let rise in a warm place until doubled, about 1-1/2 hours.

Punch the dough down. On a lightly floured surface, roll dough into a 13-in. x 9-in. rectangle. Transfer to a greased 13-in. x 9-in. baking pan. Using a sharp knife, cut dough into 16 squares. Cover and let rise until doubled, about 30 minutes.

Bake at 375° for 20 minutes or until golden brown. To serve, separate into rolls. **Yield:** 16 servings.

GERMAN CHOCOLATE RING
(Pictured below)

Anne Frederick, New Hartford, New York

This recipe is modeled after German Sweet Chocolate Cake, which is my favorite recipe, so it's no wonder I enjoy making and eating this sweet-tasting bread! It can be made ahead, too, and stored in the freezer for convenience.

1-1/4 cups flaked coconut, *divided*
   1 cup (6 ounces) semisweet chocolate
     chips, *divided*
  3/4 cup chopped pecans
    3 eggs
4-1/2 to 5 cups all-purpose flour
  1/2 cup sugar
    1 teaspoon salt
    1 package (1/4 ounce) active dry yeast
    1 cup milk
    5 tablespoons butter, *divided*

In small bowl, combine 1 cup coconut, 3/4 cup chocolate chips, pecans and 1 egg; set aside. In a large bowl, combine 1 cup flour, sugar, salt and yeast. In small saucepan, heat milk and 4 tablespoons butter to 120°-130°; add to flour mixture, beating until smooth. Add remaining eggs and enough remaining flour to form a soft dough.

Turn dough onto a lightly floured surface. Knead until smooth and elastic, about 6-8 minutes. Place in greased bowl, turning once to grease top. Cover; let rise in warm place until doubled, about 1 hour.

Punch dough down; turn onto lightly floured surface. Roll dough into 18-in. x 10-in. rectangle. Melt remaining butter and brush over dough; spread with reserved chocolate mixture.

Roll up dough jelly-roll style, starting with a long side; pinch seam to seal. Place seam side down on greased baking sheet. Pinch the ends together to form a ring.

With scissors, cut from outside edge to two-thirds of the way toward center of ring at 1-in. intervals. Separate strips slightly; twist to allow filling to show. Cover and let rise until doubled, about 1 hour.

Bake at 350° for 20-25 minutes or until golden brown. Sprinkle with the remaining chocolate chips and let stand for 5 minutes. Spread the melted chips and sprinkle with the remaining coconut. Carefully remove from pan to a wire rack to cool. **Yield:** 20-24 servings.

STREUSEL-TOPPED PLUM MUFFINS
(Pictured at right)

Betty Timmreck, Eau Claire, Michigan

Living on a fruit farm, I had fresh ingredients on hand when I found this muffin recipe. It originally called for cherries, but my husband and I agree it's delicious made with our homegrown plums.

1/2 cup butter, softened
  1 cup sugar
  2 eggs
  1 teaspoon almond extract
1/2 teaspoon vanilla extract
  2 cups all-purpose flour
  2 teaspoons baking powder
1/2 teaspoon salt
1/2 cup heavy whipping cream
1-1/2 cups chopped fresh plums
TOPPING:
  3 tablespoons brown sugar
  2 tablespoons all-purpose flour
  1 teaspoon ground cinnamon
  1 tablespoon cold butter
1/3 cup chopped walnuts
  1 tablespoon coarse sugar

In a large bowl, cream butter and sugar until light and fluffy. Add eggs, one at a time, beating well after each addition. Beat in the extracts. Combine the flour, baking powder and salt; add to creamed mixture alternately with cream. Fold in plums. Fill greased or paper-lined muffin cups three-fourths full.

For topping, in a small bowl, combine the brown sugar, flour and cinnamon; cut in butter until crumbly. Stir in walnuts. Sprinkle over the batter; sprinkle with coarse sugar.

Bake at 350° for 20-25 minutes or until a toothpick inserted near the center comes out clean. Cool for 5 minutes before removing from pans to wire racks. Serve warm. **Yield:** 15 muffins.

SATISFY YOUR *sweet tooth with these scrumptious from-scratch chocolate treats, nut-filled confections, spiced specialties and more. They're so good, you'll want to try them all!*

A LITTLE BITE OF HEAVEN. Caramel Candy Bars (p. 99).

Cookies, Bars & Candies

CARAMEL CANDY BARS

(Pictured at left)

Jeannie Klugh, Lancaster, Pennsylvania

You'll love these delicious, buttery bars. They're so rich that a small portion may be enough to satisfy your sweet tooth—but don't expect many leftovers!

1/2 cup butter, softened
1/2 cup packed brown sugar
1-1/3 cups all-purpose flour
CARAMEL LAYER:
   1 package (14 ounces) caramels
1/3 cup butter, cubed
1/3 cup evaporated milk
1-2/3 cups confectioners' sugar
   1 cup chopped pecans
CHOCOLATE DRIZZLE:
1/4 cup semisweet chocolate chips
   1 teaspoon shortening

In a large bowl, cream butter and brown sugar. Beat in flour until blended. Press into a greased 13-in. x 9-in. baking dish. Bake at 350° for 12-15 minutes or until golden brown.

For caramel layer, in a small saucepan over medium-low heat, melt caramels and butter with milk until smooth, stirring occasionally. Remove from the heat; stir in confectioners' sugar and pecans. Spread over crust.

For drizzle, in a microwave, melt chocolate chips and shortening; stir until smooth. Drizzle over caramel layer. Cover; refrigerate for 2 hours or until firm. Cut into bars. **Yield:** 2 dozen.

STRAWBERRY ALMOND BARS

Shannon Koene, Billerica, Massachusetts

I like these versatile bars because they're made from ingredients I almost always have on hand. Sometimes I substitute apricot or peach preserves for the strawberry.

1-1/4 cups all-purpose flour
1/3 cup packed brown sugar
1/2 cup cold butter, cubed
TOPPING:
3/4 cup strawberry preserves
1/4 cup butter, softened

1/2 cup all-purpose flour
1/2 cup packed brown sugar
1/2 cup quick-cooking *or* old-fashioned oats
1/2 teaspoon ground cinnamon
1/2 teaspoon almond extract
GLAZE:
1/2 cup confectioners' sugar
1/2 teaspoon almond extract
   1 to 2 teaspoons milk

In a small bowl, combine flour and brown sugar; cut in butter until mixture is crumbly. Press into a greased 9-in. square baking pan. Bake at 350° for 15-20 minutes or until lightly browned.

Spread the preserves over crust. In a small bowl, combine the butter, flour, brown sugar, oats, cinnamon and extract; sprinkle over preserves.

Bake for 20-25 minutes or until golden brown. Combine glaze ingredients; drizzle over warm bars. Cool completely on a wire rack. **Yield:** 2 dozen.

AUNT NELLIE'S PEANUT BUTTER FUDGE

Rose Goble, Winamac, Indiana

My aunt received this treasured family recipe from a former co-worker who brought it in regularly for office potlucks. She wouldn't divulge her secret recipe until after retirement.

   1 teaspoon plus 1/2 cup butter, *divided*
   1 cup chunky peanut butter
   1 package (8 ounces) process cheese (Velveeta), cubed
   1 package (2 pounds) confectioners' sugar
1-1/2 teaspoons vanilla extract

Line a 13-in. x 9-in. pan with foil and grease the foil with 1 teaspoon butter; set aside.

In a large heavy saucepan, combine the peanut butter, cheese and remaining butter. Cook and stir over medium heat until melted. Remove from the heat. Gradually stir in confectioners' sugar and vanilla until blended (mixture will be thick).

Spread into prepared pan. Chill for 2 hours or until firm.

Using foil, lift the fudge out of pan. Discard foil; cut fudge into 1-in. squares. Store in an airtight container in the refrigerator. **Yield:** 3 pounds.

RASPBERRY OAT BARS

Nourse Farms, Mary Nourse
South Deerfield, Massachusetts

These sweet, fruity bars are wonderful with a cup of hot coffee or a glass of cold milk for breakfast, a snack or afternoon break.

      2 tablespoons sugar
      2 tablespoons cornstarch
      1 package (10 ounces) frozen sweetened
        raspberries, thawed
    1/4 teaspoon almond extract
      1 cup quick-cooking oats
    3/4 cup all-purpose flour
    2/3 cup packed brown sugar
    1/4 cup whole wheat flour
    1/4 teaspoon salt
      1 teaspoon vanilla extract
    1/3 cup cold butter

In a small saucepan, combine the sugar and cornstarch. Gradually stir in the raspberries until blended. Bring to a boil; cook, while stirring, for 1-2 minutes or until thickened. Remove from the heat; stir in extract. Cool.

In a large bowl, combine the oats, flour, brown sugar, wheat flour, salt and vanilla. Cut in butter until mixture resembles coarse crumbs. Press 2-1/2 cups crumb mixture into a 9-in. square baking pan coated with cooking spray. Spread with cooled berry mixture. Sprinkle with remaining crumbs.

Bake at 350° for 25-30 minutes or until golden brown. Cool on a wire rack. Cut into bars. **Yield:** 2 dozen.

CHERRY PINEAPPLE BARS

Barbara McCollum, Waynesburg, Pennsylvania

These treats are a holiday favorite in our family. I crush the graham crackers by placing them in a plastic zippered bag and using one of my 78 rolling pins!

1-1/2 cups graham cracker crumbs
    1/2 cup butter, melted
      1 jar (10 ounces) maraschino cherries,
        drained and patted dry
      1 can (8 ounces) crushed pineapple,
        drained and patted dry
1-1/2 cups white baking chips
      1 cup flaked coconut
      1 cup chopped walnuts
      1 can (14 ounces) sweetened condensed
        milk

In a small bowl, combine the cracker crumbs and butter. Press into a greased 13-in. x 9-in. baking dish. Sprinkle with cherries, pineapple, vanilla

VANILLA WALNUT CRESCENTS
(Pictured above)

Betty Lawton, Pennington, New Jersey

Friends look forward to receiving a gift of these tasty crescents. They're my all-time favorite cookies. The pastry is tender and flaky, and the vanilla flavor comes through beautifully.

      2 cups all-purpose flour
    1/8 teaspoon salt
      1 cup cold butter, cubed
      1 egg, *separated*
    2/3 cup sour cream
    1/2 teaspoon vanilla extract
    2/3 cup finely chopped walnuts
    2/3 cup sugar
      1 teaspoon ground cinnamon

In a large bowl, combine the flour and salt; cut in butter until mixture resembles coarse crumbs. In a small bowl, whisk the egg yolk, sour cream and vanilla; add to crumb mixture and mix well. Cover and refrigerate for 4 hours or overnight.

Divide the dough into thirds. On a lightly floured surface, roll each portion into a 10-in. circle. Combine walnuts, sugar and cinnamon; sprinkle 1/4 cup over each circle. Cut each circle into 12 wedges.

Roll up each wedge from the wide end and place point side down 1 in. apart on greased baking sheets. Curve ends to form crescents. Whisk egg white until foamy; brush over crescents. Sprinkle with remaining nut mixture.

Bake at 350° for 18-20 minutes or until lightly browned. Remove to wire racks to cool. Store in an airtight container. **Yield:** 3 dozen.

chips, coconut and walnuts; drizzle with the condensed milk.

Bake at 350° for 25 minutes or until the edges are golden brown. Cool on a wire rack. Cover and refrigerate overnight. Cut into the bars. **Yield:** 2 dozen.

LEMONY BONBON COOKIES
(Pictured above)

Linda Nicholson, Palatka, Florida

These cookies were first made famous by my great grandmother. When people try one, they ask for the recipe. I make them for the holidays and other special events. The pecan on the bottom is a crunchy twist.

      1/2 cup butter, softened
      1/3 cup confectioners' sugar
        1 tablespoon lemon juice
      3/4 cup all-purpose flour
      1/3 cup cornstarch
       24 pecan halves
ICING:
    1-1/4 cups confectioners' sugar
    1-1/2 teaspoons butter, softened
        3 to 4 teaspoons lemon juice

In a small bowl, cream butter and confectioners' sugar until light and fluffy. Beat in lemon juice. Combine flour and cornstarch; gradually add to creamed mixture and mix well. Cover and chill for 2 hours.

Shape dough into 1-in. balls. Place pecan halves on two ungreased baking sheets. Top each pecan half with a ball of dough; flatten with the bottom of a small glass.

Bake at 350° for 14-16 minutes or until set. Remove to wire racks; cool completely.

For icing, combine the confectioners' sugar, butter and enough lemon juice to achieve a spreading consistency. Spread over cookies. Let stand until set. **Yield:** 2 dozen.

PASTEL TEA COOKIES
(Pictured below)

Lori Henry, Elkhart, Indiana

These glazed sugar cookies are perfect for nibbling between sips at a tea party, graduation or shower.

        1 cup butter, softened
      2/3 cup sugar
        1 egg
        1 teaspoon vanilla extract
    2-1/2 cups all-purpose flour
      1/2 teaspoon salt
    1-1/4 cups confectioners' sugar
        2 teaspoons meringue powder
        5 teaspoons water
Pastel food coloring

In a large bowl, cream the butter and sugar until light and fluffy. Beat in the egg and vanilla. Combine flour and salt; gradually add to the creamed mixture. Cover and refrigerate for 1-2 hours until dough is easy to handle.

On a lightly floured surface, roll out the dough to 1/8-in. thickness. Cut with floured 2-1/2-in. butterfly or flower cookie cutters. Place 1 in. apart on ungreased baking sheets.

Bake at 350° for 8-10 minutes or until edges are lightly browned. Remove to wire racks to cool.

For the glaze, in a small bowl, combine the confectioners' sugar and meringue powder; stir in water until smooth. Divide among small bowls; tint pastel colors. Spread over cookies; let stand until set. **Yield:** 4 dozen.

Editor's Note: Meringue powder is available from Wilton Industries. Call 1-800/794-5866 or visit *www.wilton.com*.

◆◆◆◆◆◆◆◆◆◆◆◆◆◆

SECRET TREAT MOLASSES COOKIES

(Pictured above)

Ruby Neese, Liberty, North Carolina

This recipe has been passed down in my family for generations. I've made these cookies for years, but like my mother, I only make them for special occasions. They're fun to decorate and delicious to eat with a surprise flavor inside.

  1/2 cup butter, softened
  1/2 cup packed brown sugar
    1 egg
  1/2 cup molasses
2-1/2 cups all-purpose flour
  3/4 teaspoon baking soda
  1/2 teaspoon salt
  1/2 teaspoon ground cinnamon
  1/2 teaspoon ground ginger
  1/2 cup strawberry preserves
GLAZE:
1-2/3 cups confectioners' sugar
    2 tablespoons water
  1/4 teaspoon vanilla extract

In a large bowl, cream the butter and brown sugar until light and fluffy. Beat in egg and molasses. Combine the flour, baking soda, salt, cinnamon and ginger; gradually add to creamed mixture and mix well. (The dough will be very stiff.) Cover and refrigerate for 1-2 hours or until easy to handle.

On a lightly floured surface, roll the dough to 1/8-in. thickness; cut into 2-1/4-in. to 2-1/2-in. circles. Place 1/2 teaspoon preserves on half of the circles; top with remaining circles. Pinch edges together to seal. Place on greased baking sheets.

Bake at 350° for 10 minutes or until lightly browned. Cool on wire racks. Combine the glaze ingredients and frost cooled cookies. **Yield:** about 2 dozen.

◆◆◆◆◆◆◆◆◆◆◆◆◆◆

PEACHY COOKIES

(Pictured below)

Andrea Cuteri, Coraopolis, Pennsylvania

One bite of these pretty pastries and you'll think they came fresh off the tree instead of the cookie plate. I bake them for holidays, weddings and celebrations that call for a peach of a cookie!

    2 eggs
    1 cup sugar
  3/4 cup canola oil
  1/2 cup milk
  1/2 teaspoon vanilla extract
    4 cups all-purpose flour
  3/4 teaspoon baking powder
FILLING:
    1 cup apricot preserves
  1/2 cup finely chopped pecans
    1 package (3 ounces) cream cheese, softened
    2 tablespoons unsweetened instant tea
  3/4 teaspoon ground cinnamon
COATING:
    2 packages (3 ounces *each*) lemon gelatin
    2 packages (3 ounces *each*) orange gelatin
    2 packages (3 ounces *each*) strawberry gelatin
  1/2 cup sugar
Mint leaves and additional apricot preserves

In a large bowl, beat the eggs, sugar, oil, milk and vanilla until blended. Combine flour and baking powder; gradually beat into egg mixture.

Roll into 3/4-in. balls. Place 2 in. apart on ungreased baking sheets; flatten slightly. Bake

at 325° for 13-15 minutes or until firm. Remove to wire racks.

While the cookies are warm, use a sharp knife and small spoon to cut and scoop out about 1/2 teaspoon crumbs from the bottom of each cookie; set crumbs aside (about 1-1/2 cups) for filling. Cool cookies completely.

In a small bowl, combine filling ingredients; stir in reserved crumbs. Spoon into two cookies; spread a thin amount of filling on cookie bottoms and press together to form a peach. Repeat with the remaining cookies and filling.

In a shallow bowl, combine one package each of lemon and orange gelatin powder. Place one package of strawberry gelatin powder in another bowl. Place sugar in a third bowl.

Working with one cookie at a time, spritz the cookie with water. Dip in lemon gelatin mixture, then in strawberry gelatin and then in sugar; spritz with additional water and add more gelatin as needed to create desired peach blush effect. Place on a wire rack to dry for 1 hour.

Repeat with remaining cookies and packages of gelatin. Attach mint leaves to the top of each cookie with additional preserves. Store in the refrigerator. **Yield:** about 3-1/2 dozen.

⬛⬛⬛⬛⬛⬛⬛⬛⬛⬛⬛⬛

PEANUT BUTTER BALLS

Rhonda Williams, Mayville, Michigan

It's a tradition for my sister and me to bring these chocolaty confections to functions and family gatherings.

       2 cups creamy peanut butter
    1/2 cup butter, cubed
       4 cups confectioners' sugar
       3 cups crisp rice cereal
       4 cups (24 ounces) semisweet chocolate
          chips
    1/4 cup shortening

In a small saucepan, combine the peanut butter and butter. Cook and stir over medium-low heat until smooth. Remove from the heat.

In a large bowl, combine confectioners' sugar and cereal. Pour peanut butter mixture over cereal; toss to coat. Roll into 1-in. balls; place on waxed paper-lined baking sheets. Refrigerate until chilled.

In a microwave, melt the chocolate chips and shortening; stir until smooth. Dip the balls in chocolate mixture; allow excess to drip off. Return to baking sheets; refrigerate until set. **Yield:** about 5-1/2 dozen.

Editor's Note: Reduced-fat or generic brands of peanut butter are not recommended for this recipe.

⬛⬛⬛⬛⬛⬛⬛⬛⬛⬛⬛⬛

SALTED PEANUT CHEWS

(Pictured below)

Irene Yoder, Millersburg, Ohio

I took these sweet and salty treats to an evening get-together. They disappeared fast, and soon people were asking for the recipe.

    1-1/2 cups all-purpose flour
      1/2 cup packed brown sugar
      3/4 cup butter, softened, *divided*
        3 cups miniature marshmallows
        2 cups peanut butter chips
      2/3 cup corn syrup
        2 teaspoons vanilla extract
        2 cups crisp rice cereal
        2 cups salted peanuts

In a large bowl, combine the flour, brown sugar and 1/2 cup butter. Press into an ungreased 13-in. x 9-in. baking pan. Bake at 350° for 12-15 minutes or until lightly browned.

Sprinkle with marshmallows and return to the oven for 3-5 minutes or until marshmallows begin to melt; set aside.

In a large saucepan, cook and stir the peanut butter chips, corn syrup, vanilla and remaining butter until smooth. Remove from the heat; stir in the cereal and peanuts. Pour over prepared crust, spreading to cover. Cool on a wire rack before cutting into bars. **Yield:** 2 dozen.

Christmas Cookies

EVERY COOKIE in this special section has won an award because of its exceptional flavor. If you're looking for tasty treats for your next holiday cookie exchange, look no further.

TRIPLE-CHOCOLATE PEPPERMINT TREATS

(Pictured below)

Teresa Ralston, New Albany, Ohio

Santa is sure to stop by your house if you leave these minty chocolate cookies waiting for him. They're quick and easy for the whole family to make together.

> 1 cup butter, softened
> 1 cup packed brown sugar
> 1/2 cup sugar
> 2 eggs
> 2 teaspoons vanilla extract
> 2-1/2 cups all-purpose flour
> 3/4 cup baking cocoa
> 1 teaspoon salt
> 1 teaspoon baking soda
> 1 cup (6 ounces) semisweet chocolate chips
> 1/2 cup 60% cacao bittersweet chocolate baking chips

WHITE CHOCOLATE FROSTING:

> 1/2 cup vanilla *or* white chips
> 4 ounces cream cheese, softened
> 3 cups confectioners' sugar
> 1/3 to 1/2 cup crushed peppermint candies

In a large bowl, cream butter and sugars until light and fluffy. Beat in the eggs and vanilla. Combine the flour, cocoa, salt and baking soda; gradually add to creamed mixture and mix well. Stir in the chocolate chips.

Drop by rounded teaspoonfuls 2 in. apart onto ungreased baking sheets. Bake at 375° for 8-10 minutes or until set. Cool for 2 minutes before removing to wire racks to cool completely.

For frosting, in a microwave, melt vanilla chips at 70% power for 1 minute; stir. Microwave at additional 10- to 20-second intervals, stirring until smooth; cool.

In a small bowl, beat the cream cheese and confectioners' sugar until smooth. Beat in the melted chips. Frost cookies; sprinkle with peppermint candies. **Yield:** about 6-1/2 dozen.

BROWNED-BUTTER SANDWICH SPRITZ

(Pictured above right)

Deirdre Dee Cox, Milwaukee, Wisconsin

A heavenly maple filling makes these scrumptious spritz cookies a little different. You can count on them to turn out buttery and tender.

> 1 cup plus 2 tablespoons butter, cubed
> 1-1/4 cups confectioners' sugar, *divided*
> 1 egg
> 1 egg yolk
> 2 teaspoons vanilla extract
> 2-1/4 cups all-purpose flour
> 1/2 teaspoon salt
> 1/2 cup maple syrup

In a small heavy saucepan, cook and stir the butter over medium heat for 8-10 minutes or until golden brown. Transfer to a small bowl; refrigerate until firm, about 1 hour.

3/4 cup butter, softened
1/2 cup packed brown sugar
2 eggs, *separated*
1-1/4 cups all-purpose flour
1/4 cup baking cocoa
1-1/4 cups finely chopped pecans *or* walnuts
FILLING:
4 ounces white baking chocolate, coarsely chopped
2 tablespoons butter
1/4 cup seedless raspberry jam

In a small bowl, cream butter and brown sugar until light and fluffy. Beat in egg yolks. Combine flour and cocoa; gradually add to creamed mixture and mix well. Cover and refrigerate for 1-2 hours or until easy to handle.

In a shallow bowl, whisk egg whites until foamy. Place nuts in another shallow bowl. Shape dough into 1-in. balls. Dip in egg whites, then roll in nuts.

Using a wooden spoon handle, make an indentation in center of each cookie. Place 1 in. apart on greased baking sheets. Bake at 350° for 8-10 minutes. Remove to wire racks to cool.

For the filling, in a microwave, melt white chocolate and butter at 70% power for 1 minute; stir. Microwave at additional 10- to 20-second intervals, stirring until smooth. Spoon about 1/2 teaspoon into each cookie. Top each with about 1/4 teaspoon jam. Store in an airtight container. **Yield:** about 3 dozen.

Set aside 2 tablespoons browned butter for filling. In a large bowl, beat 1/2 cup confectioners' sugar and the remaining browned butter until smooth. Beat in the egg, yolk and vanilla. Combine flour and salt; gradually add to creamed mixture and mix well.

Using a cookie press fitted with the disk of your choice, press dough 2 in. apart onto parchment paper-lined baking sheets. Bake at 375° for 8-9 minutes or until set (do not brown). Remove to wire racks to cool.

In a small heavy saucepan, bring syrup to a boil. Cool slightly. Whisk in remaining confectioners' sugar until smooth. Beat the reserved browned butter until light and fluffy. Beat in syrup mixture until smooth.

Spread 1 teaspoon of filling over the bottom of half of the cookies. Top with the remaining cookies. **Yield:** about 3 dozen.

WHITE CHOCOLATE RASPBERRY THUMBPRINTS

(Pictured at right)

Agnes Ward, Stratford, Ontario

When I pass around the cookie tray, all eyes land on these fancy thumbprints. The white chocolate filling and dab of jewel-toned jam will satisfy the most discriminating sweet tooth.

CARROT CAKE BARS

(Pictured above)

Agnes Ward, Stratford, Ontario

A friend served these moist, tender cake bars at an outdoor party, and everyone raved about the taste. Often, I'll bake a big panful and freeze some for another day. So good!

       3 eggs
1-1/4 cups canola oil
       2 cups all-purpose flour
       2 cups sugar
       2 teaspoons ground cinnamon
       1 teaspoon baking powder
   1/2 teaspoon baking soda
   1/4 to 1/2 teaspoon salt
       1 jar (6 ounces) carrot baby food
       1 container (3-1/2 ounces) applesauce
          baby food
       1 container (3-1/2 ounces) apricot baby
          food
   1/2 cup chopped walnuts, optional
FROSTING:
       1 package (8 ounces) cream cheese,
          softened
   1/2 cup butter, softened
       1 teaspoon vanilla extract
3-3/4 cups confectioners' sugar

In a large bowl, beat eggs and oil for 2 minutes. Combine flour, sugar, cinnamon, baking powder, baking soda and salt; add to the egg mixture. Add baby foods; mix well. Stir in the walnuts if desired. Transfer to a greased 15-in. x 10-in. x 1-in. baking pan.

Bake at 350° for 20-25 minutes or until a toothpick inserted near the center comes out clean. Cool on a wire rack.

For frosting, in a small bowl, beat cream cheese and butter until light and fluffy. Beat in vanilla. Gradually beat in confectioners' sugar. Frost; cut into bars. Store in the refrigerator. **Yield:** 3 dozen.

TAKE-ALONG BREAKFAST COOKIES

(Pictured below)

Pam Crockett, Huntsville, Utah

Paired with fresh fruit, these wholesome cookies are perfect for an energizing breakfast when you're on the go. Although they're called breakfast cookies, they're delicious any time of day.

   1/2 cup butter, softened
   1/2 cup peanut butter
       1 cup packed brown sugar
       1 egg
       3 tablespoons milk
       1 teaspoon vanilla extract
       1 cup old-fashioned oats
   3/4 cup whole wheat flour
   1/2 cup nonfat dry milk powder
   1/4 cup toasted wheat germ
   1/2 teaspoon salt
   1/4 teaspoon baking soda
   1/4 teaspoon baking powder
       1 cup golden raisins
       3 tablespoons sesame seeds

In a large bowl, cream the butter, peanut butter and brown sugar until light and fluffy. Beat in the egg, milk and vanilla. Combine the oats, flour, milk powder, wheat germ, salt, baking soda and baking powder; gradually add to creamed mixture and mix well. Stir in raisins.

Drop by 1/4 cupfuls 4 in. apart onto a greased baking sheet. Flatten into 3-in. circles. Sprinkle with sesame seeds.

Bake at 375° for 10-12 minutes or until edges are lightly browned. Cool for 5 minutes before removing to a wire rack. **Yield:** 1 dozen.

Chocolate Chip Cheese Bars

(Pictured above)

Teri Lindquist, Gurnee, Illinois

This is my most requested dessert recipe. Everyone loves these yummy bars with their soft cream cheese filling...and they couldn't be easier to prepare.

1 tube (18 ounces) refrigerated chocolate chip cookie dough
1 package (8 ounces) cream cheese, softened
1/2 cup sugar
1 egg

Cut cookie dough in half. For crust, press half of the dough onto the bottom of a greased 8-in. square baking pan.

In a large bowl, beat the cream cheese, sugar and egg until smooth. Spread over crust. Crumble remaining dough over top.

Bake at 350° for 35-40 minutes or until a toothpick inserted near the center comes out clean. Cool on a wire rack. Refrigerate leftovers. **Yield:** 12-16 servings.

Editor's Note: 2 cups of your favorite chocolate chip cookie dough can be substituted for the refrigerated dough.

Double-Drizzle Pecan Cookies

(Pictured at right)

Paula Marchesi, Lenhartsville, Pennsylvania

These chewy, toasted pecan treats are a must with my cookie munchers every holiday. Using caramel and chocolate drizzles makes them doubly delicious and so pretty on the plate.

1/2 cup butter, softened
1-1/2 cups packed brown sugar
1 egg
1 teaspoon vanilla extract
1-1/2 cups all-purpose flour
1-1/2 teaspoons baking powder
1/4 teaspoon salt
1-1/4 cups chopped pecans, toasted

CARAMEL DRIZZLE:

1/2 cup packed brown sugar
1/4 cup heavy whipping cream
1/2 cup confectioners' sugar

CHOCOLATE DRIZZLE:

1 ounce semisweet chocolate
1 tablespoon butter

In a large bowl, cream the butter and brown sugar until light and fluffy. Beat in egg and vanilla. Combine the flour, baking powder and salt; gradually add to creamed mixture and mix well.

Shape dough into 1-in. balls; roll in pecans. Place 2 in. apart on ungreased baking sheets; flatten slightly. Bake at 350° for 8-10 minutes or until lightly browned. Cool for 2 minutes before removing to wire racks to cool completely.

For caramel drizzle, in a small saucepan, bring brown sugar and cream to a boil. Remove from the heat; whisk in confectioners' sugar. Immediately drizzle over cookies.

For chocolate drizzle, in a microwave, melt chocolate and butter; stir until smooth. Drizzle over the cookies. Let stand until set. Store in an airtight container. **Yield:** about 3-1/2 dozen.

In a small bowl, cream the butter, shortening and sugars until light and fluffy. Beat in eggs and extracts. Stir in sour cream. Combine the flour, salt and baking soda; gradually add to creamed mixture and mix well. Fold in coconut.

Drop by tablespoonfuls 2 in. apart onto lightly greased baking sheets. Bake at 375° for 8-10 minutes or until set. Remove to wire racks to cool.

For frosting, in a small heavy saucepan, cook butter over medium heat for 5-7 minutes or until golden brown. Pour into a small bowl; beat in the confectioners' sugar, milk and extracts. Frost cookies; dip in coconut. Let stand until completely dry. Store in an airtight container. **Yield:** about 5-1/2 dozen.

CHOCOLATE-CHERRY CHEESECAKE BARS
(Pictured below)

Darlene Brenden, Salem, Oregon

I've had this recipe longer than I can remember. I like to make it for Valentine's Day and Christmas. The pretty bars also look colorful for a party or shower.

  1 cup all-purpose flour
1/2 cup packed brown sugar
1/3 cup cold butter, cubed
1/2 cup finely chopped walnuts
  1 package (8 ounces) cream cheese, softened
1/2 cup sugar
1/3 cup baking cocoa
  1 egg, lightly beaten
1/4 cup milk
1/2 teaspoon vanilla extract
1/2 cup chopped maraschino cherries
Additional maraschino cherries, halved

COCONUT CLOUDS
(Pictured above)

Donna Scofield, Yakima, Washington

Coconut lovers will have extra reason to celebrate when they taste these cake-like drop cookies. The generous frosting and coconut topping make them a hit at holiday cookie exchanges.

1/4 cup butter, softened
1/4 cup shortening
  1 cup sugar
1/2 cup packed brown sugar
  2 eggs
  1 teaspoon coconut extract
  1 teaspoon vanilla extract
  1 cup (8 ounces) sour cream
2-3/4 cups all-purpose flour
  1 teaspoon salt
1/2 teaspoon baking soda
  1 cup flaked coconut, toasted
FROSTING:
1/3 cup butter, cubed
  3 cups confectioners' sugar
  3 tablespoons evaporated milk
  1 teaspoon coconut extract
  1 teaspoon vanilla extract
  2 cups flaked coconut, toasted

Cookies, Bars & Candies

Place the flour, brown sugar and butter in a food processor; cover and process until fine crumbs form. Stir in walnuts. Set aside 3/4 cup for topping.

Press the remaining crumb mixture onto the bottom of an ungreased 8-in. square baking dish. Bake at 350° for 10 minutes or until set.

Meanwhile, in a small bowl, beat the cream cheese, sugar and cocoa until smooth. Add the egg, milk and vanilla; beat on low speed just until combined. Stir in chopped cherries. Pour over crust; sprinkle with reserved crumb mixture.

Bake for 20-25 minutes or until center is almost set. Cool on a wire rack for 1 hour. Refrigerate for at least 2 hours.

Cut into bars; top each with a cherry half. Store in the refrigerator. **Yield:** 15 bars.

COCONUT BROWNIES

Carol Lipp, Timber Lake, South Dakota

My children and grandchildren are the light of my life. I always try to have homemade cookies or brownies on hand for them when they visit. This recipe is one of their favorites.

- 1 cup butter, softened
- 2 cups sugar
- 4 eggs
- 1 teaspoon vanilla extract
- 1-1/2 cups all-purpose flour
- 1/2 cup plus 2 tablespoons baking cocoa
- 1/2 cup flaked coconut

In a large bowl, cream butter and sugar until light and fluffy. Add eggs, one at a time, beating well after each addition. Beat in vanilla. Combine the flour and cocoa; gradually beat into creamed mixture just until blended. Stir in coconut.

Spread into a greased 13-in. x 9-in. baking pan. Bake at 350° for 22-25 minutes or until a toothpick inserted near the center comes out with moist crumbs (do not overbake). Cool on a wire rack. **Yield:** 1-1/2 dozen.

QUICKLY SHAPING COOKIES

Instead of scooping up cookie dough one teaspoonful at a time, pat the dough into a rectangle on a baking sheet and freeze until almost solid. Remove from the freezer, and slice the dough horizontally and vertically at even intervals, forming a grid. Pick up and roll the individual pieces for baking.

DIPPED CHERRY COOKIES
(Pictured above)

Ruth Anne Dale, Titusville, Pennsylvania

Our seven children and four grandkids voted this festive, flavorful cookie a "keeper." We gave a batch to our mail carrier, in thanks for trudging through so much snow, and she asked for the recipe.

- 2-1/2 cups all-purpose flour
- 3/4 cup sugar, *divided*
- 1 cup cold butter, cubed
- 1/2 cup finely chopped maraschino cherries, drained
- 12 ounces white baking chocolate, finely chopped, *divided*
- 1/2 teaspoon almond extract
- 2 teaspoons shortening
- Coarse sugar and red edible glitter

In a large bowl, combine flour and 1/2 cup sugar; cut in butter until crumbly. Knead in the cherries, 2/3 cup white chocolate and extract until dough forms a ball.

Shape into 3/4-in. balls. Place 2 in. apart on ungreased baking sheets. Flatten slightly with a glass dipped in remaining sugar. Bake at 325° for 10-12 minutes or until edges are lightly browned. Remove to wire racks to cool.

In a microwave, melt the shortening and remaining white chocolate at 70% power for 1 minute and stir. Microwave at additional 10- to 20-second intervals, stirring until smooth.

Dip half of each cookie into the chocolate and allow the excess to drip off. Sprinkle with coarse sugar and edible glitter. Place on waxed paper until set. Store in an airtight container. **Yield:** about 4 dozen.

Editor's Note: Edible glitter is available from Wilton Industries. Call 1-800/794-5866 or visit *www.wilton.com*.

DREAMY SWEETS, from decadent cakes to home-style pies, are here for the taking. You simply won't be disappointed with these fabulous dinner finales.

PICTURE-PERFECT PIE. Butterscotch Peach Pie (p. 111).

Dazzling Desserts

APPLE DUMPLINGS

*College Hill Presbyterian Church Women's
Association, Beaver Falls, Pennsylvania*

*Luscious dumplings are a popular fund-raiser for the
College Hill Presbyterian Church Women's Association. We up our apple order by a bushel each year.*

    8 cups all-purpose flour
    3 tablespoons baking powder
4-1/2 teaspoons salt
1-1/2 pounds butter-flavored shortening
    2 cups milk
  24 medium tart apples, peeled and cored
1-1/2 cups sugar
    1 teaspoon ground cinnamon
  1/2 cup butter, *divided*
SYRUP:
2-1/2 cups packed brown sugar
1-1/2 cups water
    1 cup butter, cubed
    1 teaspoon ground cinnamon

In a large bowl, combine flour, baking powder and
salt; cut in shortening until crumbly. Gradually
add milk, tossing with a fork until dough forms a
ball. Divide into 24 portions. Cover; refrigerate
for at least 1 hour or until easy to handle.

On a well-floured surface, roll each portion of
dough into a 7-in. square. Place an apple on each
square. Combine the sugar and cinnamon; place
1 tablespoonful into the core of each apple. Dot
each with 1 teaspoon butter.

Gently bring up corners of pastry to center;
pinch edges to seal. Place in four greased 13-in. x
9-in. baking dishes. Bake at 350° for 15 minutes.

Meanwhile, in a large saucepan, combine the
syrup ingredients. Bring to a boil; cook and stir
until smooth and blended. Pour over apples.

APPLES FOR BAKING

Firm-fleshed apples are best for baking whole.
Varieties include Empire, Fuji, Golden Delicious, Jonagold, Rome Beauty and Royal Gala.
Select apples that are firm and have a smooth,
unblemished skin that is free from bruises.

Bake 35-40 minutes longer or until apples are
tender and pastry is golden brown. Serve warm.
Yield: 24 servings.

BUTTERSCOTCH PEACH PIE
(Pictured at left)

Barbara Moyer, Tiffin, Ohio

*When peach season arrives, this old-fashioned pie
is sure to be on the table. The recipe has been in our
family for well over 60 years, and I still make it
every summer. Butterscotch buffs love it.*

    2 cups all-purpose flour
    1 teaspoon salt
  3/4 cup shortening
    4 to 5 tablespoons cold water
FILLING:
  3/4 cup packed brown sugar
    2 tablespoons all-purpose flour
  1/3 cup light corn syrup
    3 tablespoons butter, melted
    2 tablespoons lemon juice
  1/4 teaspoon almond extract
    8 medium peaches, peeled and sliced

In a large bowl, combine flour and salt; cut in
shortening until crumbly. Gradually add water,
tossing with a fork until the dough forms a ball.
Cover and refrigerate for 30 minutes or until
easy to handle.

For filling, in a small saucepan, combine brown
sugar and flour. Stir in the corn syrup and butter
until blended. Bring to a boil; cook and stir for
2 minutes or until thickened. Remove from the
heat; stir in lemon juice and extract. Place the
peaches in a large bowl; add syrup mixture and
toss to coat.

Divide the dough in half so one ball is slightly
larger than the other. Roll out the larger ball to fit
a 9-in. pie plate. Transfer pastry to plate; trim
pastry even with edge. Add the filling. Roll out
remaining pastry; make a lattice crust. Trim, seal
and flute edges. Cover edges loosely with foil.

Bake at 375° for 25 minutes. Uncover and bake
20-25 minutes longer or until crust is golden
brown and filling is bubbly. Cool on a wire rack.
Yield: 8 servings.

SPICED PLUM PIE
(Pictured above)
Lucille Mead, Ilion, New York

The subtle tastes of orange and nutmeg bring out the fresh flavor of plums in this comforting pie. Be sure to have a slice while it's still warm with a scoop of vanilla ice cream.

Pastry for double-crust pie (9 inches)
- 4-1/2 cups sliced fresh plums
- 2/3 cup sugar
- 1/4 cup all-purpose flour
- 1 teaspoon ground cinnamon
- 1/4 teaspoon salt
- 1/4 teaspoon ground nutmeg
- 1 egg, lightly beaten
- 1/2 cup orange juice
- 1 teaspoon grated orange peel
- 2 tablespoons butter
Vanilla ice cream, optional

Line a 9-in. pie plate with bottom pastry; trim even with edge. Arrange plums in crust. In a small bowl, combine the sugar, flour, cinnamon, salt and nutmeg. Stir in the egg, orange juice and peel. Pour over plums; dot with butter.

Roll out remaining pastry to fit top of pie; place over filling. Trim, seal and flute edges. Cut slits in pastry.

Bake at 400° for 45-50 minutes or until crust is golden brown and filling is bubbly (cover edges with foil during the last 15 minutes to prevent overbrowning if necessary). Cool on a wire rack for 10 minutes before cutting. Serve warm with ice cream if desired. **Yield:** 8 servings.

COCONUT FUDGE CAKE
(Pictured below)
Johnnie McLeod, Bastrop, Louisiana

A big piece of this moist cake is a chocolate- and coconut-devotee's dream. You should see my husband, children and grandkids smile when I serve it.

- 1 tablespoon shortening
- 1 package (8 ounces) cream cheese, softened
- 2-1/4 cups sugar, *divided*
- 3 eggs
- 2 teaspoons vanilla extract, *divided*
- 1 cup (6 ounces) semisweet chocolate chips
- 1/2 cup flaked coconut
- 1 cup buttermilk
- 1 cup canola oil
- 1 cup cold brewed coffee
- 3 cups all-purpose flour
- 3/4 cup baking cocoa
- 2 teaspoons baking powder
- 1-1/2 teaspoons baking soda
- 1-1/2 teaspoons salt
- 1/2 cup chopped pecans

CHOCOLATE GLAZE:
- 1 cup confectioners' sugar
- 3 tablespoons baking cocoa
- 2 to 3 tablespoons hot water
- 2 tablespoons butter, melted
- 2 teaspoons vanilla extract

Grease a 10-in. fluted tube pan with shortening and lightly coat with flour; set aside. In a small bowl, beat the cream cheese, 1/4 cup sugar, 1 egg and 1 teaspoon vanilla until smooth. Fold in chocolate chips and coconut; set aside.

In a large bowl, combine the buttermilk, oil, coffee, and remaining eggs and vanilla. Combine the flour, cocoa, baking powder, baking soda, salt and remaining sugar; add to buttermilk mixture, beating just until combined. Fold in pecans.

Pour half of the batter into prepared pan. Spoon the reserved cream cheese mixture over batter to within 1/2 in. of edges; top with the remaining batter.

Bake at 350° for 60-70 minutes or until a toothpick inserted near the center comes out clean. Cool for 20-25 minutes before removing from pan to a wire rack to cool completely.

In a small bowl, combine glaze ingredients until smooth. Drizzle over cake. **Yield:** 12-16 servings.

PINEAPPLE-BLUEBERRY GELATIN SALAD

Sandra Goodwin, Apex, North Carolina

My husband has a green thumb, and our blueberry bushes are proof of his fruitful endeavors. This is one of our family's favorite blueberry dishes.

      2 packages (3 ounces *each*) grape gelatin
      2 cups boiling water
      1 can (20 ounces) crushed pineapple
      2 cups fresh blueberries
      1 package (8 ounces) cream cheese, softened
  1/2 cup sour cream
  1/2 cup sugar
      1 teaspoon vanilla extract
  1/2 cup chopped pecans

In a large bowl, dissolve gelatin in boiling water. Drain pineapple, reserving juice in a measuring cup; add enough water to measure 1 cup. Stir into gelatin. Add pineapple and blueberries. Transfer to an 11-in. x 7-in. dish; cover and refrigerate until firm.

In a small bowl, beat the cream cheese, sour cream, sugar and vanilla until smooth. Spread over gelatin. Cover and refrigerate until serving. Just before serving, sprinkle with the pecans. **Yield:** 8 servings.

PICNIC FARE

When taking gelatin salad to picnics, pour it into individual plastic containers. To make each serving special, sprinkle with jimmies or marshmallows—kids always enjoy this. Plus, this type of preparation prevents spills that can occur when serving from a larger bowl.

CINNAMON BLUEBERRY CRUMBLE

(Pictured above)

Lori Sulewski, Ringoes, New Jersey

This is my favorite blueberry recipe. Its cookie topping tastes delicious with the warm berry filling.

      4 cups fresh blueberries
  1/2 cup sugar
      2 tablespoons cornstarch
      1 tablespoon all-purpose flour
      1 teaspoon ground cinnamon
      1 teaspoon grated lemon peel
      1 teaspoon lemon juice
  1/2 teaspoon ground nutmeg
  1/4 teaspoon salt
TOPPING:
  2/3 cup crushed reduced-fat vanilla wafers (about 20 wafers)
      1 tablespoon all-purpose flour
      2 teaspoons packed brown sugar
  3/4 teaspoon ground cinnamon
      1 tablespoon butter, melted
Whipped cream and shredded lemon peel, optional

Place the blueberries in a large bowl. Combine the sugar, cornstarch, flour, cinnamon, lemon peel and juice, nutmeg and salt; sprinkle over the blueberries and toss to coat. Transfer to a greased 8-in. square baking dish.

For the topping, in a small bowl, combine the wafer crumbs, flour, brown sugar and cinnamon. Stir in the butter until blended. Sprinkle over the blueberry mixture.

Bake at 350° for 40-50 minutes or until filling is bubbly and topping is golden brown. Serve warm. Garnish with whipped cream and lemon peel if desired. **Yield:** 6 servings.

LAYERED STRAWBERRY SHORTCAKE
(Pictured above)

West Virginia Strawberry Festival
Helen Heater, Buckhannon, West Virginia

This dessert is so popular, I entered it in the local Strawberry Festival. The judges loved the tender shortcake layered with berries and whipped cream. It is a real people pleaser.

> 4 cups sliced fresh strawberries
> 1/2 cup sugar
> 2 cups all-purpose flour
> 1 teaspoon baking powder
> 1/2 teaspoon salt
> 1/2 teaspoon baking soda
> 1/3 cup shortening
> 3/4 cup buttermilk
> 2 tablespoons butter, melted
> 1 cup heavy whipping cream
> 1/4 cup honey

In a small bowl, combine strawberries and sugar; cover and refrigerate until serving.

In a large bowl, combine flour, baking powder, salt and baking soda. Cut in the shortening until mixture resembles coarse crumbs. Stir in buttermilk just until moistened. Turn onto a lightly floured surface; knead 8-10 times.

Divide the dough in half. On two parchment paper-lined baking sheets, gently pat each portion into an 8-in. circle; brush with the butter. Bake at 400° for 13-15 minutes or until golden brown. Remove to wire racks to cool.

In a large bowl, beat cream until it begins to thicken. Add honey; beat until stiff peaks form. Place one shortcake on a serving platter; layer with half of the strawberries and whipped cream. Top with remaining shortcake, berries and cream. Serve immediately. Refrigerate leftovers. **Yield: 8 servings.**

RED-WHITE-AND-BLUE BERRY DELIGHT

Constance Fennell, Grand Junction, Michigan

Loaded with fresh strawberries and blueberries, this luscious gelatin treat is perfect for a Fourth of July celebration or summer get-together.

> 1/2 cup sugar
> 2 envelopes unflavored gelatin
> 4 cups white cranberry-peach juice drink, *divided*
> 1 tablespoon lemon juice
> 2 cups fresh strawberries, halved
> 2 cups fresh blueberries

CREAM:
- 1/2 cup heavy whipping cream
- 1 tablespoon sugar
- 1/4 teaspoon vanilla extract

In a large saucepan, combine sugar and gelatin. Add 1 cup cranberry-peach juice; cook and stir over low heat until the gelatin is completely dissolved, about 5 minutes. Remove from the heat; stir in the lemon juice and the remaining cranberry-peach juice.

Place the strawberries in an 8-cup ring mold coated with cooking spray; add 2 cups gelatin mixture. Refrigerate until set but not firm, about 30 minutes. Set aside remaining gelatin mixture.

Stir blueberries into remaining gelatin mixture; spoon over the strawberry layer. Refrigerate overnight. Unmold onto a serving platter.

In a small bowl, beat cream until it begins to thicken. Add sugar and vanilla; beat until stiff peaks form. Serve with gelatin. **Yield:** 8 servings.

BLUEBERRY COBBLER

Diane Cain, Hixton, Wisconsin

All nine varieties of blueberries we grow on our fruit farm taste yummy in this easy cobbler. Cut a juicy piece and celebrate summer!

- 2 cups fresh blueberries
- 1/2 cup sugar
- 2 tablespoons butter, melted
- 2/3 cup all-purpose flour
- 1-1/2 teaspoons baking powder
- 1/4 teaspoon salt
- 2/3 cup milk
- Whipped cream, optional

Sprinkle blueberries into a well-greased 8-in. square baking dish. In a small bowl, combine sugar and butter until crumbly. Combine the flour, baking powder and salt; add to the sugar mixture alternately with milk. Spread over blueberries.

Bake at 350° for 40-45 minutes until golden brown and a toothpick inserted near the center comes out clean. Serve warm with whipped cream if desired. **Yield:** 9 servings.

CHOOSING BLUEBERRIES

Look for fresh blueberries that are firm, dry, plump and smooth-skinned and relatively free from leaves and stems. Berries should be deep purple-blue to blue-black; reddish berries aren't ripe, but may be used in cooking.

FROZEN PEACH PIES
(Pictured below)

Athena Russell, Florence, South Carolina

A refreshing, peachy filling and a buttery graham cracker crust are the perfect pair. I've found that this pie can be frozen up to three days.

- 2-1/2 cups graham cracker crumbs
- 1/2 cup plus 2 tablespoons butter, melted
- 1/4 cup sugar
- 1 can (14 ounces) sweetened condensed milk
- 1/4 cup lemon juice
- 1/4 cup orange juice
- 1 package (16 ounces) frozen unsweetened sliced peaches
- 1 tablespoon grated lemon peel
- 1-1/2 cups heavy whipping cream

In a small bowl, combine the graham cracker crumbs, butter and sugar; press onto the bottom and up the sides of two greased 9-in. pie plates. Bake at 350° for 10-12 minutes or until lightly browned. Cool on wire racks.

In a blender, combine the milk, lemon juice, orange juice, peaches and lemon peel; cover and process until smooth. Transfer to a large bowl. In a large bowl, beat cream until stiff peaks form; fold into peach mixture.

Spoon into the crusts. Cover and freeze for at least 4 hours or until firm. Remove from the freezer 15 minutes before serving. **Yield:** 2 pies (8 servings each).

Place springform pan in a large baking pan; add 1 in. of hot water to larger pan. Bake at 350° for 45-50 minutes or until center is just set and top appears dull.

Remove pan from water bath. Cool on a wire rack for 10 minutes. Carefully run a knife around the edge of pan to loosen; cool 1 hour longer. Refrigerate overnight. Remove sides of pan before slicing. Serve with whipped cream and lime if desired. **Yield:** 12 servings.

WHITE CHOCOLATE LIME CHEESECAKE

(Pictured above)

Wisconsin Cheese Festival
Jean Landreman, Little Chute, Wisconsin

If this fest had a beauty contest, this cheesecake would've won! It turned heads and thrilled taste buds with its spectacular flavors.

- 1/3 cup butter, softened
- 1/3 cup sugar
- 1 cup all-purpose flour
FILLING:
- 4 packages (8 ounces *each*) cream cheese, softened
- 1 cup sugar
- 1 teaspoon vanilla extract
- 4 eggs, lightly beaten
- 1/4 cup lime juice
- 1 package (10 to 12 ounces) vanilla *or* white chips, melted and cooled
Whipped cream and lime wedges, optional

Place a greased 9-in. springform pan on a double thickness of heavy-duty foil (about 18 in. square). Securely wrap foil around pan; set aside.

Cream butter and sugar until light and fluffy. Gradually add flour; mix well. Press onto bottom of prepared pan. Place on a baking sheet. Bake at 350° for 12 minutes or until set. Cool on a wire rack.

For filling, in a large bowl, beat the cream cheese, sugar and vanilla until well blended. Add eggs; beat on low speed just until combined. Transfer half of the mixture to another bowl; stir in lime juice. Stir melted chips into remaining cream cheese mixture; pour over crust. Top with lime filling.

BROWNIE CHUNK ICE CREAM

(Pictured below)

Agnes Ward, Stratford, Ontario

Each time I make brownies, half the batch goes to friends and the rest ends up in this ice cream. For crunch, I sometimes add a half cup of chopped nuts.

- 3 cups half-and-half cream
- 3/4 cup sugar, *divided*
- 3 tablespoons baking cocoa
- 6 egg yolks
- 6 ounces semisweet chocolate, finely chopped
- 1 package fudge brownie mix (8-inch square pan size)

In a large saucepan, heat the cream to 175°; stir in 1/2 cup sugar until dissolved. In a bowl, combine cocoa and remaining sugar; whisk in egg yolks until smooth. Whisk in a small amount of the hot cream mixture. Return all to the pan, whisking constantly. Cook and stir over low heat until mixture reaches at least 160° and coats the back of a metal spoon.

Remove from the heat; stir in the chocolate until melted. Cool quickly by placing the pan in a bowl of ice water; let stand for 30 minutes, stirring frequently.

Transfer to a bowl; press plastic wrap onto the surface of custard. Refrigerate for several hours or overnight.

Prepare and bake the brownies according to package directions. Cool on a wire rack; cut into 1/2-in. cubes.

Fill cylinder of ice cream freezer two-thirds full with custard; freeze according to manufacturer's directions. Stir in half of the brownie cubes. Refrigerate remaining custard until ready to freeze. Add remaining brownies. When ice cream is frozen, transfer to a freezer container; freeze for 2-4 hours before serving. **Yield:** about 1-1/2 quarts.

DATE PECAN PIE

Marie Delffs, Normandy, Tennessee

At our house, we call this "oh-so-good pie." It's rather like a traditional Southern pecan pie without being overly sweet.

Pastry for single-crust pie (9 inches)
- 1/2 cup butter, cubed
- 1 cup sugar
- 2-1/2 teaspoons vinegar
- 1 teaspoon ground cinnamon
- 1/2 teaspoon ground nutmeg
- 4 eggs, lightly beaten
- 1 cup finely chopped dates
- 1/2 cup chopped pecans
- 1 cup heavy whipping cream, whipped

Line a 9-in. pie plate with pastry; trim and flute edges. Line the pastry shell with a double thickness of heavy-duty foil. Bake at 450° for 8 minutes. Remove the foil; bake 5 minutes longer. Cool on a wire rack.

In a small saucepan, melt butter. Remove from the heat; whisk in the sugar, vinegar, cinnamon and nutmeg. Stir in the eggs, dates and pecans. Pour into crust.

Bake at 375° for 35-40 minutes or until set. Cool on a wire rack. Serve with whipped cream. Refrigerate leftovers. **Yield:** 6-8 servings.

LEMON COCONUT CUPCAKES
(Pictured above right)

Debra Henderson, Booneville, Arkansas

Lemon plus coconut equals big smiles in this cupcake equation. These zesty gems are a hit with everyone.

- 3/4 cup butter, softened
- 1 cup sugar
- 3 eggs
- 3 teaspoons grated lemon peel
- 1/2 teaspoon vanilla extract
- 1-1/2 cups all-purpose flour
- 1/2 teaspoon baking powder
- 1/2 teaspoon baking soda
- 1/4 teaspoon salt
- 1/2 cup sour cream
- 1/2 cup flaked coconut

FROSTING:
- 4 ounces cream cheese, softened
- 2 tablespoons butter, softened
- 1 teaspoon grated lemon peel
- 1/4 teaspoon vanilla extract
- 1/4 teaspoon lemon juice
- 1-1/4 cups confectioners' sugar
- 3/4 cup flaked coconut, *divided*

Shredded lemon peel, optional

In a large bowl, cream butter and sugar until light and fluffy. Add eggs, one at a time, beating well after each addition. Stir in the lemon peel and vanilla. Combine the flour, baking powder, baking soda and salt; add to creamed mixture alternately with sour cream. Beat just until combined. Fold in coconut.

Fill paper-lined muffin cups three-fourths full. Bake at 350° for 18-22 minutes or until a toothpick inserted near the center comes out clean. Cool for 10 minutes before removing from pans to wire racks to cool completely.

In a small bowl, beat the cream cheese, butter, grated lemon peel, vanilla and lemon juice until fluffy. Gradually beat in the confectioners' sugar until smooth; stir in 1/4 cup coconut. Frost the cupcakes; sprinkle with the remaining coconut. Garnish with shredded lemon peel if desired. **Yield:** 15 cupcakes.

Cupcake Caper

THESE SCRUMPTIOUS, pint-sized cakes are more popular than ever with kids and adults alike. Here are three wonderful recipes to peak the interest of cupcake lovers everywhere.

★★★★★★★★★★★★★

CLOWN CUPCAKES

(Pictured below)

Taste of Home Test Kitchen

Throwing a children's party can be a real circus if you serve these colorful clown cupcakes. Set up a decorating table and let kids create funny faces on the cupcakes using their favorite candies.

    1 package (18-1/4 ounces) yellow cake mix
    3 cans (16 ounces *each*) vanilla frosting, **divided**
Yellow, red and blue paste food coloring
   24 ice cream sugar cones
Assorted candies: M&M's miniature baking bits, red shoestring licorice and cherry sour ball candies

Prepare and bake cake batter according to package directions for cupcakes. Cool completely on wire racks. Divide two cans of frosting among three bowls; tint with yellow, red and blue food coloring.

For clown hats, use a serrated knife or kitchen scissors to cut 2 in. from the open end of each cone. Frost cones with tinted frosting; decorate with baking bits. Place on waxed paper for 30 minutes or until frosting is set.

Frost cupcakes with remaining vanilla frosting. Leaving room for the hat on each cupcake, make a clown face and hair with candies. Pipe a matching ruffle on each. Carefully position a hat on each cupcake. **Yield:** 2 dozen.

★★★★★★★★★★★★★

CINNAMON CUPCAKES

(Pictured above right)

Judy Learned, Boyertown, Pennsylvania

My from-scratch cinnamon cupcakes take a little work. But the results speak for themselves when snackers say, "Yum!"

   3/4 cup shortening
1-1/2 cups sugar
    4 egg whites
    1 teaspoon vanilla extract
2-1/4 cups cake flour
    2 teaspoons baking powder
  1/2 teaspoon salt
  3/4 cup milk
TOPPING:
    2 tablespoons sugar
  1/2 teaspoon ground cinnamon
CINNAMON FROSTING:
  1/4 cup shortening
    1 teaspoon vanilla extract
  1/4 teaspoon ground cinnamon
2-1/4 cups confectioners' sugar
    3 tablespoons milk
Additional ground cinnamon

In a small bowl, cream the shortening and sugar until light and fluffy. Beat in the egg whites and vanilla. Combine the flour, baking powder and

1/2 cup baking cocoa
1 teaspoon baking soda
1/4 teaspoon salt
1/2 cup buttermilk
1/2 cup strong brewed coffee

CHOCOLATE GANACHE:
4 ounces semisweet chocolate, coarsely chopped
1/2 cup heavy whipping cream
1/2 teaspoon vanilla extract

In a small bowl, cream butter and sugar until light and fluffy. Beat in egg and vanilla. Combine the flour, cocoa, baking soda and salt; gradually add to creamed mixture alternately with buttermilk and coffee, beating well after each addition.

Fill paper-lined muffin cups two-thirds full. Bake at 350° for 25-30 minutes or until a toothpick inserted near the center comes out clean. Cool for 10 minutes before removing from pans to wire racks to cool completely.

In a small saucepan, melt chocolate with cream over low heat; stir until blended. Remove from the heat. Stir in the vanilla. Transfer to a bowl; cover and refrigerate until the mixture reaches spreading consistency, stirring occasionally. Frost cupcakes. **Yield:** 14 cupcakes.

salt; gradually add to creamed mixture alternately with milk, beating well after each addition.

Fill paper-lined muffin cups two-thirds full. For topping, combine sugar and cinnamon; sprinkle 1/4 teaspoon over each cupcake.

Bake at 350° for 18-20 minutes or until a toothpick inserted near the center comes out clean. Cool for 10 minutes before removing from pans to wire racks to cool completely.

For the frosting, in a small bowl, cream the shortening, vanilla and cinnamon. Gradually beat in confectioners' sugar. Add milk; beat until light and fluffy. Frost the cupcakes; sprinkle with additional cinnamon. **Yield:** 17 cupcakes.

RICH CHOCOLATE CUPCAKES
(Pictured at right)

Taste of Home Test Kitchen

This small indulgence will make you feel like a kid again. Our Test Kitchen topped each sweet handful with a decadent ganache that grown-ups will appreciate, too.

1/2 cup butter, softened
1 cup sugar
1 egg
1 teaspoon vanilla extract
1-1/2 cups all-purpose flour

PEACHES AND CREAM TORTE
(Pictured below)

Elva Roberts, Summerside, Prince Edward Island

This is the dessert I make when I'm craving something cool and fruity. It's a lovely ending to any meal. The cream cheese adds zing to the fluffy filling.

>   2 cups graham cracker crumbs
>   1/3 cup packed brown sugar
>   1/2 cup butter, melted
> FILLING:
>   1 can (29 ounces) sliced peaches
> 1-1/4 cups sugar, *divided*
>   2 tablespoons cornstarch
>   1 package (8 ounces) cream cheese,
>   softened
>   2 cups heavy whipping cream

In a small bowl, combine graham cracker crumbs and brown sugar; stir in butter. Set aside 1/4 cup for topping. Press the remaining crumb mixture onto the bottom and 1 in. up the sides of a greased 9-in. springform pan.

Place pan on a baking sheet. Bake at 350° for 10 minutes. Cool on a wire rack.

Drain the peaches, reserving syrup in a 2-cup measuring cup. Add enough water to measure 1-1/2 cups. In a large saucepan, combine 1/4 cup sugar and cornstarch; stir in the syrup mixture until smooth. Add the peaches. Bring to a boil over medium heat; cook and stir for 2 minutes or until thickened. Cool to room temperature, stirring occasionally.

Meanwhile, in a large bowl, beat cream cheese and remaining sugar until smooth. In a small bowl, beat cream until stiff peaks form; fold into cream cheese mixture.

Spread half of the the cream cheese mixture over crust. Top with half of the peach mixture; repeat layers. Sprinkle with the reserved crumb mixture. Cover and refrigerate for 8 hours or overnight. Remove sides of pan before slicing. **Yield:** 12 servings.

BLACK WALNUT COCONUT CAKE
(Pictured at right)

Margaret Bright, Coeburn, Virginia

I've been making cakes for over 60 years, and this is one of my favorites. I'm often asked to bring it to the monthly senior citizens' fellowship meal at my church. My children and grandchildren think it's special, too.

>   2 cups sugar
>   1 cup buttermilk
>   1 cup canola oil
>   4 eggs
>   2 teaspoons coconut extract
>   3 cups all-purpose flour
>   1/2 teaspoon baking powder
>   1/2 teaspoon baking soda
>   1/2 teaspoon salt
>   1 cup flaked coconut
>   1 cup chopped black walnuts
> SYRUP:
>   1 cup sugar
>   1/2 cup water
>   2 tablespoons butter
>   1 teaspoon coconut extract

In a large bowl, beat the sugar, buttermilk, oil, eggs and extract until well blended. Combine the flour, baking powder, baking soda and salt; gradually beat into sugar mixture until blended. Stir in the coconut and walnuts.

Transfer to a greased and floured 10-in. fluted tube pan. Bake at 325° for 60-70 minutes or until a toothpick inserted near the center comes out clean. Cool for 10 minutes.

Meanwhile, for syrup, in a small saucepan, bring the sugar and water to a boil over medium heat. Cook and stir for 5 minutes or until slightly reduced. Remove from the heat; stir in the butter and extract.

Remove cake from pan to a wire rack. Poke holes in warm cake with a skewer; slowly pour syrup over cake. Cool completely before cutting. **Yield:** 12 servings.

ORANGE-DATE NUT CAKE
(Pictured below)

Theresa Switzer, Mt. Dora, Florida

One of my fondest memories as a child was the scent of this cake cooling on my mom's dining room table. For those who like dates, nuts and oranges, it is heavenly.

    1 cup chopped dates
2-1/2 cups all-purpose flour, *divided*
    1 cup butter, softened
    1 cup sugar
    2 eggs
  1/4 cup grated orange peel
    1 teaspoon baking powder
  1/2 teaspoon baking soda
  1/2 teaspoon salt
    1 cup buttermilk
    1 cup chopped walnuts *or* pecans
ORANGE GLAZE:
    1 cup orange juice
    1 cup confectioners' sugar
    1 teaspoon vanilla extract

Toss dates with 1/4 cup flour; set aside. In a large bowl, cream butter and sugar until light and fluffy. Add eggs, one at a time, beating well after each addition. Stir in orange peel. Combine the baking powder, baking soda, salt and remaining flour; add to creamed mixture alternately with buttermilk. Stir in dates and nuts.

Transfer to a greased and floured 10-in. fluted tube pan. Bake at 350° for 50-55 minutes or until a toothpick inserted near center comes out clean.

Meanwhile, combine the glaze ingredients in a small saucepan. Bring to a boil. Remove from the heat; stir in vanilla. Cool for 30 minutes.

Cool cake on a wire rack for 10 minutes before inverting onto a serving plate. Poke holes in cake top. Drizzle glaze over top and sides of cake; cool completely before serving. **Yield:** 12 servings.

CHERRY-CHIP ICE CREAM SANDWICHES
(Pictured above)

Sally Hook, Montgomery, Texas

You can make these marvelous ice cream treats days ahead. Just wrap and freeze! My kids created them one afternoon after I made the ice cream.

1-1/2 cups milk
  1/2 cup sugar
Dash salt
    1 cup heavy whipping cream
    1 teaspoon vanilla extract
  2/3 cup chopped dried cherries
  1/2 cup miniature semisweet chocolate chips
   10 whole chocolate graham crackers

In a large saucepan over medium heat, cook and stir the milk, sugar and salt until sugar is dissolved. Remove from the heat; stir in cream and vanilla. Transfer to a bowl; refrigerate until chilled.

Line a 13-in. x 9-in. pan with waxed paper; set aside. Fill cylinder of ice cream freezer with milk mixture; freeze according to manufacturer's directions. Stir in the cherries and chocolate chips. Spread into the prepared pan; cover and freeze overnight.

Cut or break graham crackers in half. Using waxed paper, lift ice cream out of pan; discard waxed paper. Cut the ice cream into squares the same size as the graham cracker halves; place ice cream between the cracker halves. Wrap the sandwiches in plastic wrap. Freeze until serving. **Yield:** 10 servings.

CARAMEL-GLAZED APPLE CAKE
(Pictured below)

Shirley Knighton, Robbinsville, North Carolina

My mother made this family favorite from scratch and it was the most requested birthday cake. Us kids could hardly wait for apple harvest to begin because we knew what would be baking in the oven. The tempting aroma brought us right into the kitchen.

    1 cup all-purpose flour
  1/2 cup sugar
  1/4 teaspoon baking soda
  1/4 teaspoon salt
    1 egg
  1/2 cup canola oil
  1/2 teaspoon vanilla extract
    1 cup chopped peeled tart apple
  1/3 cup chopped walnuts
  1/4 cup flaked coconut, chopped
GLAZE:
  1/3 cup packed brown sugar
    3 tablespoons butter
    1 tablespoon milk

In a large bowl, combine the flour, sugar, baking soda and salt. Whisk the egg and oil; add to dry ingredients and beat until well blended. Stir in vanilla. Fold in the apple, walnuts and coconut.

Spread into a greased 8-in. fluted tube pan. Bake at 350° for 45-50 minutes or until a toothpick inserted near the center comes out clean. Cool for 10 minutes before removing from pan to a wire rack.

In a small saucepan, combine glaze ingredients; bring to a boil. Remove from the heat; drizzle over cake. **Yield:** 6 slices.

VIENNESE PLUM CAKE
(Pictured above)

Lorraine Dyda, Rancho Palos Verdes, California

This is one of my husband's all-time favorite desserts. It was passed on to me by his mother, who knew how much he loved this one. The cake is moist and tender with a streusel-like topping and is also good made with fresh blueberries.

  1/2 cup butter, softened
  1/2 cup plus 1 tablespoon sugar, *divided*
    2 eggs
    1 teaspoon vanilla extract
    1 cup all-purpose flour
    1 teaspoon baking powder
  1/4 teaspoon salt
    3 cups sliced fresh plums (about
      1-3/4 pounds)
  1/4 teaspoon ground cinnamon
TOPPING:
  1/2 cup all-purpose flour
  1/4 cup sugar
  1/4 cup cold butter, cubed
    3 tablespoons chopped walnuts, optional

In a small bowl, cream butter and 1/2 cup sugar until light and fluffy. Add eggs, one at a time, beating well after each addition. Beat until light and fluffy, about 4 minutes. Beat in the vanilla. Combine the flour, baking powder and salt; add to creamed mixture and mix well.

Transfer to a greased 9-in. square baking dish. Top with the plums. Combine the cinnamon and remaining sugar; sprinkle over plums.

For topping, in a small bowl, combine the flour and sugar; cut in butter until mixture resembles coarse crumbs. Stir in walnuts if desired. Sprinkle over the plums.

Bake at 350° for 50-55 minutes or until topping is golden brown and plums are tender. Cool on a wire rack. **Yield:** 9 servings.

Turn cake onto a kitchen towel dusted with 1 tablespoon confectioners' sugar. Gently peel off waxed paper. Roll up the cake in the towel jelly-roll style, starting with a short side. Cool completely on a wire rack.

For filling, in a large saucepan, combine sugar and cornstarch; stir in water until smooth. Cook and stir over medium-high heat until thickened and bubbly. Reduce heat; cook and stir 2 minutes longer. Remove from the heat. Stir a small amount of hot mixture into egg; return all to the pan, stirring constantly. Bring to a gentle boil; cook and stir 2 minutes longer.

Remove from the heat. Gently stir in lemon juice, peel and food coloring if desired. Cool to room temperature without stirring.

Unroll the cake; spread the filling to within 1/2 in. of edges. Roll up again. Place seam side down on a serving plate; sprinkle with additional confectioners' sugar. **Yield:** 10 servings.

◆◆◆◆◆◆◆◆◆◆◆◆◆◆

LEMON ANGEL CAKE ROLL
(Pictured above)

Taste of Home Test Kitchen

Tart and delicious, this pretty cake roll will tickle any lemon lover's fancy. Its feathery, angel food texture enhances its guilt-free goodness.

   9 egg whites
1-1/2 teaspoons vanilla extract
 3/4 teaspoon cream of tartar
   1 cup plus 2 tablespoons sugar
 3/4 cup cake flour
   1 tablespoon confectioners' sugar
FILLING:
   1 cup sugar
   3 tablespoons cornstarch
   1 cup water
   1 egg, lightly beaten
 1/4 cup lemon juice
   1 tablespoon grated lemon peel
Yellow food coloring, optional
Additional confectioners' sugar

Place the egg whites in a large bowl; let stand at room temperature for 30 minutes. Meanwhile, line a 15-in. x 10-in. x 1-in. baking pan with waxed paper; lightly coat paper with cooking spray and set aside.

Add vanilla and cream of tartar to egg whites; beat on medium until soft peaks form. Beat in the sugar, 2 tablespoons at a time, on high until stiff glossy peaks form and sugar is dissolved. Fold in flour, about 1/4 cup at a time.

Carefully spread batter into prepared pan. Bake at 350° for 15-20 minutes or until cake springs back when lightly touched. Cool for 5 minutes.

◆◆◆◆◆◆◆◆◆◆◆◆◆◆

PINEAPPLE CHEESE PIE
(Pictured below)

Barbara Gaggiano, Mission Viejo, California

I cut this recipe out of a magazine over 40 years ago when I was a new cook and wanted recipes that were quick and easy. It is always a hit with guests, and, other than the whipping cream, I can keep most of the ingredients on hand.

 2/3 cup graham cracker crumbs
4-1/2 teaspoons sugar
   3 tablespoons butter, melted
FILLING:
   4 ounces cream cheese, softened
   2 tablespoons sugar
 1/2 cup heavy whipping cream, whipped
   1 can (8 ounces) unsweetened crushed
       pineapple, well drained

Dazzling Desserts

Combine the graham cracker crumbs, sugar and butter; press onto the bottom and up the sides of an ungreased 7-in. pie pan. Refrigerate while preparing filling.

In a small bowl, beat the cream cheese and sugar until smooth. Fold in whipped cream and pineapple. Spoon into crust. Refrigerate for at least 3 hours or until firm. **Yield:** 4 servings.

▰▰▰▰▰▰▰▰▰▰▰▰

BLUEBERRY CITRUS CAKE

(Pictured above)

Shirley Cooper, Salemburg, North Carolina

My husband and I grow blueberries for market, and this cake is my favorite way to use them. With fresh berries, this cake is enhanced by a light, citrusy frosting. I bring this beauty to all potlucks.

    1 package (18-1/4 ounces) yellow cake mix
    3 eggs
    1 cup orange juice
    1/3 cup canola oil
  1-1/2 cups fresh blueberries
    1 tablespoon grated lemon peel
    1 tablespoon grated orange peel

CITRUS FROSTING:
    1 package (3 ounces) cream cheese,
      softened
  1/4 cup butter, softened
    3 cups confectioners' sugar
    2 tablespoons orange juice
    2 teaspoons grated orange peel
    1 teaspoon grated lemon peel
    2 cups whipped topping

In a large bowl, combine the yellow cake mix, eggs, orange juice and oil; beat on low speed for 30 seconds. Beat on medium speed for 2 minutes. Fold in the blueberries, lemon peel and orange peel. Pour into two greased and floured 9-in. round baking pans.

Bake at 350° for 20-25 minutes or until a toothpick inserted near the center comes out clean. Cool for 10 minutes before removing from pans to wire racks to cool completely.

For frosting, in a small bowl, combine the cream cheese and butter until fluffy. Add confectioners' sugar, orange juice and peels; beat until blended. Fold in whipped topping.

Spread frosting between layers and over the top and sides of cake. Refrigerate until serving. **Yield:** 12 servings.

In a large bowl, combine the eggs, cream, brown sugar, vanilla, salt and nutmeg. Stir in the remaining butter and reserved raisin mixture. Gently stir in bread; let stand for 15 minutes or until bread is softened.

Transfer to prepared dish. Bake, uncovered, at 350° for 35-40 minutes or until a knife inserted near the center comes out clean.

For sauce, in a small saucepan, combine the brown sugar, cornstarch and salt; gradually add water. Bring to a boil; cook and stir for 1-2 minutes or until thickened. Remove from the heat; stir in butter and vanilla. Serve with bread pudding. **Yield:** 12 servings.

AMERICANA PEANUT CHEESECAKE

Rosemary Corte, Canton, Georgia

Need an easy, creamy no-bake cheesecake? As a peanut farmer, I recommend you try this recipe. It's the ultimate indulgence!

    1 cup graham cracker crumbs
  3/4 cup plus 2 tablespoons chopped salted
       peanuts, *divided*
  1/3 cup butter, melted
    4 packages (3 ounces *each*) cream cheese,
       softened
  2/3 cup creamy peanut butter
    1 can (14 ounces) sweetened condensed
       milk
  1/3 cup lemon juice
    1 teaspoon vanilla extract
1-1/2 cups whipped topping

In a small bowl, combine cracker crumbs, 3/4 cup peanuts and butter. Press onto the bottom and 1 in. up the sides of a greased 9-in. springform pan. Cover and refrigerate for 20 minutes.

Meanwhile, in a large bowl, beat cream cheese and peanut butter until light and fluffy. Gradually beat in milk; stir in lemon juice and vanilla. Fold in whipped topping. Pour over crust. Sprinkle with remaining peanuts. Cover and refrigerate for at least 8 hours. **Yield:** 12 servings.

NEW ORLEANS BREAD PUDDING
(Pictured above)

Linda Wiese, Payette, Idaho

For an extra-special treat, try this sweet and buttery bread pudding. The cowboys we serve it to say it tastes like true Southern comfort food.

  1/2 cup raisins
  1/4 cup brandy *or* unsweetened apple juice
  1/2 cup butter, melted, *divided*
    1 tablespoon sugar
    4 eggs, lightly beaten
    2 cups half-and-half cream
    1 cup packed brown sugar
    2 teaspoons vanilla extract
  1/2 teaspoon salt
  1/2 teaspoon freshly ground nutmeg
   10 slices day-old French bread (1 inch
       thick), cubed
SAUCE:
  1/2 cup packed brown sugar
    2 tablespoons cornstarch
Dash salt
    1 cup cold water
    1 tablespoon butter
    2 teaspoons vanilla extract

In a small saucepan, combine raisins and brandy; bring to a boil. Remove from heat; cover. Set aside. Brush a shallow 2-1/2-qt. baking dish with 1 tablespoon butter; sprinkle with sugar. Set aside.

LEMON JUICE
When a recipe calls for juice from a fresh lemon, you can use either fresh, frozen or bottled in equal amounts. When lemons are in season or you have extra on hand, juice them and freeze the juice in ice cube trays.

CHOCOLATE SHOOFLY PIE
(Pictured above)

Gwen Brounce Widdowson
Fleetwood, Pennsylvania

If you like traditional shoofly pie, you'll agree the chocolate version is even better! I sometimes serve it with vanilla ice cream, but it's just as good on its own.

Pastry for single-crust pie (9 inches)
1/2 cup semisweet chocolate chips
1-1/2 cups all-purpose flour
1/2 cup packed brown sugar
3 tablespoons butter-flavored shortening
1 teaspoon baking soda
1-1/2 cups water
1 egg, lightly beaten
1 cup molasses

Line a 9-in. deep-dish pie plate with pastry. Trim to 1/2 in. beyond edge of plate; flute the edges. Sprinkle chocolate chips into shell; set aside.

In a large bowl, combine the flour and brown sugar; cut in shortening until crumbly. Set aside 1 cup for topping. Add the baking soda, water, egg and molasses to remaining crumb mixture and mix well. Pour over the chips. Sprinkle with the reserved crumb mixture.

Bake at 350° for 45-55 minutes or until a knife inserted near the center comes out clean. Cool on a wire rack for 20 minutes before cutting. Serve warm. **Yield:** 6-8 servings.

RASPBERRY PEAR TART
(Pictured at right)

Bernice Janowski, Stevens Point, Wisconsin

Fetch the forks! Guests will be eager to dig into this festive tart. Destined to become a favorite holiday dessert, it looks and smells as delightful as it tastes.

1-2/3 cups all-purpose flour
2/3 cup sugar
2/3 cup cold butter, cubed
1/3 cup chopped macadamia nuts
FILLING:
3 medium pears, peeled and thinly sliced
1/2 cup sugar
2 tablespoons cornstarch
1 teaspoon ground cinnamon
1 teaspoon grated lemon peel
2 cups fresh *or* frozen raspberries
TOPPING:
1/2 cup all-purpose flour
1/2 cup packed brown sugar
1 teaspoon grated lemon peel
1/4 cup cold butter, cubed
1/3 cup chopped macadamia nuts

In a large bowl, combine the flour and sugar; cut in butter until mixture resembles coarse crumbs. Stir in nuts. Press onto the bottom and up the sides of an ungreased 11-in. fluted tart pan with removable bottom.

For filling, combine pears, sugar, cornstarch, cinnamon and lemon peel. Add the raspberries; toss gently. Pour into the crust. Bake at 425° for 25 minutes.

For topping, in a small bowl, combine the flour, brown sugar and lemon peel; cut in butter until crumbly. Stir in nuts. Sprinkle over filling.

Bake 15-20 minutes longer or until the filling is bubbly and the topping is golden brown. Cool on a wire rack. Refrigerate any leftovers. **Yield:** 12-16 servings.

SOUR CREAM CHERRY PIE

(Pictured below)

Betty Wingo, Marshall, Arkansas

If I can beat the birds to our cherry tree, I make this luscious pie. Otherwise, strawberries or blueberries can be substituted. It's especially good served warm with vanilla bean ice cream.

> 3 cups pitted frozen tart cherries, thawed, drained and patted dry
> 1 unbaked pastry shell (9 inches)
> 1 tablespoon butter
> 1-3/4 cups plus 2 tablespoons sugar, *divided*
> 1 cup all-purpose flour
> 1/2 teaspoon salt
> 2 eggs, lightly beaten
> 1 cup (8 ounces) sour cream
> 1 tablespoon lemon juice

Arrange cherries evenly in the pastry shell. Dot with butter. In a large bowl, combine 1-3/4 cups sugar, flour and salt. Stir in the eggs, sour cream and lemon juice; mix well. Spread evenly over cherries. Sprinkle with remaining sugar.

Bake at 400° for 10 minutes. Reduce heat to 350°; bake 30 minutes longer or until topping is set. Cool for 1 hour on a wire rack. Refrigerate for 3-4 hours before cutting. Refrigerate the leftovers. **Yield:** 8 servings.

■■■■■■■■■■■■■

HOT FUDGE SAUCE

(Pictured above)

Karen Willoughby, Oviedo, Florida

This fudgy sauce is scrumptious spooned over French vanilla ice cream and sprinkled with toasted pecans. Actually, I could eat the topping all by itself!

> 1/2 cup semisweet chocolate chips
> 6 tablespoons evaporated milk
> 6 tablespoons light corn syrup
> 1/4 cup butter, cubed
> 1/2 teaspoon vanilla extract

In a small heavy saucepan, combine the chocolate chips, milk and corn syrup. Cook and stir over low heat until chips are melted and mixture is smooth.

Stir in the butter until melted. Cook and stir 5 minutes longer. Remove from the heat; stir in vanilla. **Yield:** about 1 cup.

SPICED HOT FUDGE

For special ice cream sundaes, add 1/4 teaspoon *each* of ground cloves and ground cinnamon to 1-1/2 cups of hot fudge topping. The aromatic spices add a nice flavor to the sauce.

※※※※※※※※※※

FRUITS OF THE FOREST PIE

(Pictured above)

Mary Lou Timpson, Colorado City, Arizona

Five kinds of nuts are squirreled away in this pie that is deliciously sweet. There's a crunch in every bite.

- 1/3 **cup coarsely chopped macadamia nuts**
- 1/3 **cup chopped hazelnuts**
- 1 **unbaked pastry shell (9 inches)**
- 1/2 **cup salted cashew halves**
- 1/2 **cup pecan halves**
- 1/3 **cup slivered almonds**
- 4 **eggs**
- 1 **cup light corn syrup**
- 1/2 **cup sugar**
- 1/4 **cup packed brown sugar**
- 2 **tablespoons butter, melted**
- 1 **teaspoon vanilla extract**
- 1/4 **teaspoon salt**

Sprinkle the macadamia nuts and hazelnuts into the pastry shell. Arrange the cashews, pecans and almonds over the chopped nuts.

Beat eggs, corn syrup, sugars, butter, vanilla and salt until well blended. Pour over the nuts.

Bake at 350° for 45-50 minutes or until a knife inserted near the center comes out clean. (Cover the edges with foil during the last 10 minutes to prevent overbrowning if necessary.) Cool on a wire rack. Store in the refrigerator. **Yield:** 8 servings.

※※※※※※※※※※

BUTTERMILK TORTE

(Pictured at right)

Carol Ledvina, Mishicot, Wisconsin

My family lived on a farm and we were always very busy with chores. This luscious dessert was one of our top picks because it was so easy to make.

- 3/4 **cup butter-flavored shortening**
- 1-3/4 **cups sugar,** *divided*
- 2 **eggs,** *separated*
- 1 **teaspoon vanilla extract**
- 2-1/2 **cups all-purpose flour**
- 1 **teaspoon baking soda**
- 1 **teaspoon ground cinnamon**
- 1/2 **teaspoon salt**
- 1-1/4 **cups buttermilk**
- 1/4 **teaspoon cream of tartar**
- 1/2 **cup semisweet chocolate chips**
- 1/2 **cup flaked coconut**

Grease the bottom only of a 10-in. springform pan; set aside. In a large bowl, cream shortening and 1-1/2 cups sugar until light and fluffy. Beat in egg yolks and vanilla. Combine flour, baking soda, cinnamon and salt; add to creamed mixture alternately with buttermilk, beating well after each addition. Transfer to prepared pan.

Bake at 325° for 50-55 minutes or until a toothpick inserted near the center comes out clean. Remove from the oven; increase heat to 375°.

In a small bowl, beat egg whites and cream of tartar on medium speed until soft peaks form. Gradually add remaining sugar, 1 tablespoon at a time, beating on high until stiff glossy peaks form.

Spread evenly over warm cake, sealing edges to sides of pan. Sprinkle chips and coconut over the top. Bake for 15 minutes or until coconut and meringue are golden brown. Run a knife around edge of pan; remove sides. Cool completely on a wire rack. Refrigerate leftovers. **Yield:** 12 servings.

BANANA SPLIT ICE CREAM CAKE

(Pictured below)

Gladys McCollum Abee, McKee, Kentucky

Every time they visit, my children and grandkids request this fantastic frozen dessert. It takes time to assemble, but it's worth the effort when I see all those smiling faces.

>   12 ice cream sugar cones, finely crushed
>   1/2 cup finely chopped walnuts
>   6 tablespoons butter, melted

CAKE:

> 1-3/4 quarts low-fat vanilla frozen yogurt,
>   softened, *divided*
>   2 medium ripe bananas, mashed
>   1 teaspoon banana extract, optional
>   1 jar (16 ounces) hot fudge ice cream
>   topping
>   1 cup chopped walnuts
>   1 cup strawberry ice cream topping
>   1 carton (8 ounces) frozen whipped
>   topping, thawed

In a small bowl, combine crushed cones, walnuts and butter; press onto the bottom of a greased 9-in. springform pan.

In another small bowl, combine 3 cups yogurt, bananas and extract if desired. Spread over crust. In a small bowl, combine the fudge topping and walnuts; spread over yogurt. Cover and freeze for 2 hours or until firm.

Top with the remaining yogurt; spread with strawberry topping. Cover and freeze for 8 hours or overnight until firm. Garnish with whipped topping. **Yield:** 12 servings.

ITALIAN CREAM CAKE

(Pictured above)

Marilyn Morel, Keene, New Hampshire

Here's a scrumptious cake that melts in your mouth and makes you say, "Thanks a million!"

>   1/2 cup butter, softened
>   1/2 cup shortening
>   2 cups sugar
>   5 eggs
>   1 teaspoon vanilla extract
>   2 cups all-purpose flour
>   1 teaspoon baking soda
>   1/4 teaspoon salt
>   1 cup buttermilk
>   1 cup chopped pecans
>   1/2 cup flaked coconut

CREAM CHEESE FROSTING:

>   2 packages (one 8 ounces, one 3 ounces)
>   cream cheese, softened
>   1/2 cup butter, softened
> 3-3/4 cups confectioners' sugar
>   1 teaspoon vanilla extract
>   1 cup coarsely chopped pecans

In a large bowl, cream the butter, shortening and sugar until light and fluffy. Add eggs, one at a time, beating well after each addition. Stir in vanilla. Combine the flour, baking soda and salt; add to the creamed mixture alternately with the buttermilk. Fold in pecans and coconut.

Pour into three greased and floured 9-in. round baking pans. Bake at 350° for 20-25 minutes or until a toothpick inserted near the center comes out clean. Cool for 10 minutes before removing from pans to wire racks to cool completely.

For frosting, in a large bowl, beat cream cheese and butter until fluffy. Add confectioners' sugar and vanilla; beat until smooth.

Spread frosting between layers and over top and sides of cake. Press pecans onto sides of cake. Store in the refrigerator. **Yield:** 12 servings.

CANDY APPLE WALNUT PIE
(Pictured below)

Serita Bratcher, Morrison, Tennessee

The South is known for apple pies, but this one is not your typical apple pie! The filling contains red-hot candies, and instead of a regular double crust, you simply crumble a frozen pastry shell and sprinkle it over the top. You can peel the apples if you wish or leave them unpeeled.

> 6 cups sliced tart apples
> 2/3 cup chopped walnuts
> 1/2 cup red-hot candies
> 1/3 cup plus 2 tablespoons sugar, *divided*
> 1/3 cup all-purpose flour
> 2 frozen deep-dish pastry shells (9 inches)

In a large bowl, combine apples, walnuts, red-hots, 1/3 cup sugar and flour; toss to coat. Spoon into one pastry shell. Crumble the remaining pastry shell into 1/2-in. pieces; toss with the remaining sugar. Sprinkle over filling.

Place on a baking sheet. Bake at 375° for 50-60 minutes or until the filling is bubbly and crust is golden brown. Cool completely on a wire rack before cutting. **Yield:** 6-8 servings.

BUTTERFLY CAKE
(Pictured above)

Taste of Home Test Kitchen

Our home economists predict the colorful cake they created will set taste buds aflutter and give your next gathering a springtime lift.

> 1 package (18-1/4 ounces) yellow cake mix
> 1 individual cream-filled sponge cake
> 1 can (16 ounces) chocolate frosting
> Red shoestring licorice
> Assorted candies of your choice

Prepare the cake batter according to package directions. Pour into two greased and floured 9-in. round baking pans. Bake at 350° for 25-30 minutes or until a toothpick inserted near center comes out clean. Cool for 10 minutes before removing from pans to wire racks to cool completely.

Cut one cake in half widthwise. (Save the second cake for another use or make two butterflies.) Cut a notch from the center of each cut side to show definition between the upper and lower wings. Let cake stand for 2 hours.

On a round platter, position cake halves (with notched edges facing out) on each side of sponge cake. With a knife, cut the corners of wings so they are rounded. Frost top and sides of butterfly with chocolate frosting.

Cut licorice into two small pieces; push ends into top of sponge cake for antennae. Decorate with assorted candies. **Yield:** 8 servings.

FROSTING A CAKE

To keep crumbs from mixing into the cake frosting, first spread a very thin layer of frosting over the top and sides. If the frosting is thick, thin with a teaspoon or two of milk or cream.

SUNNY ORANGE LAYER CAKE
(Pictured below)

Donna Gaston, Coplay, Pennsylvania

If you like orange flavor, you'll love this made-from-scratch cake. No one will ever believe gelatin is the secret ingredient in both the cake and the frosting.

  2/3 cup shortening
1-1/2 cups sugar
    3 eggs
    1 tablespoon grated orange peel
2-1/2 cups cake flour
    1 package (3 ounces) orange gelatin
2-1/2 teaspoons baking powder
    1 teaspoon salt
  3/4 cup orange juice
  1/3 cup 2% milk
FROSTING:
    1 package (8 ounces) cream cheese, softened
  1/2 cup butter, softened
1-1/2 cups confectioners' sugar
    2 tablespoons orange gelatin powder
    2 teaspoons vanilla extract

In a large bowl, cream shortening and sugar until light and fluffy. Add eggs, one at a time, beating well after each addition. Beat in orange peel.

Combine flour, gelatin, baking powder and salt; add to creamed mixture alternately with orange juice and milk, beating well after each addition.

Pour into two greased and floured 9-in. round baking pans. Bake at 350° for 25-30 minutes or until a toothpick inserted near the center comes out clean. Cool for 10 minutes before removing from pans to wire racks to cool completely.

In a large bowl, beat cream cheese and butter until light and fluffy. Beat in the confectioners' sugar, gelatin powder and vanilla until blended.

Place one cake layer on a serving plate; spread with frosting. Top with remaining cake layer; frost top and sides of cake. Store in the refrigerator. **Yield:** 14 servings.

▰▰▰▰▰▰▰▰▰▰▰

CHOCOLATE MALT CHEESECAKE

Anita Moffett, Rewey, Wisconsin

For a change of pace, substitute pretzel crumbs for the graham cracker crumbs in this irresistible cheesecake. They make a surprisingly good crust and add a real flavor boost!

    1 cup graham cracker crumbs (about 16 squares)
  1/4 cup sugar
  1/3 cup butter, melted
FILLING:
    3 packages (8 ounces *each*) cream cheese, softened
    1 can (14 ounces) sweetened condensed milk
  3/4 cup chocolate malt powder
    4 eggs, lightly beaten
    1 cup semisweet chocolate chips, melted and cooled
    1 teaspoon vanilla extract
Confectioners' sugar and chocolate curls, optional

Combine the cracker crumbs, sugar and butter. Press onto the bottom of a greased 9-in. springform pan; set aside.

For filling, in a large bowl, beat cream cheese and milk until smooth. Add malt powder; beat well. Add eggs; beat on low speed until combined. Stir in melted chocolate and vanilla. Pour into crust. Place pan on a baking sheet.

Bake at 325° for 60-65 minutes or until center is almost set. Cool on a wire rack for 10 minutes. Carefully run a knife around edge of pan to loosen; cool 1 hour longer. Refrigerate overnight.

Remove the sides of the pan. Garnish with confectioners' sugar and chocolate curls if desired. Refrigerate leftovers. **Yield:** 12-14 servings.

APPLE BUTTER PUMPKIN PIE
(Pictured above)

Virginia Moore, Fairdale, Kentucky

Two autumn standards—apple and pumpkin—are joined together in this delightful pie. Topped with a crown of golden pastry "leaves," this dessert is sure to impress.

  1 cup apple butter
  1 cup canned pumpkin
1/2 cup packed brown sugar
3/4 teaspoon ground cinnamon
3/4 teaspoon ground nutmeg
1/2 teaspoon salt
1/4 teaspoon ground ginger
  3 eggs, lightly beaten
3/4 cup evaporated milk
  1 unbaked pastry shell (9 inches)

Additional pie pastry, optional
Whipped cream, optional

In a large bowl, combine apple butter, pumpkin, brown sugar, cinnamon, nutmeg, salt and ginger. Add eggs. Gradually beat in milk until smooth. Pour into pastry shell.

Bake at 425° for 35-40 minutes or until set (cover the edges loosely with foil if necessary to prevent overbrowning). Cool on a wire rack.

If decorative cutouts are desired, roll additional pastry to 1/8-in. thickness; cut out with 1-in. to 1-1/2-in. leaf-shaped cookie cutters. With a sharp knife, score leaf veins on cutouts if desired.

Place on an ungreased baking sheet. Bake at 400° for 6-8 minutes or until golden brown. Remove to a wire rack to cool. Arrange around edge of pie. Garnish with the whipped cream if desired. Refrigerate leftovers. **Yield:** 8 servings.

Editor's Note: This recipe was tested with commercially prepared apple butter.

Run a knife around side and center tube of pan. Serve cake with remaining puree; garnish with the whipped topping and fresh strawberries if desired. **Yield:** 12 servings.

LEMON NOODLE KUGEL
(Pictured below)

Romaine Smith, Garden Grove, Iowa

Comforting kugel is a traditional dessert at our family's Polish Christmas Eve supper. Rich with butter, sugar, sour cream and cinnamon, it suits any special-occasion meal.

>   5 cups uncooked egg noodles
>   2 tablespoons butter
>   4 eggs
>   2 cups (16 ounces) sour cream
>   2 cups (16 ounces) 4% cottage cheese
>   1 cup milk
>   3/4 cup plus 1-1/2 teaspoons sugar, *divided*
> 1-1/2 teaspoons lemon extract
>   1 teaspoon vanilla extract
>   1/2 teaspoon ground cinnamon

Cook noodles according to package directions; drain and return to the pan. Toss with the butter; set aside.

In a large bowl, beat eggs, sour cream, cottage cheese, milk, 3/4 cup sugar and extracts until well blended. Stir in noodles.

Transfer to a 13-in. x 9-in. baking dish coated with cooking spray. Combine cinnamon and remaining sugar; sprinkle over noodle mixture.

Bake, uncovered, at 350° for 55-60 minutes or until a thermometer reads 160°. Let stand for 10 minutes before cutting. Serve warm or cold. Refrigerate leftovers. **Yield:** 12 servings.

STRAWBERRY MARBLE CAKE
(Pictured above)

Margery Richmond, Fort Collins, Colorado

Perfect for special occasions, this strawberry swirl cake makes a pretty presentation at the end of a meal. I also serve it with afternoon tea, and it's a quick sell at any bake sale.

> 1-1/2 cups egg whites (about 10)
>   1 package (10 ounces) frozen
>   unsweetened strawberries, thawed
>   and drained
> 1-1/2 cups sugar, *divided*
> 1-1/4 cups cake flour
> 1-1/2 teaspoons cream of tartar
>   1/2 teaspoon salt
>   1 teaspoon vanilla extract
>   1 teaspoon almond extract
> Red food coloring, optional
> Whipped topping and sliced fresh strawberries,
>   optional

Let egg whites stand at room temperature for 30 minutes. In a food processor, puree strawberries; strain puree and discard seeds. Set aside.

Sift together 3/4 cup sugar and the flour twice; set aside. Add cream of tartar and salt to egg whites; beat on medium speed until soft peaks form. Gradually beat in the remaining sugar, 2 tablespoons at a time, on high until stiff glossy peaks form and sugar is dissolved. Gradually fold in flour mixture, about 1/2 cup at a time.

Transfer half of the batter to another bowl; fold in extracts. Fold 1/4 cup strawberry puree into remaining batter; add food coloring if desired.

Gently spoon batters, alternating colors, into an ungreased 10-in. tube pan. Cut through with a knife to swirl. Bake at 350° for 45-50 minutes or until lightly browned and the top appears dry. Immediately invert pan; cool completely, about 1 hour.

GOOSEBERRY DESSERT
(Pictured above)

Betty Janzen, Clemson, South Carolina

A Mennonite friend gave me this delicious recipe when I got married. Most of us grow our own gooseberries here in South Carolina, and I enjoy trying a variety of dishes and desserts with them.

1-1/2 cups all-purpose flour
1/4 cup sugar
1-1/2 teaspoons baking powder
1/8 teaspoon salt
1/2 cup cold butter, cubed
1 egg
1/4 cup milk
FILLING:
1 cup sugar
2 tablespoons quick-cooking tapioca
2 cans (15 ounces *each*) gooseberries, drained
TOPPING:
1 tablespoon milk
3 tablespoons sugar
1/2 teaspoon ground cinnamon

In a large bowl, combine the flour, sugar, baking powder and salt; cut in the butter until crumbly. In a small bowl, whisk egg and milk. Gradually add to flour mixture, tossing with a fork until dough forms a ball. Cover and refrigerate for 20 minutes or until easy to handle.

For filling, in a large bowl, combine sugar and tapioca. Gently stir in gooseberries; let stand for 15 minutes. Divide dough in half. Roll out each portion to an 8-in. square. Place one portion in the bottom of a greased 8-in. square baking dish. Top with filling and remaining pastry.

Cut slits in pastry; brush with milk. Combine sugar and cinnamon; sprinkle over the top. Bake at 375° for 30-35 minutes or until lightly browned. Serve warm. **Yield:** 9 servings.

GINGER FRUIT CRISP
(Pictured below)

Elmor Stabile, Canmore, Alberta

Our B&B guests tell us this fun breakfast crisp is one of the most enjoyable parts of their stay. There is seldom a crumb left.

1/3 cup packed brown sugar
2 tablespoons plus 1-1/2 teaspoons cornstarch
2 cups sliced fresh plums
1 cup sliced peeled peaches
1 cup sliced nectarines
TOPPING:
1 cup crushed gingersnap cookies (about 20 cookies)
1/2 cup old-fashioned oats
1/3 cup packed brown sugar
1/2 teaspoon ground ginger
1/2 teaspoon ground cinnamon
1/4 teaspoon salt
1/3 cup cold butter, cubed
1/2 cup sliced almonds
Whipped cream, optional

In a large bowl, combine the brown sugar and cornstarch. Add plums, peaches and nectarines; gently toss to coat. Transfer to a greased 8-in. square baking dish.

For topping, combine the gingersnap crumbs, oats, brown sugar, ginger, cinnamon and salt. Cut in butter until crumbly. Stir in almonds; sprinkle over fruit.

Bake at 350° for 30-35 minutes or until filling is bubbly and topping is browned. Serve warm with whipped cream if desired. **Yield:** 9 servings.

THE PERFECT PORTION *for two is easy with the trimmed-back fare found in this chapter. These delicious dishes are sure to satisfy any hearty appetite.*

SIZED JUST RIGHT. Cornish Hens (p. 137).

Cooking for Two

CORNISH HENS
(Pictured at left)

Mae Highhouse, Newport, Kentucky

I like this recipe for Cornish hens because it's easy to prepare and a delicious entree for two. The basting ingredients result in beautifully browned hens, sealing in the juices so that they are moist, tender and quite flavorful.

 2 Cornish game hens (20 ounces *each*)
 1/4 cup unsweetened apple juice
 3 tablespoons reduced-sodium soy sauce
 1 tablespoon browning sauce, optional

Place hens on a rack in a shallow baking pan. Combine the apple juice, soy sauce and browning sauce if desired; pour over hens.

Bake, uncovered, at 350° for 50-60 minutes or until a meat thermometer reads 180°, basting occasionally with pan juices. **Yield:** 2 servings.

INDIVIDUAL HAM LOAVES

Gladys May, Dunfermline, Illinois

I found this recipe in a 1989 Fulton County Illinois Homemaker's cookbook. When I make it I usually double or triple the recipe and then freeze individual loaves. They're great to have on hand for unexpected guests, and they make your meal look and taste special.

 1/4 cup milk
 2 tablespoons beaten egg
 1/2 cup graham cracker crumbs
 1 tablespoon finely chopped onion
1-1/4 teaspoons ground mustard
 1/4 teaspoon salt
 1/8 teaspoon pepper
 1/4 pound ground fully cooked ham
 1/4 pound ground beef
 1/4 pound ground pork
GLAZE:
 1/4 cup packed brown sugar
 2 tablespoons unsweetened pineapple
  juice
 1 tablespoon cider vinegar
 1/4 teaspoon ground mustard

In a small bowl, combine the milk, egg, cracker crumbs, onion, mustard, salt and pepper. Crumble the ham, beef and pork over mixture and mix well. Shape into two 4-1/2-in. x 2-1/2-in. loaves.

Place in a greased 8-in. square baking dish. Bake, uncovered, at 350° for 25 minutes.

Meanwhile, in a small bowl, combine brown sugar, pineapple juice, vinegar and mustard. Spread half of the mixture over the loaves; bake 5 minutes longer. Spread with remaining mixture. Bake 5-10 minutes longer or until a meat thermometer reads 160°. **Yield:** 2 servings.

LEMONY ROASTED SWEET POTATOES

Joan Parks, Boise, Idaho

These sweet potatoes became a family tradition when I was a child and are now one of my family's favorites. I hope they become a tradition for your family, too.

 2 medium sweet potatoes, peeled
  and cubed
 2 teaspoons butter, melted
 1 teaspoon lemon juice
 1/4 teaspoon salt
 1/4 cup packed brown sugar
 1/2 teaspoon grated lemon peel

Place sweet potatoes in a greased 1-qt. baking dish. Combine the butter, lemon juice and salt; drizzle over sweet potatoes. Sprinkle with brown sugar and lemon peel.

Bake, uncovered, at 350° for 40-45 minutes or until potatoes are tender, stirring every 15 minutes. Stir before serving. **Yield:** 3 servings.

SWEET POTATOES OR YAMS?

There are two common varieties of sweet potato. One has pale skin, light yellow flesh and a dry mealy texture. The other, also known as a yam, has dark skin, orange flesh and a moist texture. True yams are different than sweet potatoes, and although uncommon in North America, are interchangeable with sweet potatoes in most recipes.

In a large skillet over medium heat, cook pork in oil for 2-3 minutes on each side or until meat is no longer pink. Remove and keep warm.

Add the onion and garlic to the pan; cook and stir until tender. Serve with the pork. **Yield:** 2 servings.

MANDARIN-WALNUT LETTUCE SALAD
(Pictured below)

Valerie Gee, Depew, New York

The sweetened walnuts add a nice crunch to this salad and a taste that is compatible with oranges. The dressing is sweet, tangy and light...just right for the simple ingredients of the salad.

    4-1/2 teaspoons sugar
    1-1/2 teaspoons water
        3 tablespoons chopped walnuts
    4-1/2 teaspoons olive oil
    2-1/4 teaspoons tarragon vinegar
Dash salt
    2-1/2 cups torn Boston lettuce
        2/3 cup mandarin oranges

In a small saucepan over medium-low heat, bring sugar and water to a boil, stirring constantly. Add walnuts; cook and stir for 2-3 minutes or until lightly browned. Spread onto a piece of greased foil; set aside.

In a small bowl, whisk the oil, vinegar and salt. In a salad bowl, combine lettuce and oranges. Drizzle with dressing and sprinkle with walnuts; toss to coat. **Yield:** 2 servings.

PARMESAN PORK MEDALLIONS
(Pictured above)

Angela Ciocca, Saltsburg, Pennsylvania

I was so happy to find this recipe. I've served it countless times for family and friends. It takes little preparation and adapts easily to serve any number.

    1/2 pound pork tenderloin
      2 tablespoons seasoned bread crumbs
      1 tablespoon grated Parmesan cheese
    1/4 teaspoon salt
Dash pepper
      2 teaspoons canola oil
    1/4 cup chopped onion
      1 garlic clove, minced

Cut the pork into four slices; flatten to 1/4-in. thickness. In a shallow bowl, combine the bread crumbs, Parmesan cheese, salt and pepper. Add pork, one slice at a time, and turn to coat.

FLATTENING PORK TENDERLOIN

When flattening slices of pork tenderloin, it's best to put them inside a heavy-duty resealable plastic bag or between two sheets of plastic wrap to prevent messy splatters. Using the smooth side of a meat mallet to gently pound the pork will prevent the meat from shredding.

Cooking for Two

▄▀▄▀▄▀▄▀▄▀▄▀▄▀▄▀▄▀

ALMOND CHOCOLATE CAKES
(Pictured above)

Mary Lou Wayman, Salt Lake City, Utah

I serve this variation of chocolate cake often and it is always a hit. It is almost like a steamed pudding, served warm and topped with whipped cream or ice cream. The chocolate-praline flavor comes through nicely.

1/3 cup packed brown sugar
2 tablespoons butter, melted
2 tablespoons half-and-half cream
1/4 cup finely chopped almonds
BATTER:
1/2 cup sugar
2 tablespoons butter, softened
1 egg
1/4 teaspoon vanilla extract
1/2 cup all-purpose flour
2 tablespoons baking cocoa
1/2 teaspoon baking powder
1/4 teaspoon baking soda
1/3 cup milk

Combine the brown sugar, butter and cream; divide between two greased 10-oz. ramekins or custard cups. Sprinkle with almonds.

In a small bowl, beat sugar and butter until crumbly, about 2 minutes. Beat in the egg and vanilla. Combine flour, cocoa, baking powder and baking soda; add to sugar mixture alternately with milk, beating well after each addition. Divide between ramekins. Place on a baking sheet.

Bake at 350° for 20-25 minutes or until a toothpick inserted near the center comes out clean. Cool for 5 minutes before inverting onto dessert plates. Serve warm. **Yield:** 2 servings.

▄▀▄▀▄▀▄▀▄▀▄▀▄▀▄▀▄▀

CHICKEN WITH COUNTRY GRAVY
(Pictured below)

Linda Foreman, Locust Grove, Oklahoma

My mother, grandson and I put our heads together and after several tries, we came up with our version of oven-fried chicken. We tweaked the recipe ingredients until the gravy was tasty and the chicken was nicely browned and tender.

2 tablespoons butter
2 tablespoons canola oil
1/4 cup all-purpose flour
1/4 teaspoon paprika
Dash *each* seasoned salt, garlic powder,
  salt and pepper
2 chicken leg quarters
GRAVY:
1 tablespoon all-purpose flour
2/3 cup milk
1/4 teaspoon salt
1/4 tablespoon pepper

Place the butter and oil in a large ovenproof skillet. Place in a 425° oven for 5 minutes. Meanwhile, in a shallow bowl, combine flour and seasonings; add chicken, one piece at a time, and turn to coat.

Carefully place chicken, skin side down, in the hot skillet. Bake, uncovered, for 30 minutes. Turn pieces over; bake 20-30 minutes longer or until a meat thermometer reads 180°. Remove and keep warm.

For gravy, transfer 1 tablespoon of drippings from the skillet to a small saucepan; stir in flour until smooth. Gradually stir in the milk, salt and pepper. Bring to a boil; cook and stir for 2 minutes or until thickened. Serve with the chicken. **Yield:** 2 servings.

NOODLE RICE PILAF
(Pictured above)

Anne Jones, Pinehurst, North Carolina

My friend shared this recipe with me several years ago. It is a good side dish that complements chicken, pork and beef. It's a big hit whenever I serve it.

    2 tablespoons butter
1/2 cup uncooked long grain rice
1/4 cup uncooked egg noodles *or* vermicelli, crushed
1-1/3 cups chicken broth

In a small saucepan, melt the butter. Add the rice and noodles; cook and stir for 3-4 minutes or until lightly browned. Stir in the broth. Bring to a boil. Reduce the heat; cover and simmer for 20-25 minutes or until rice is tender and broth is absorbed. **Yield:** 2 servings.

CRANBERRY SHORT RIBS
(Pictured at far right)

Cathy Wylie, Dawson City, Yukon

This recipe originally came from my mother-in-law. Living in the Yukon, I sometimes substitute moose for the beef, and I pick wild cranberries in the fall. I prepare this comfort food often during the long winter, and we never tire of it.

1-1/2 pounds bone-in beef short ribs
1/2 teaspoon salt, *divided*
1/4 teaspoon pepper
    1 tablespoon all-purpose flour
    1 tablespoon brown sugar
1/8 teaspoon ground mustard

Dash ground cloves
3/4 cup water
    2 teaspoons cider vinegar
1-1/2 to 2 teaspoons grated lemon peel
1/2 cup fresh cranberries

Sprinkle ribs with 1/4 teaspoon salt and pepper. Place ribs in a greased 8-in. square baking dish. Cover and bake at 350° for 1-1/4 hours.

In a small saucepan, combine the flour, brown sugar, mustard, cloves and remaining salt. Stir in the water, vinegar and lemon peel until smooth. Add cranberries. Bring to a boil; cook and stir for 2 minutes or until thickened.

Drain ribs; top with the cranberry mixture. Bake 15-25 minutes longer or until meat is tender. **Yield:** 2 servings.

SOFT HONEY COOKIES
(Pictured at right)

Rochelle Friedman, Brooklyn, New York

This old-fashioned cookie has a honey-cinnamon flavor and a tender texture that resembles cake. It has been a family favorite for years and I wanted to share the recipe with others.

1/4 cup sugar
    2 tablespoons canola oil
    1 egg
    3 tablespoons honey
3/4 teaspoon vanilla extract
    1 cup plus 2 tablespoons all-purpose flour
1/4 teaspoon baking powder
1/4 teaspoon ground cinnamon
1/8 teaspoon salt

Beat sugar and oil until blended. Beat in egg; beat in honey and vanilla. Combine flour, baking powder, cinnamon and salt; gradually add to sugar mixture and mix well (dough will be stiff). Cover and refrigerate for at least 2 hours.

Drop dough by tablespoonfuls 2 in. apart onto a greased baking sheet. Bake at 350° for 8-10 minutes or until bottoms are lightly browned. Cool for 1 minute before removing from pan to a wire rack. Store in an airtight container. **Yield:** 16 cookies.

SPICED PEAR LETTUCE SALAD
(Pictured above right)

Jessie Apfel, Berkeley, California

I like to serve this pretty salad in the fall. The colors are bright, the texture fresh and the flavors delightful. It compliments roasted entrees and is very good with grilled meats, too.

2 tablespoons water
2 tablespoons orange juice
1-1/2 teaspoons honey
1/2 teaspoon ground cinnamon
1/8 teaspoon ground allspice
1/8 teaspoon ground ginger
Dash salt
1 medium ripe pear, sliced
2-1/2 cups torn mixed salad greens
1/2 cup chopped tomato
2 tablespoons chopped red onion
2 tablespoons raisins

In a small saucepan, combine the water, orange juice, honey, cinnamon, allspice, ginger and salt. Bring to a boil. Reduce the heat and simmer, uncovered, for 5 minutes. Add the pear slices and simmer 5-8 minutes longer or just until the pears are tender.

Divide salad greens between two bowls; top with the tomato, onion, raisins and pear slices. Drizzle with warm dressing; serve immediately. **Yield:** 2 servings.

NOODLES AND KRAUT
(Pictured above)

Joanne Keller, Mukwonago, Wisconsin

I sampled this recipe at a 25th anniversary party and was told it was a family favorite, courtesy of a Polish grandmother. I shared the recipe with my sister-in-law's family, and she told me her five-year-old son loved it so much that he would eat it cold for breakfast! Every time our family gathers now, someone brings this dish.

2 cups uncooked egg noodles
1/4 cup butter, cubed
1/4 cup chopped onion
1 cup sauerkraut, rinsed and well drained

Cook the egg noodles according to package directions; drain.

In a small skillet, melt butter. Add onion; saute until tender. Add noodles and sauerkraut; cook and stir over medium heat for 2 minutes. Reduce the heat; simmer, uncovered, for 10-15 minutes, stirring occasionally. **Yield:** 3 servings.

HEARTY VEGGIE SANDWICHES
(Pictured below)

Caroline Munoz, Austin, Minnesota

My sister and I developed this sandwich one day when we had some spicy everything bagels left over. I have often served it to my friends as a casual lunch. The total lack of fussiness for the sandwich allows me to spend quality time with our guests.

    2 tablespoons mayonnaise
    2 teaspoons Dijon mustard
    2 bagels, split
    2 lettuce leaves
    1 medium ripe avocado, peeled and sliced
    2 large slices tomato
    1 slice sweet onion, separated into rings
Salt and pepper to taste

In a small bowl, combine the mayonnaise and mustard; spread over cut sides of bagels. On bagel bottoms, layer lettuce, avocado, tomato and onion. Sprinkle with salt and pepper. Replace bagel tops. **Yield:** 2 servings.

FISH CHOWDER
(Pictured above)

Margaret Jean, Ayer, Massachusetts

This recipe came from a book that was included with a set of pots and pans we purchased about 30 years ago. Living in New England, we love fish in any dish, and this is something we especially enjoy.

    1 bacon strip, diced
    2 tablespoons chopped onion
    2 tablespoons chopped celery
    2/3 cup condensed cream of potato soup, undiluted
    1/2 cup water
    1/8 teaspoon pepper
Dash salt
    1/2 pound haddock fillets, cut into 1-inch pieces
    1/2 cup milk
 1-1/2 teaspoons butter
Oyster crackers, optional

In a small saucepan, saute the bacon, onion and celery until vegetables are tender. Add the soup, water, pepper and salt. Bring to a boil; reduce the heat. Add the haddock; cover and simmer for 8-12 minutes or until fish flakes easily with a fork. Stir in milk and butter; heat through. Serve with oyster crackers if desired. **Yield:** 2 servings.

STEAMED BROWN BREAD

Myrtle Oliver, Portland, Maine

Folks in our region cherish old recipes which have been passed down to them from generation to generation. Nothing beats homemade brown bread accompanied by a pot of beans.

    2/3 cup all-purpose flour
    2/3 cup old-fashioned oats
    2/3 cup cornmeal
    2 teaspoons baking soda
    1/2 teaspoon salt

1-1/3 cups buttermilk
1/2 cup molasses

In a large bowl, combine the flour, oats, cornmeal, baking soda and salt. Combine buttermilk and molasses; stir into dry ingredients. Pour into two greased 10-oz. ramekins or custard cups; cover with foil.

Place ramekins on a rack in a deep kettle; add 1 in. of hot water to kettle. Bring to a gentle boil; cover and steam for 35-45 minutes or until a toothpick inserted near the center comes out clean, adding more water as needed.

Remove ramekins from the kettle; let stand for 5 minutes before removing the bread from ramekins. **Yield:** 2 servings.

***

BRUSSELS SPROUTS WITH LEEKS
(Pictured below)

Patricia Mickelson, San Jose, California

This is a dish I've made a few times for my husband and me. Since we both love brussels sprouts, I often experiment with different combinations to enhance the taste. We found leeks give the sprouts a special flavor.

  10 brussels sprouts, trimmed and halved
   1 medium leek (white portion only), thinly sliced
   1 tablespoon butter
Dash salt

In a large saucepan, bring 1 in. of water and the brussels sprouts to a boil. Reduce heat; cover and simmer for 8 minutes.

Add leek; cover and simmer 2-4 minutes longer or until vegetables are tender. Drain; stir in butter and salt. **Yield:** 2 servings.

***

GREEN GRAPE SALAD
(Pictured above)

Marjorie Green, South Haven, Michigan

This is an easy, great salad for any time of the year. The combination of the flavors and textures of the fruits and the crunch from the nuts, topped with blue cheese salad dressing, make it tasty and flavorful.

   1 cup green grapes, halved
   1 large firm banana, sliced
 1/2 cup chopped walnuts
 1/4 cup blue cheese salad dressing
   3 tablespoons mayonnaise
   2 teaspoons honey

In a small bowl, combine the grapes, banana and walnuts. Whisk the salad dressing, mayonnaise and honey; pour over grape mixture and toss to coat. Chill until serving. **Yield:** 2 servings.

MIX IT UP

Use any variety of fruits and nuts for the Green Grape Salad to suit your individual taste. Instead of bananas and grapes, use strawberries, pears or apples. And instead of walnuts, use pecans or cashews.

SPECIAL CAULIFLOWER

(Pictured above)

Rita Reinke, Wauwatosa, Wisconsin

I found this recipe in a local paper, and it has become my favorite topping for cauliflower. I like it because the glaze adds color and also enhances the flavor with a little zip. It works well with any entree.

    2 cups fresh cauliflowerets
    1 tablespoon plain yogurt
    1 tablespoon mayonnaise
  1/2 teaspoon Dijon mustard
  1/8 teaspoon dill weed
  1/8 teaspoon salt
  1/8 teaspoon garlic powder
  1/4 cup shredded cheddar cheese

Place cauliflower in a steamer basket; place in a small saucepan over 1 in. of water. Bring to a boil; cover and steam for 6-8 minutes or until crisp-tender.

Meanwhile, in a small bowl, combine yogurt, mayonnaise, mustard, dill, salt and garlic powder.

Transfer the cauliflower to an ungreased 3-cup baking dish; top with yogurt mixture and cheese. Bake, uncovered, at 350° for 5 minutes or until heated through and the cheese is melted. **Yield:** 3 servings.

ABOUT CAULIFLOWER

Look for cauliflower with compact florets that are free from spots. The leaves should be crisp and green. Tightly wrap an unwashed head of cauliflower and refrigerate for up to 5 days. Before using, wash and remove the leaves at the base and trim the stem.

RED SNAPPER FOR TWO

(Pictured below)

Joy Adcock, Amarillo, Texas

This is a fast and easy recipe that is also healthy. Add a tossed salad and some hard bread and you have a tasty gourmet meal. Plus, the cook can even plate the meal from the casserole dish, leaving only two cooking utensils to clean.

  1/4 cup chopped onion
    1 garlic clove, minced
    2 teaspoons olive oil
  1/2 cup chopped fresh mushrooms
    1 medium tomato, chopped
  1/4 cup white wine *or* chicken broth
  1/4 teaspoon salt
  1/4 teaspoon dried basil
  1/4 teaspoon dried oregano
Dash pepper
    2 red snapper fillets (8 ounces *each*)
    2 teaspoons grated Parmesan cheese
    1 tablespoon minced fresh parsley

In a small saucepan, saute the onion and garlic in oil for 1 minute. Stir in the mushrooms and tomato; cook 3 minutes longer. Stir in the wine, salt, basil, oregano and pepper. Bring to a boil. Reduce heat; simmer, uncovered, for 7-11 minutes or until sauce is thickened.

Place fish in a greased 13-in. x 9-in. baking dish; top with sauce. Sprinkle with cheese. Bake, uncovered, at 400° for 12-18 minutes or until fish flakes easily with a fork. Sprinkle with the parsley. **Yield:** 2 servings.

Cooking for Two

BAVARIAN STEW

(Pictured above)

Barbara Pizzi, Sycamore, Illinois

This dish has delighted guests as well as family. I don't remember where this recipe came from, but it has been a family mainstay of ours for many years. It's an excellent German recipe, similar to sauerbraten, but you don't have to marinate the meat for several days. The beef is very flavorful and tender.

   3/4 **pound beef stew meat, cut into**
        3/4-inch cubes
     1 **tablespoon canola oil**
1-1/4 **cups beef broth**
   1/3 **cup thinly sliced onion**
     1 **bay leaf**
   1/2 **teaspoon caraway seeds**
   1/8 **teaspoon pepper**
   1/4 to 1/3 **cup white vinegar**
   1/2 **teaspoon sugar**
   1/4 **medium head red cabbage, cut into**
        2 wedges
   1/4 to 1/3 **cup crushed gingersnap cookies**
        (about 8 cookies)

In a large saucepan, cook the beef in oil until browned; drain. Stir in broth, onion, bay leaf, caraway seeds and pepper. Bring to a boil. Reduce heat; cover and simmer for 1-1/4 hours or until meat is almost tender.

Combine the vinegar and sugar; stir into beef mixture. Place the cabbage on top of the meat mixture. Bring to a boil. Reduce the heat; cover and simmer for 18-22 minutes or until meat and cabbage are tender.

Remove beef and cabbage; keep warm. Discard bay leaf. Stir gingersnaps into cooking liquid; cook and stir until thickened. Stir in beef. Serve with cabbage. **Yield:** 2 servings.

POACHED PEARS WITH RASPBERRY SAUCE

(Pictured below)

Dawn Bryant, Thedford, Nebraska

This elegant dessert for two has a wonderful vanilla flavor that is very satisfying. With an extremely simple raspberry sauce adding a dash of bright color, it is very impressive.

    1 **cup water**
 1/2 **cup sugar**
 1/4 **cup white wine *or* white cranberry juice**
    2 **medium pears, peeled and halved**
    3 **tablespoons seedless raspberry**
       spreadable fruit
 1/2 **teaspoon vanilla extract**
Fresh raspberries and mint leaves, optional

In a small saucepan, bring the water, sugar and wine to a boil. Reduce the heat; carefully add pears. Cover and simmer for 5-10 minutes or until tender. Remove pears and reserve cooking liquid.

In a small bowl, combine spreadable fruit and vanilla. Stir in enough cooking liquid to form a sauce consistency. Cover and refrigerate sauce and pears separately until chilled.

Remove sauce from the refrigerator 15 minutes before serving. Place two pear halves on each dessert plate; top with sauce. Garnish with the raspberries and mint if desired. **Yield:** 2 servings.

CHICKEN PICCATA
(Pictured below)

Carol Cottrill, Rumford, Maine

This is a flavorful dish. With the lemon juice, the salt isn't missed. I usually serve this with rice or pasta, but it takes longer to cook either one of these than it does the chicken!

>   2 boneless skinless chicken breast halves
>   (4 ounces *each*)
>   2 tablespoons all-purpose flour
>   1/4 teaspoon salt
>   1/8 teaspoon pepper
>   1 tablespoon canola oil
>   2 tablespoons white wine *or*
>   reduced-sodium chicken broth
>   1 garlic clove, minced
>   1/3 cup reduced-sodium chicken broth
>   1 tablespoon lemon juice
> 1-1/2 teaspoons capers
> 1-1/2 teaspoons butter
>   2 thin lemon slices

Flatten chicken to 1/2-in. thickness. In a shallow bowl, combine the flour, salt and pepper. Add chicken, one piece at a time, and turn to coat.

In a small skillet, brown the chicken in oil for 2-3 minutes on each side or until no longer pink. Remove and keep warm.

Add wine and garlic to the pan; cook and stir for 30 seconds. Add the broth, lemon juice and capers. Bring to a boil; cook for 1-2 minutes or until slightly thickened. Stir in butter and lemon slices. Return chicken to the pan; heat through. **Yield:** 2 servings.

STRAWBERRY CREAM PUFFS
(Pictured above)

Suzette Jury, Keene, California

My family loves to cook, and this recipe came from a collection of recipes that have been handed down from generation to generation. These cream puffs were a favorite for holidays, but are good anytime. It's a nice departure from strawberry shortcake, and the best part is you can make the shells ahead of time and freeze them.

>   1/4 cup water
>   2 tablespoons butter
>   1/4 teaspoon sugar
> Dash salt
>   1/4 cup all-purpose flour
>   1 egg
> FILLING:
> 1-1/4 cups sliced fresh strawberries
>   3 teaspoons sugar, *divided*
>   1/2 cup heavy whipping cream
>   1/4 teaspoon confectioners' sugar
> Additional sliced fresh strawberries, optional

In a small saucepan, bring the water, butter, sugar and salt to a boil. Add flour all at once and stir until a smooth ball forms. Remove from the heat; let stand for 5 minutes. Add egg and beat well. Continue beating until mixture is smooth and shiny. Drop by rounded tablespoonfuls 3 in. apart onto a greased baking sheet.

Bake at 400° for 25-30 minutes or until golden brown. Remove to a wire rack. Immediately split puffs open; remove tops and set aside. Discard soft dough from inside. Cool puffs.

For filling, in a small bowl, combine the strawberries and 2 teaspoons sugar. Cover and refrigerate for 30 minutes.

In a small bowl, beat the heavy cream and the remaining sugar until stiff peaks form. Fold in the strawberry mixture.

Fill cream puffs just before serving. Sprinkle with the confectioners' sugar. Garnish with the additional strawberries if desired. **Yield:** 3 servings.

SIMPLE LETTUCE SALAD
(Pictured below)

Susan Davis, Vale, North Carolina

My mother often fixed this salad when I was a child. I grew up on a farm and most of our food came right from the garden. We especially liked this in the spring, when early leaf lettuce appeared. After a long winter of cooked vegetables, this was a real treat.

- 2 cups torn leaf lettuce
- 1 hard-cooked egg, chopped
- 1 green onion, sliced
- 2 tablespoons mayonnaise
- 1 teaspoon cider vinegar
- 1/8 teaspoon pepper

In a salad bowl, combine the lettuce, egg and onion. In a small bowl, whisk the mayonnaise, vinegar and pepper. Pour over salad and toss to coat. **Yield:** 2 servings.

SCALLOPED POTATOES
(Pictured above)

Lillian Julow, Gainesville, Florida

I found I could cut down the prep time of this potato dish by first simmering them on top of the stove in an ovenproof skillet and then slipping it into the oven to finish them nicely with a brown crust.

- 2 cups thinly sliced peeled potatoes (about 2 large)
- 2 teaspoons all-purpose flour
- Dash *each* salt, pepper and ground nutmeg
- 2 teaspoons butter
- 2/3 to 1 cup half-and-half cream
- 1/3 cup shredded Gouda cheese

Place half of the potatoes in a greased small ovenproof skillet and sprinkle with 1 teaspoon flour. Repeat layers. Sprinkle with salt, pepper and nutmeg. Dot with butter.

Add enough cream to fill skillet about three-fourths full. Bring to a boil over medium-high heat. Reduce heat; simmer, uncovered, for 15-20 minutes or until most of the liquid is absorbed.

Carefully place the skillet in the oven. Bake, uncovered, at 350° for 10-15 minutes or until bubbly and potatoes are tender. Sprinkle with cheese; bake 5 minutes longer or until cheese is melted. **Yield:** 2 servings.

FRUITED POPPY SEED COLESLAW

(Pictured at left)

Mildred Bell, Millen, Georgia

This recipe was served at a church dinner in a pretty round crystal bowl. It has a unique look as well as taste.

- 1/2 cup chopped green cabbage
- 1/4 cup chopped red cabbage
- 1/4 cup chopped Red Delicious apple
- 1/4 cup chopped fresh pear
- 2 tablespoons golden raisins
- 2 tablespoons canola oil
- 1 tablespoon sugar
- 2 teaspoons red wine vinegar
- 1/2 teaspoon finely chopped onion
- 1/2 teaspoon poppy seeds
- 1/8 teaspoon salt
- 1/8 teaspoon ground mustard
- 2 tablespoons salted peanuts

In a small bowl, combine cabbage, apple, pear and raisins. In another bowl, whisk oil, sugar, vinegar, onion, poppy seeds, salt and mustard. Pour over the cabbage mixture and toss to coat. Cover and refrigerate for at least 30 minutes. Just before serving, sprinkle with peanuts. **Yield:** 2 servings.

APRICOT-PISTACHIO CHICKEN SALAD SANDWICHES

(Pictured above)

Lesley Pew, Lynn, Massachusetts

I ordered an entree similar to this at the local museum cafe and liked it so much I decided to make something similar. I like to serve it as a chilled salad during the summer. It's really good on a hot day.

- 1-1/2 cups shredded rotisserie chicken
- 1/3 cup chopped dried apricots
- 2 tablespoons mayonnaise
- 2 tablespoons sour cream
- 4 teaspoons coarsely chopped pistachios
- 1 teaspoon prepared horseradish
- 1 teaspoon whole grain mustard
- 1 teaspoon honey
Dash salt
Dash white pepper
Dash hot pepper sauce
- 4 slices sourdough bread
- 2 Bibb lettuce leaves
- 2 slices tomato
- 2 slices sweet onion

In a small bowl, combine the first 11 ingredients. Spread over two slices of bread; top with lettuce, tomato, sweet onion and the remaining bread. **Yield:** 2 servings.

SOFT BUTTERMILK SUGAR COOKIES

(Pictured above left)

Traci Rowlett, Lawrenceburg, Indiana

Gatherings are very important to my family, so we have lots of recipes that are favorites.

- 1-1/4 cups sugar, *divided*
- 1/4 teaspoon ground cinnamon
- 1/2 cup shortening
- 2 eggs
- 2 teaspoons vanilla extract
- 2 cups all-purpose flour
- 2 teaspoons baking powder
- 1 teaspoon salt
- 1/2 teaspoon baking soda
- 1/2 cup buttermilk

Combine 1/4 cup sugar and cinnamon; set aside. In a large bowl, cream shortening and remaining sugar until light and fluffy. Beat in eggs and vanilla. Combine flour, baking powder, salt and baking soda; add to creamed mixture alternately with buttermilk. Beat well after each addition.

Drop by tablespoonfuls onto greased baking sheets. Sprinkle with reserved cinnamon-sugar. Bake at 375° for 8-10 minutes or until the edges begin to brown. Remove to wire racks. Store in an airtight container. **Yield:** about 2-1/2 dozen.

Cooking for Two

CUCUMBER SALAD
(Pictured above)

Yulia Bagwell, Philadelphia, Pennsylvania

This is a good salad for those who are watching their weight...very light but filling. Go easy on the dressing as too much will spoil the natural flavors of the salad.

- 1-1/2 cups thinly sliced cucumbers
- 2 tablespoons sour cream
- 2 tablespoons prepared ranch salad dressing
- 1 green onion, chopped
- 1 teaspoon minced fresh parsley, *divided*
- 1 teaspoon snipped fresh dill, *divided*
- 1 hard-cooked egg, sliced

Arrange cucumbers on a serving plate. In a small bowl, combine the sour cream, ranch, onion, 1/2 teaspoon parsley and 1/2 teaspoon dill. Spoon over the cucumbers. Garnish with egg slices and sprinkle with the remaining parsley and dill. **Yield:** 2 servings.

◆◆◆◆◆◆◆◆◆◆◆◆

HINT-OF-MINT LEMONADE

Laura Mae Newcomer, Bowdoin, Maine

We always have a plentiful supply of fresh mint leaves in the garden, so this makes a very refreshing drink on warm summer days.

- 2/3 cup water
- 1/3 cup sugar
- 1 fresh mint sprig
- 3 tablespoons lemon juice
- 3 tablespoons orange juice
- 1 teaspoon grated orange peel
- 1-3/4 cups cold water
- Crushed ice
- Lemon slices and additional mint, optional

In a small saucepan, bring water and sugar to a boil. Reduce the heat; cover and simmer for 5 minutes. Remove from the heat; stir in the mint, lemon juice, orange juice and peel. Cover and let stand for 1 hour.

Strain and discard the mint and orange peel. Stir in cold water; serve over ice. Garnish with lemon slices and additional mint if desired. **Yield:** 2 servings.

◆◆◆◆◆◆◆◆◆◆◆◆

CHERRY COBBLER
(Pictured below)

Eleanor Jacoby, Eureka, Kansas

Berries, peaches or any fruit you like can be used for this simple recipe, but the cheery bright color of cherries makes it just right for gray winter days.

- 1 cup canned pitted tart cherries
- 1/3 cup plus 3 tablespoons sugar, *divided*
- 1/2 cup all-purpose flour
- 1/2 teaspoon baking powder
- 1 tablespoon cold butter
- 1/4 cup milk

In a small saucepan over medium heat, bring the cherries and 1/3 cup sugar to a boil. Remove from the heat; set aside.

In a small bowl, combine flour, baking powder and remaining sugar. Cut in butter until mixture resembles coarse crumbs. Stir in milk just until moistened. Spread into a greased 3-cup baking dish; pour cherries over the top.

Bake at 375° for 25-30 minutes or until bubbly and the edges are golden brown. Serve warm. **Yield:** 3 servings.

CHICKEN ASPARAGUS PASTA
(Pictured at right)

Taralynn Plastina, McHenry, Illinois

We enjoy this dish often in the spring when asparagus is fresh on the market. It's a favorite with family and friends and a welcome surprise to those who think they don't like asparagus.

    2/3 cup cut fresh asparagus (1-inch pieces)
    4 teaspoons canola oil, *divided*
    1/2 teaspoon salt
    1/4 teaspoon pepper
    4 ounces uncooked fettuccine
    1/2 pound boneless skinless chicken breast,
         cut into 1/2-inch cubes
    1 garlic clove, minced
    2 tablespoons lemon juice
    1 tablespoon grated lemon peel
    1 tablespoon butter
    2 tablespoons grated Parmesan cheese

Place the asparagus in an ungreased 2-qt. baking dish; drizzle with 2 teaspoons oil and sprinkle with the salt and pepper. Bake, uncovered, at 400° for 10-12 minutes or until the asparagus is tender, stirring occasionally.

Meanwhile, cook the fettuccine according to package directions. In a large skillet over medium heat, cook the chicken and garlic in remaining oil until chicken is no longer pink.

Stir in the lemon juice, peel and butter; heat through. Remove from the heat. Drain fettuccine; toss with the chicken mixture and asparagus. Sprinkle with Parmesan cheese. **Yield:** 2 servings.

HEAVENLY ICE CREAM DREAM
(Pictured at right)

Winola Holliday, Bogalusa, Louisiana

My daughter created this recipe after she tried this dessert at a restaurant in England, where she is stationed in the U.S. Air Force. The delight in this sundae is the surprise at the bottom of the dish.

    3 tablespoons chopped pecans
    3 tablespoons graham cracker crumbs
    2 tablespoons semisweet chocolate chips
    2 tablespoons flaked coconut, toasted
    1 tablespoon butter, melted
    1 cup vanilla ice cream
    2 tablespoons caramel ice cream topping
    2 tablespoons hot fudge ice cream topping

In a small bowl, combine the first five ingredients. Set aside 1 tablespoon for topping; divide the remaining mixture between two dessert dishes.

Top with ice cream. Drizzle with caramel and hot fudge toppings and sprinkle with reserved pecan mixture. **Yield:** 2 servings.

STRAWBERRY, ONION AND ROMAINE SALAD
(Pictured at right)

Norma Miedema, Litchville, North Dakota

The combination of berries, onions and a raspberry-based dressing may seem odd, but it is delicious and different. This salad is very tasty and refreshing at picnics and summer meals...a recipe that has been shared many times with family and friends.

    2 cups torn romaine
    1/2 cup sliced fresh strawberries
    1/4 cup thinly sliced red onion
    2 tablespoons slivered almonds
DRESSING:
    1/4 cup mayonnaise
    1 tablespoon sugar
    1 tablespoon half-and-half cream
    1 tablespoon raspberry vinegar
    1 teaspoon red raspberry preserves
    1/2 teaspoon poppy seeds

In a serving bowl, combine romaine, strawberries, onion and almonds. In a small bowl, whisk the dressing ingredients; serve with the salad. **Yield:** 2 servings.

BREADSTICK BRAIDS
(Pictured at right)

Mary Relyea, Canastota, New York

These tender, flavorful bread sticks are not only attractive, they taste every bit like they were made from scratch. It's a very nice use of a frozen dough product and, of course, very convenient because you only need three ingredients to make the breadsticks.

    4 frozen bread dough dinner rolls, thawed
    2 tablespoons beaten egg
    1 teaspoon poppy, sesame *and/or* caraway
         seeds

Cut a dinner roll into three pieces; roll each piece into a 9-in. rope. Place three ropes together; braid. Pinch the ends to seal and tuck under. Repeat with remaining ropes.

Place 2 in. apart on a greased baking sheet. Cover and let rise until doubled, about 20 minutes. Brush breadsticks with egg; sprinkle with seeds.

Bake at 375° for 10-14 minutes or until golden brown. **Yield:** 4 breadsticks.

Meals in Minutes

A hot home-cooked meal is just moments away with these recipes that can be made in half an hour or less.

Filet Mignon On the Go

DOES FALL find you on the go with after-school activities and more? Well, your family is sure to fall for this complete menu with recipes from three super cooks...all ready in just 30 minutes!

Blanche Stevens of Anderson, Indiana serves Mushroom Beef Tenderloin with toasted French bread. It's quick to fix but seems special. A tasty mushroom sauce complements the juicy beef.

"Lemony Brussels Sprouts is a fast and refreshing way to serve little cabbages," shares Joyce Guth of Mohnton, Pennsylvania. "My youngest son loves them!"

And Ruth Peterson of Jenison, Michigan, says, "I always have the ingredients for this delicious Rapid Raspberry Torte on hand so I can make the dessert at a moment's notice."

MUSHROOM BEEF TENDERLOIN

    3/4 pound fresh mushrooms, sliced
      5 tablespoons butter, *divided*
      2 teaspoons all-purpose flour
      1 teaspoon salt
    1/4 teaspoon pepper
      1 cup heavy whipping cream
      1 tablespoon minced fresh parsley
      6 beef tenderloin steaks (1-1/2 inches
        thick and 4 ounces *each*)

In a large skillet, saute mushrooms in 3 tablespoons butter for 6-8 minutes or until tender. Stir in the flour, salt and pepper until blended. Gradually add the cream. Bring to a gentle boil; cook and stir for 1-2 minutes or until thickened. Stir in parsley; set aside and keep warm.

Meanwhile, in another large skillet, heat the remaining butter over medium-high heat. Cook steaks for 6-7 minutes on each side or until meat reaches desired doneness (for medium-rare, a meat thermometer should read 145°; medium, 160°; well-done, 170°). Serve with the mushroom sauce. **Yield:** 6 servings.

LEMONY BRUSSELS SPROUTS

    1-1/2 pounds fresh brussels sprouts (about
          2-1/2 cups), trimmed
        1 teaspoon lemon juice
      1/8 teaspoon salt
      1/8 teaspoon pepper
      1/3 cup butter, cubed
        2 garlic cloves, minced

Cut an "X" in the core of each brussels sprout. Place in a saucepan; add 1 in. of water. Bring to a boil. Reduce heat; cover and simmer for 10-12 minutes or until crisp-tender. Drain. In a large skillet, saute the sprouts, lemon juice, salt and pepper in butter for 2-3 minutes or until flavors are blended. Add garlic; cook 1 minute longer. **Yield:** 6 servings.

RAPID RASPBERRY TORTE

    3/4 cup heavy whipping cream
      1 tablespoon confectioners' sugar
      2 snack-size cups (3-1/2 ounces *each*)
        lemon pudding
      1 loaf (10-3/4 ounces) frozen pound
        cake, thawed
    1/3 cup raspberry jam, *divided*

In a small bowl, beat the cream until soft peaks form. Add confectioners' sugar; beat until stiff peaks form. Place pudding in a bowl; fold in whipped cream.

Cut cake horizontally into three layers. Place bottom layer on a serving plate; top with half the jam. Repeat layers. Top with third cake layer. Cut into slices; dollop with pudding mixture. **Yield:** 7-10 servings.

Editor's Note: This recipe was tested with Hunt's Snack Pack lemon pudding.

Pork Chops Are Super Fast

FOR THOSE who love to cook, spending time in the kitchen preparing an elaborate meal is a joy. Still, there are some days when you need to pull together a satisfying supper in just minutes. Here's an example of a quick and easy meal that looks like you spent all day preparing.

This complete menu is made up of family favorites from four great cooks. You can have everything for a delicious, wholesome dinner ready to serve in just 30 minutes.

A tempting and beautiful glaze makes Mustard-Apricot Pork Chops an impressive main dish that looks like you fussed over it. "This recipe is so simple and good," says Sheila Townsend of West Des Moines, Iowa. These tender chops are nice to serve during the week as well as for special dinners or company on weekends.

Asparagus with Almonds will please the palates of everyone—even those who generally don't care for asparagus, assures Eileen Bechtel of Wainwright, Alberta. "I look forward to spring each year so I can make this tasty side dish." And for those who love asparagus, it's such an effortless, delectable vegetable dish to make.

Fruit Parfaits are a refreshing fruity treat, and you can use whatever flavor of gelatin you like. Spring City, Tennessee cook Erlene Cornelius shares the recipe. And because it calls for canned fruit, you can rely on it as a scrumptious dessert any time of year.

Tina Christensen's Vanilla-Almond Coffee is a warming accompaniment to the meal. It pairs well with dessert in her Addison, Illinois home.

MUSTARD-APRICOT PORK CHOPS

  1/3 cup apricot preserves
    2 tablespoons Dijon mustard
    4 pork loin chops (1/2 to 3/4 inch thick
      and 8 ounces *each*)
    3 green onions, chopped
Hot cooked rice

In a small saucepan over low heat, cook and stir preserves and mustard until preserves are melted; set aside.

Place the pork chops on a lightly greased broiler pan; broil 4 in. from heat for 5 minutes. Brush with half of the glaze; turn the pork chops. Broil 5 minutes longer; brush with the remaining glaze. Broil 2-4 minutes more or until a meat thermometer reads 160°. Top with onions. Serve with the rice. **Yield:** 4 servings.

ASPARAGUS WITH ALMONDS

    2 tablespoons sliced almonds
    4 teaspoons olive oil, *divided*
    1 pound fresh asparagus, cut into
      2-inch pieces
  1/4 cup water
    1 teaspoon sugar
  1/4 teaspoon salt
Dash pepper
    1 teaspoon lemon juice

In a large skillet, saute sliced almonds in 1 teaspoon of olive oil until lightly browned; remove and set aside. In the same skillet, saute asparagus in the remaining olive oil for 1 minute. Add the water, sugar, salt and pepper; bring to a boil. Reduce heat; cover and simmer asparagus for 3-4 minutes or tender. Drain. Sprinkle with lemon juice; top with toasted almonds. **Yield:** 3-4 servings.

FRUIT PARFAITS

    1 can (15 ounces) fruit cocktail
    1 package (3 ounces) lemon gelatin
    8 ice cubes (1-1/2 cups crushed ice)

Drain the fruit cocktail, reserving syrup. Divide the fruit among four parfait glasses and set aside. Add water to the syrup to measure 3/4 cup; pour into a saucepan. Bring to a boil.

Place the gelatin in a blender; carefully add the syrup. Cover and blend on low until the gelatin is dissolved, about 30 seconds. Add the ice; cover and blend until dissolved, about 1 minute. Pour over the fruit. Cover and refrigerate until set, about 15 minutes. **Yield:** 4 servings.

VANILLA-ALMOND COFFEE

    1 pound ground coffee
    2 tablespoons almond extract
    2 tablespoons vanilla extract

Place the ground coffee in a large jar with tight-fitting lid. Add the almond and vanilla extracts. Cover, making sure the lid is tight, and shake well. Store in the refrigerator. Prepare the coffee as usual. **Yield:** 1 pound.

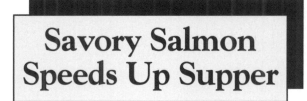

Savory Salmon Speeds Up Supper

WITH TWO busy youngsters and a demanding split-shift job as a waitress, Denise Blackman has little time on weeknights for making the meals she serves to her own family. That's why Denise counts on a helpful husband...and on "Meals in Minutes" menus!

"With my changeable work schedule, I need recipes that are quick to fix and easy enough for my husband to prepare when I have to work in the evening," declares Denise.

Fast doesn't rule out fresh ingredients, however. Denise prefers using them whenever possible, especially when produce is at its peak season and most affordable and flavorful. And, when she has more time on the weekends, she loves to cook dishes that are a bit more complicated.

The meal pictured here is a favorite with the Blackman family. It features fresh salmon, which is a seafood that's a mealtime mainstay in Denise's home area of Port Cartier, Quebec. (If fresh salmon isn't readily available where you live, Denise assures that other fish varieties will also work well for this recipe.) Not only is salmon naturally rich in flavor, it's a heart-healthy choice for a main dish.

Enjoy summer's garden greens in a crisp, fresh salad crowned with creamy, delicious blue cheese dressing. And take advantage of seasonal squash and tiny red potatoes for the speedy, delicious vegetable side dish.

But be sure to save room for dessert—fresh berries topped with a dollop of orangy whipped cream are a perfect ending to an extra-simple meal that goes from start to finish in a snap!

It's easy to see with Denise Blackman's super convenient, well-rounded meal that creating a tasty supper for your family doesn't have to be a chore. With these four delicious recipes, cooking can actually be a joy!

FISH FILLETS IN GARLIC BUTTER

> 2 tablespoons butter
> 2 small garlic cloves, minced
> 4 fish fillets (about 6 ounces *each*)
>   (salmon *or* whitefish *or* cod)
> 1/4 cup thinly sliced green onions
Lemon wedges

In a skillet, melt the butter over medium heat. Saute the garlic 1 minute. Place the fish fillets over the minced garlic, cover and cook over low heat 3 minutes. Carefully turn the fish; sprinkle with the green onions. Cover and continue to cook until the fish flakes easily with a fork, about 2-3 minutes. Squeeze the lemon over the fish. Serve immediately. **Yield:** 4 servings.

SUMMER SQUASH AND POTATO SAUTE

> 2 tablespoons butter
> 2 medium summer squash, sliced
> 2 small red potatoes, thinly sliced
Minced fresh parsley
Salt and pepper to taste

In a large skillet, melt the butter over medium heat. Add the summer squash and red potatoes, and saute until tender. Sprinkle with the minced parsley, salt and pepper to taste. Serve immediately. **Yield:** 4 servings.

BLUE CHEESE DRESSING

> 1/4 cup crumbled blue cheese
> 3/4 cup sour cream, *divided*
> 2 tablespoons canola oil
> 1 tablespoon lemon juice
> 1 to 1-1/2 teaspoons Worcestershire
>   sauce, optional
Salt and pepper to taste

Mash the blue cheese with a fork. Add 2 tablespoons sour cream; beat until smooth. Stir in oil, lemon juice, Worcestershire if desired, salt and pepper. Serve over mixed greens. Refrigerate leftover dressing. **Yield:** 1 cup.

STRAWBERRIES ROMANOFF

> 1 quart fresh strawberries, hulled
> 1/2 cup confectioners' sugar
> 1 cup heavy whipping cream
> 1/4 cup orange juice

Sprinkle the strawberries with sugar. Cover and refrigerate for 15-20 minutes. Just before serving, whip the cream until almost stiff. Gently stir in the orange juice.

Fold in the strawberry mixture or serve individually by placing the strawberries in small bowls topped with the flavored whipped cream. **Yield:** 4-6 servings.

Fast and Delicious Can't Be Beat

SURPRISE YOUR family with a special dinner in the middle of the week. It's easy with this fast fare from our Test Kitchen.

Cranberry Pork Chops capture the flavors of the season. Dried cranberries add a touch of sweetness and autumn appeal to this tasty skillet supper. If you don't have pork chops on hand, simply use four boneless, skinless chicken breast halves instead.

Simple seasonings dress up Garlic Green Beans. This savory vegetable dish is a wonderful accompaniment to pork, beef and poultry. In season, fresh garden green beans can be substituted for the frozen.

To make the meal a bit more special, make your own pilaf with Lemon Rice Pilaf. The lemon adds such a fresh flavor and will become a favorite in your household.

The aroma of Apricot Crisp baking is unbeatable. During the week, homemade fruit crisp is a treat you likely don't have time to prepare. But these individual crisps call for canned fruit and bake for a mere 15 minutes.

And it's easy to rouse sleepy taste buds with big cups of this anything-but-average cup of joe from our Test Kitchen. Brewed with lemon peel then stirred into mugs with a pineapple-sugar mixture, the spiced coffee adds zest to everyday routines.

CRANBERRY PORK CHOPS

    4 bone-in pork loin chops (1/2 inch thick
      and 8 ounces *each*)
    2 tablespoons butter
    1 cup chicken broth, *divided*
  1/2 teaspoon dried rosemary, crushed
  1/4 cup sliced green onions
  1/4 cup dried cranberries
  1/8 teaspoon pepper
    3 teaspoons cornstarch
Hot cooked rice

In a large skillet, brown the pork chops in the butter for 3 minutes on each side. Add 1/2 cup chicken broth and dried rosemary to the skillet. Reduce heat and cover. Simmer for 5 minutes or until a meat thermometer reaches 160°. Remove the pork chops to a serving dish and keep warm.

In the same skillet, add onions, cranberries and

pepper. In a small bowl, whisk cornstarch and remaining broth until smooth; gradually add to skillet. Bring to a boil; cook and stir for 2 minutes or until thickened. Serve with pork and rice. **Yield:** 4 servings.

GARLIC GREEN BEANS

  1/2 cup water
  1/2 teaspoon chicken bouillon granules,
      optional
    1 package (16 ounces) frozen whole
      green beans
    1 to 2 garlic cloves, minced
    1 tablespoon butter
  1/4 teaspoon seasoned salt

In a saucepan, bring the water and the chicken bouillon if desired to a boil. Add the green beans. Reduce heat; cover and simmer for 10-12 minutes or until the beans are tender.

In a large skillet, saute the minced garlic in butter for 1 minute. Drain beans; add to skillet. Sprinkle with seasoned salt and toss to coat. **Yield:** 4 servings.

LEMON RICE PILAF

    1 cup uncooked jasmine *or* long grain
      white rice
    1 cup sliced celery
    1 cup thinly sliced green onions
    2 tablespoons butter
    1 tablespoon grated lemon peel
    1 teaspoon salt
  1/4 teaspoon pepper

Cook the rice according to package directions. Meanwhile, in a skillet over medium heat, saute celery and onions in butter until tender. Add rice, lemon peel, salt and pepper; toss lightly. Cook and stir until heated through. **Yield:** 4-6 servings.

CITRUS SPICED COFFEE

  3/4 cup ground coffee
    1 teaspoon grated lemon peel
    1 cup water
  3/4 cup packed brown sugar
    3 cinnamon sticks (3 inches)
    2 fresh orange slices
    2 tablespoons unsweetened pineapple
      juice
  1/2 teaspoon vanilla extract

Place coffee grounds in a filter or basket of a coffeemaker; add lemon peel. Prepare nine cups brewed coffee according to the manufacturer's directions.

In a small saucepan, combine water, brown sugar, cinnamon sticks, orange slices, pineapple juice and vanilla. Cook and stir over medium heat until sugar is dissolved. Strain; discard cinnamon and oranges. Pour sugar mixture into mugs; add coffee. Stir. **Yield:** 9 servings.

APRICOT CRISP

3 cans (15-1/4 ounces *each*) apricot
  halves, drained
2 tablespoons brown sugar
1/2 teaspoon ground ginger

TOPPING:
1/4 cup all-purpose flour
  3 tablespoons brown sugar
  3 tablespoons quick-cooking oats
  2 tablespoons flaked coconut
1/4 cup cold butter, cubed

In a large bowl, combine the apricots, brown sugar and ginger. Divide among four greased 8-oz. baking dishes.

For topping, in a small bowl, combine the flour, brown sugar, oats and coconut. Cut in the cold butter until mixture resembles coarse crumbs. Sprinkle over the apricots. Bake at 400° for 15 minutes or until the filling is bubbly and top is golden brown. **Yield:** 4 servings.

Editor's Note: Crisp may be baked in an 8-in. square baking dish for 23-25 minutes.

Our Most Memorable Meals

All-time family favorites still bring folks together around the table for lasting dinner memories.

Simple, Elegant And Easy

GARLIC-BUTTER BAKED SALMON

Deborah Oedekoven, Spearfish, South Dakota

My husband discovered this recipe in 1995. The salmon bakes up tender, moist and flavorful.

> 2 whole garlic bulbs
> 4 teaspoons olive oil, *divided*
> 3 tablespoons butter
> 6 salmon fillets (6 ounces *each*)
> 1/4 teaspoon salt
> 1/4 teaspoon pepper
> 2 to 3 tablespoons lemon juice
> 1 teaspoon minced fresh parsley
> 1/4 teaspoon minced fresh rosemary

Remove papery outer skin from garlic (do not peel or separate cloves). Cut top off garlic bulbs. Brush with 1 teaspoon oil. Wrap each in heavy-duty foil.

Bake at 425° for 30-35 minutes or until softened. Cool for 10-15 minutes.

Squeeze softened garlic into a food processor; add butter and remaining oil. Cover and process until blended; set aside.

Place salmon in a greased 15-in. x 10-in. x 1-in. baking pan. Sprinkle with the salt and pepper; drizzle with lemon juice. Spoon 1 tablespoon garlic butter over each fillet. Bake, uncovered, at 425° for 8-10 minutes or until fish flakes easily with a fork. Sprinkle with herbs. **Yield:** 6 servings.

ROASTED VEGGIE MEDLEY

Candice Garcia, Winter Haven, Florida

This colorful blend of fall veggies is tender and sweet, and it is an eye-catching addition to any autumn menu.

> 1-1/2 cups pearl onions
> 2 cups fresh baby carrots
> 3 medium turnips (about 3/4 pound), peeled and cut into 1/2-inch wedges
> 10 fresh thyme sprigs
> 1 tablespoon olive oil
> 2 teaspoons maple syrup, *divided*
> 1/4 teaspoon salt
> 1/8 teaspoon pepper
> 2 teaspoons cider vinegar
> 2 tablespoons minced fresh parsley, *divided*

In a large saucepan, bring 4 cups water to a boil. Add pearl onions; boil for 3 minutes. Drain and rinse in cold water; peel.

Place the onions, carrots and turnips in a large resealable plastic bag; add the thyme sprigs, oil, 1 teaspoon syrup, salt and pepper. Seal bag and shake to coat. Arrange the vegetables in a single layer in a greased 15-in. x 10-in. x 1-in. baking pan. Bake, uncovered, at 425° for 30-35 minutes or until vegetables are tender, stirring twice.

Discard thyme. Transfer vegetables to a serving bowl. Drizzle with the vinegar, remaining syrup and 1 tablespoon parsley; toss to coat. Sprinkle with remaining parsley. **Yield:** 6 servings.

PEAR SORBET WITH RASPBERRY SAUCE

Laurie Fisher, Evans, Colorado

I clipped this recipe out of the newspaper several years ago and then modified it to suit my family's taste. It's a timeless dessert.

> 2 pounds pears, peeled and halved
> 2 cups water
> 1-1/2 cups sugar
> 5-1/2 teaspoons lemon juice, *divided*
> 1 package (10 ounces) frozen sweetened raspberries, thawed

In a large saucepan, combine pears, water, sugar and 4-1/2 teaspoons lemon juice. Cook and stir over medium heat for 15-20 minutes or until pears are tender. Cool slightly.

In a blender, process pear mixture for 1-2 minutes or until smooth. Transfer to a 13-in. x 9-in. dish. Cover and freeze for 45 minutes or until edges begin to firm; stir. Freeze 2 hours longer or until firm. Just before serving, process again in a blender for 2-3 minutes or until smooth.

For sauce, press the raspberries through a sieve; discard seeds. Stir in remaining lemon juice. Serve with sorbet. **Yield:** 10 servings.

NUTTY WHOLE WHEAT BREAD

Caryl Miller, Muscoda, Wisconsin

This bread is delicious for morning toast and for French toast. It's actually very simple to make.

1-1/8 teaspoons active dry yeast
  1/2 cup warm water (110° to 115°)
  1/2 cup warm milk (110° to 115°)
    4 teaspoons honey
    1 tablespoon olive oil
1-1/2 cups whole wheat flour
    1 cup all-purpose flour
  1/2 teaspoon salt
  1/4 teaspoon pepper, optional
    3 tablespoons chopped pecans, toasted
    1 tablespoon cornmeal
    1 tablespoon milk

In a large bowl, dissolve yeast in warm water. Add the warm milk, honey and oil. Combine flours, salt and pepper if desired; add 1-1/2 cups to yeast mixture. Beat on medium speed for 3 minutes. Stir in pecans and remaining flour mixture to form a stiff dough.

Turn onto a floured surface; knead until smooth and elastic, about 6-8 minutes. Place in a greased bowl, turning once to grease top. Cover and let rise in a warm place until doubled, about 1 hour.

Sprinkle cornmeal over a greased baking sheet. Punch dough down. Shape into a round loaf; place on prepared baking sheet. Cover and let rise until doubled, about 30 minutes.

Brush milk over loaf. Bake at 350° for 45-50 minutes or until bread sounds hollow when tapped. Remove from pan to a wire rack to cool. **Yield:** 1 loaf (16 slices).

Festive and Fun Picnic Fare

Fabulous Cherry Ribs

Margaret Smith, Superior, Wisconsin

My husband and I love to cook and we're always looking for something a little different. These ribs are a refreshing change from the traditional tomato-based barbecue sauces. A friend gave me this recipe years ago, and it has been a family favorite since.

4 pounds pork spareribs, cut into serving-size pieces
1 can (21 ounces) cherry pie filling
1 small onion, chopped
2 tablespoons olive oil
1/4 cup soy sauce
2 teaspoons spicy brown mustard
1 teaspoon ground ginger
1 teaspoon Worcestershire sauce

Place ribs in two ungreased 13-in. x 9-in. baking pans. Cover and bake at 350° for 1-1/2 to 2 hours or until meat is tender.

Meanwhile, place the pie filling in a food processor; cover and process until smooth.

In a small saucepan, saute onion in oil until tender. Stir in the pie filling, soy sauce, mustard, ginger and Worcestershire sauce.

Bring to a boil. Reduce the heat; simmer, uncovered, for 10-15 minutes or until slightly thickened, stirring occasionally. Remove from the heat. Set aside 1 cup for serving.

Grill ribs, covered, over medium heat for 6-8 minutes on each side or until lightly browned, brushing occasionally with remaining sauce. Warm the reserved sauce; serve with ribs. **Yield:** 4 servings.

BLT Caesar Salad

Rachelle McCalla, Wayne, Nebraska

With the addition of cold cooked chicken, this salad makes a great meal all by itself. As is, it's a nice idea for a twist on Caesar salad, which is always lighter than your standard BLT.

3 cups torn romaine
2 plum tomatoes, chopped
4 bacon strips, cooked and crumbled
1/4 cup creamy Caesar salad dressing
1/2 cup salad croutons

In a large bowl, combine romaine, tomatoes and bacon. Divide among four salad plates; drizzle with dressing and top with croutons. **Yield:** 4 servings.

Horseradish Potatoes

Madelaine Fletcher, Catonsville, Maryland

This is a great dish for spring and early summer when the chives are first coming up and are young and tender. Because of the tang from the horseradish and mustard, it is a compatible side dish to ham or corned beef.

1-1/4 pounds red potatoes (about 5 medium), sliced
1/2 cup sour cream
4-1/2 teaspoons minced chives
3-1/2 teaspoons prepared horseradish
1 tablespoon minced fresh parsley
1 teaspoon lemon juice
1/2 teaspoon Dijon mustard
1/4 teaspoon salt
1/8 teaspoon pepper
Lettuce leaves, optional

Place the potatoes in a large saucepan and cover with water. Bring to a boil. Reduce the heat; cover and cook for 12-15 minutes or until tender. Meanwhile, combine the sour cream, chives, horseradish, parsley, lemon juice, mustard, salt and pepper.

Drain potatoes and cool slightly. Add dressing and gently stir to coat. Serve in a lettuce-lined bowl if desired. **Yield:** 4 servings.

Blueberry Buckle

Maureen Carr, Carman, Manitoba

This recipe is a family favorite, served warm as dessert, plain or with a scoop of ice cream. My gang also likes it cold as a coffee cake. But the lemon sauce topping makes this traditional dessert a little different, enhancing the flavor of the blueberries.

2 cups all-purpose flour
1/3 cup sugar
2 teaspoons baking powder
1/4 teaspoon salt
1 egg
1/2 cup milk
1/2 cup butter, melted
2 cups fresh *or* frozen blueberries, thawed

TOPPING:
- 1/2 cup sugar
- 1/3 cup all-purpose flour
- 1/2 teaspoon ground cinnamon
- 1/4 cup cold butter, cubed

LEMON SAUCE:
- 1/3 cup sugar
- 1 tablespoon cornstarch
- 1 teaspoon grated lemon peel
- 1 cup water
- 1 tablespoon butter
- 1 tablespoon lemon juice

In a large bowl, combine the flour, sugar, baking powder and salt. In a small bowl, whisk the egg, milk and butter; add to the dry ingredients just until moistened. Spread into a greased 8-in. square baking dish. Top with blueberries.

For topping, in a small bowl, combine sugar, flour and cinnamon; cut in butter until crumbly. Sprinkle over blueberries.

Bake at 350° for 45-55 minutes or until golden brown and a toothpick inserted near the center comes out clean.

In a small saucepan, combine sugar, cornstarch and lemon peel; gradually stir in water until smooth. Bring to a boil over low heat, stirring constantly. Cook and stir 1 minute longer or until thickened. Remove from the heat; stir in butter and lemon juice. Serve warm with buckle.
Yield: 9 servings (1 cup sauce).

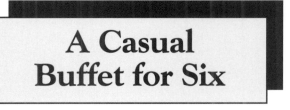

A Casual Buffet for Six

MARINATED PORK TENDERLOIN

Lisa Peters, Dewitt, New York

My sister, who has always had a knack for tossing spices and ingredients together, introduced this dish to our family at a barbecue she hosted. She worked at the ingredients until she came up with a recipe she could share with all of us. It's a healthy alternative to steak, easy to prepare and can be made ahead of time.

> 3/4 cup canola oil
> 1/3 cup soy sauce
> 1/4 cup white vinegar
> 2 tablespoons lemon juice
> 2 tablespoons Worcestershire sauce
> 1 tablespoon minced fresh parsley
> 1 garlic clove, minced
> 1/4 teaspoon salt
> 1/4 teaspoon pepper
> 2 pork tenderloins (1 pound *each*)
> MUSTARD SAUCE:
> 1/2 cup mayonnaise
> 2 tablespoons Dijon mustard
> 2 teaspoons prepared horseradish
> 1 teaspoon Worcestershire sauce
> 1/8 teaspoon crushed red pepper flakes, optional

In a large resealable plastic bag, combine the first nine ingredients; add the pork. Seal bag and turn to coat; refrigerate overnight.

Drain and discard marinade. Prepare grill for indirect heat. Coat grill rack with cooking spray before starting the grill. Grill pork, covered, over indirect medium-hot heat for 25-40 minutes or until a meat thermometer reads 160°. Let stand for 5 minutes before slicing.

In a small bowl, combine the sauce ingredients; serve with pork. **Yield:** 6 servings (2/3 cup sauce).

ALMOND GREEN BEANS

Mary Lou Wayman, Salt Lake City, Utah

This simple, quick way of preparing beans makes it an easy recipe to turn to at the last minute. Cooking the beans in the basic ingredients results in a flavorful, impressive side dish.

> 1/4 cup butter, cubed
> 1-1/4 teaspoons chicken bouillon granules
> 1/4 teaspoon celery seed
> 1/8 teaspoon pepper
> 1-1/4 pounds fresh green beans, trimmed
> 1-1/4 teaspoons soy sauce
> 1/2 cup slivered almonds, toasted

In a large skillet, melt butter; add the bouillon, celery seed and pepper. Stir in the beans. Cover and cook over medium heat for 9-11 minutes or until crisp-tender, stirring occasionally. Stir in soy sauce and almonds. **Yield:** 6 servings.

ZESTY CHEESE SPREAD

Brigitte Lehnert, Newark, California

I usually make this spread a day before I plan on serving it, since it needs time for the flavors to meld. But it also keeps well for a few weeks. It's an appetizer that can be served with snack rye bread or assorted crackers.

> 2 teaspoons ground mustard
> 2 teaspoons hot water
> 1 package (8 ounces) cream cheese, softened
> 1/2 cup butter, softened
> 1 tablespoon minced shallot
> 1 teaspoon capers, drained
> 1 teaspoon minced fresh parsley
> 1/2 teaspoon paprika
> Assorted crackers

In a small bowl, combine the mustard and water; let stand for 10 minutes. In a small bowl, beat the cream cheese and butter until smooth. Beat in the shallot, capers, parsley, paprika and mustard mixture until blended.

Transfer to a serving bowl; cover and refrigerate for 4 hours or overnight. Serve with crackers. **Yield:** 1-1/4 cups.

PINEAPPLE CHIFFON CAKE

Cheryl Tichenor, Elgin, Illinois

I was looking for a unique recipe that I could enter in a competition at the local county fair. It seemed that unusual cakes and pies won, so I looked through my mother's old recipes and found this. I love pineapple, so I gave this a try. It was a big hit with my husband and brought me a blue ribbon at the fair!

> 8 egg whites
> 2-1/4 cups cake flour

1-1/2 cups sugar
3 teaspoons baking powder
1/2 teaspoon salt
5 egg yolks
2/3 cup unsweetened pineapple juice
1/2 cup canola oil
2 teaspoons grated lemon peel
1/2 teaspoon cream of tartar

GLAZE:
2 cups confectioners' sugar
2 tablespoons butter, melted
2 to 3 tablespoons unsweetened pineapple juice

Let the egg whites stand at room temperature for 30 minutes. In a large bowl, combine the flour, sugar, baking powder and salt. In a small bowl, whisk the egg yolks, pineapple juice, oil and lemon peel. Add to dry ingredients; beat until well blended.

In another bowl, beat egg whites and cream of tartar until stiff peaks form; fold into batter. Gently spoon into an ungreased 10-in. tube pan. Cut through the batter with a knife to remove air pockets.

Bake on the lowest oven rack at 325° for 55-60 minutes or until top springs back when lightly touched. Immediately invert pan; cool completely, about 1 hour.

Run a knife around the side and center tube of pan. Remove the cake to a serving plate. Combine confectioners' sugar, butter and enough pineapple juice to achieve a glaze consistency. Drizzle over top of cake, allowing some glaze to drip down the sides. **Yield:** 12 servings.

SPECIAL SLOW-COOKED BEEF

Juli George, Grandville, Michigan

This hearty entree is easy to prepare for Sunday dinner. While the beef is slow cooking, the cook has lots of time to attend to the other details. The olives and sun-dried tomatoes add a special touch. With mashed potatoes or hot egg noodles on the side, it's comfort food that is perfect for the cool months ahead.

> 1 boneless beef chuck roast (3 pounds), cubed
> 1 tablespoon canola oil
> 1 tablespoon Italian seasoning
> 1 teaspoon salt
> 1 garlic clove, minced
> 1/2 cup sliced ripe olives, drained
> 1/3 cup oil-packed sun-dried tomatoes, drained and chopped
> 1 cup beef broth
> 1/2 cup fresh pearl onions, peeled
> 1 tablespoon cornstarch
> 2 tablespoons water

In a large skillet, brown meat in oil in batches; drain. Transfer to a 5-qt. slow cooker.

Sprinkle with Italian seasoning, salt and garlic; top with olives and tomatoes. Add broth and onions. Cover and cook on low for 6-8 hours or until meat is tender.

With a slotted spoon, remove beef and onions to a serving platter and keep warm. Pour cooking juices into a small saucepan; skim fat.

Combine the cornstarch and water until smooth, then gradually stir into the cooking juices. Bring to a boil; cook and stir for 2 minutes or until thickened. Spoon over beef mixture. **Yield:** 8 servings.

PEELING PEARL ONIONS

To peel pearl onions, place them in boiling water for about 2 minutes. Transfer them to a bowl of ice water and allow to cool. Cut off the root end of each onion, then slip off the skin. It should come off easily.

MASHED POTATO SPINACH BAKE

Fauneil Bennett, Wayne, Nebraska

I like this potato recipe because it's a make-ahead dish, and when the company rings the bell, it can be placed in the oven. Of Swedish origin, it was first served to my husband and me when we visited our daughter in Michigan and this was part of her Easter meal. She had received it from a friend.

> 6 medium potatoes, peeled and quartered
> 1 package (10 ounces) fresh spinach, torn
> 3/4 cup sour cream
> 1/4 cup butter, cubed
> 2 teaspoons minced chives
> 1-1/2 teaspoons salt
> 1 teaspoon sugar
> 1/4 teaspoon pepper
> 1/4 teaspoon dill weed
> 1 cup (4 ounces) shredded cheddar cheese

Place potatoes in a large saucepan and cover with water. Bring to a boil. Reduce heat; cover and cook for 15-20 minutes or until tender. Meanwhile, cook spinach in a small amount of water until wilted; drain well.

Drain the potatoes; place in a large bowl and mash. Stir in the spinach, sour cream, butter, chives and seasonings.

Transfer to a greased 2-1/2-qt. baking dish. Sprinkle with cheese. Bake, uncovered, at 400° for 20-25 minutes or until heated through. **Yield:** 8 servings.

BLACK-EYED PEA SOUP

Erin Walstead, Orange, California

This soup is easy and delicious. It can be made in little time. Once you try it, it will become a favorite.

> 3 bacon strips, diced
> 1 medium onion, finely chopped
> 1 garlic clove, minced
> 2 cans (14-1/2 ounces *each*) beef broth
> 1 can (10 ounces) diced tomatoes and green chilies, undrained
> 1/4 teaspoon salt
> 1/4 teaspoon pepper
> 2 cans (15-1/2 ounces *each*) black-eyed peas, rinsed and drained

In a large saucepan, cook bacon over medium heat until crisp. Using a slotted spoon, remove to paper towels to drain.

In the drippings, saute onion until tender. Add garlic; cook 1 minute longer. Stir in the broth, tomatoes, salt and pepper. Bring to a boil. Stir in black-eyed peas and bacon; heat through. **Yield:** 6 servings.

━━━━━━━━━━━━

CRANBERRY APPLE CRISP

Susie Van Etten, Chapmansboro, Tennessee

Both my sister-in-law and I make this treat for Thanksgiving and Christmas. We are aware that the other will have it on her menu, but we make it anyway. It's a family favorite, which has become a tradition for holiday meals.

6 cups chopped peeled tart apples (about 7 medium)

1/2 cup fresh or frozen cranberries, thawed
2 tablespoons maple syrup
1 teaspoon lemon juice
1 cup all-purpose flour
1 cup sugar
1/2 teaspoon salt
1 egg, lightly beaten
1/2 cup butter, melted
1-1/2 teaspoons ground cinnamon
Vanilla ice cream

In a large bowl, combine apples and cranberries. Add syrup and lemon juice; toss to coat. Transfer to a greased 11-in. x 7-in. baking dish.

In a small bowl, combine the flour, sugar and salt. Stir in egg until blended. Sprinkle over fruit. Drizzle with butter; sprinkle with cinnamon.

Bake, uncovered, at 350° for 40-45 minutes or until topping is golden brown and fruit is tender. Serve warm with ice cream. **Yield:** 8 servings.

This Dinner Is Simply Divine

✦✦✦✦✦✦✦✦✦✦✦✦✦

RED FLANNEL STEW

Kathy Padgett, Diamond City, Arkansas

When I was child, every Saturday night was "Red Flannel Night." Grandpa and I wore our red flannel underwear to supper and Grandma, the cook, dressed in a long calico dress and sunbonnet. We'd eat Red Flannel Stew spooned over fluffy biscuits. Grandma learned to make the stew from earlier generations.

    2 whole fresh beets, washed, trimmed
      and halved
    6 cups water, *divided*
    1 pound corned beef brisket, trimmed
      and cut into 1-inch pieces
    4 small carrots, sliced
    1 large potato, cubed
    1 small turnip, peeled and cubed
    1 small onion, chopped
    1 teaspoon *each* dried parsley flakes, basil
      and thyme
  1/4 teaspoon salt
  1/8 teaspoon pepper

In a large saucepan, bring the halved beets and 4 cups water to a boil. Reduce heat; simmer, uncovered, for 20-25 minutes or until tender. Drain, reserving 2 cups cooking liquid. Peel and dice beets; set aside.

In the same pan, combine the corned beef, carrots, potato, turnip, onion, seasonings, remaining water and reserved cooking liquid. Bring to a boil. Reduce heat; cover and simmer for 1-1/4 to 1-1/2 hours or until meat and vegetables are tender. Stir in the diced beets; heat through. **Yield:** 5 servings.

✦✦✦✦✦✦✦✦✦✦✦✦✦

PEAR SPINACH SALAD

Lois Telloni, Lorain, Ohio

When I take a dish to a potluck gathering and everyone asks for the recipe, I know I have a winner. This refreshing salad is good with any entree, presents itself well and is an interesting combination of tastes.

    1 can (15-1/4 ounces) sliced pears
    4 cups fresh baby spinach

    2 green onions, thinly sliced
    1 medium grapefruit, peeled and
      sectioned
    3 bacon strips, cooked and crumbled
    2 tablespoons white wine vinegar
    2 tablespoons canola oil
  1-1/2 teaspoons lime juice
    1 tablespoon minced fresh parsley
    1 teaspoon sugar
  1/4 teaspoon salt
  1/8 teaspoon grated lime peel
Dash cayenne pepper

Drain the sliced pears, reserving 2 tablespoons of the juice. In a salad bowl, combine the spinach and green onions. Top with the pears, grapefruit and cooked bacon.

In a small bowl, whisk the white wine vinegar, canola oil, lime juice, minced parsley, sugar, salt, grated lime peel, cayenne pepper and reserved pear juice. Pour over the salad; gently toss to coat. **Yield:** 5 servings.

✦✦✦✦✦✦✦✦✦✦✦✦✦

CHEESE POKE MUFFINS

Katrina Rivera, Pittsfield, Massachusetts

These easy-to-make, savory treats are extra special because each little muffin has a bubbling center of creamy cheese, which is irresistible. They make a wonderful side to any main dish, or they can also be served at breakfast with eggs. Yum!

  3/4 cup all-purpose flour
  3/4 cup yellow cornmeal
    2 teaspoons sugar
    1 teaspoon baking powder
    1 teaspoon salt
    1 egg
  1/2 cup plus 2 tablespoons milk
  1/3 cup canola oil
  1/2 cup finely chopped process cheese
      (Velveeta)
    2 tablespoons butter, softened

In a large bowl, combine the flour, cornmeal, sugar, baking powder and salt. In a small bowl, whisk the egg, milk and canola oil. Stir into the dry ingredients just until moistened. To prevent the muffins from turning tough, do not overmix.

Fill eight greased muffin cups one-fourth full with the batter. Combine the chopped cheese and butter; spoon over the batter. Top with the remaining batter.

Bake at 400° for 15-18 minutes or until a toothpick inserted near the center comes out clean. Cool for 5 minutes before removing from pan to a wire rack. Serve warm. **Yield:** 8 muffins.

CHOCOLATE RASPBERRY SQUARES

Marilyn Swisher, Berrien Center, Michigan

This elegant bar cookie is loaded with wonderful flavors and effortless to assemble. A special touch is to sprinkle the bars with confectioners' sugar.

1-1/2 cups all-purpose flour
1-1/2 cups quick-cooking *or* old-fashioned
    oats
  1/2 cup sugar
  1/2 cup packed brown sugar
  1/4 teaspoon salt
    1 cup cold butter, cubed

  3/4 cup seedless raspberry jam
    1 package (11-1/2 ounces) semisweet
    chocolate chunks
  1/4 cup chopped walnuts

In a large bowl, combine the flour, oats, sugars and salt. Cut in butter until mixture resembles coarse crumbs. Set aside 1 cup for topping; press remaining crumb mixture into a greased 9-in. square baking pan. Spread with jam; sprinkle with chocolate chunks.

Combine walnuts and reserved crumb mixture; sprinkle over top. Bake at 375° for 30-35 minutes or until lightly browned and bubbly. Cool on a wire rack. Cut into squares. **Yield:** 16 servings.

The Best of Country Cooking 2010   169

Make Lunch Special Again

▰▰▰▰▰▰▰▰▰▰▰▰

CHICKEN SALAD PITAS

Jessie Sarrazin, Livingston, Montana

This colorful chicken salad is ideal as a luncheon tradition or can be easily packed for a picnic. The combination of flavors is refreshing…one of our family's favorite warm-weather entrees.

     3 cups cubed cooked chicken
 1/2 cup chopped cucumber
 1/2 cup halved seedless red grapes
 1/2 cup chopped carrots
 1/4 cup chopped walnuts
 1/4 cup mayonnaise
 1/4 cup ranch salad dressing
     4 pita breads (6 inches), halved
     8 lettuce leaves

In a large bowl, combine the chicken, cucumber, grapes, carrots and walnuts. Combine mayonnaise and ranch dressing. Pour over chicken mixture; toss to coat.

Line the pita halves with lettuce; spoon about 1/2 cup chicken salad into each. Refrigerate until serving. **Yield:** 4 servings.

▰▰▰▰▰▰▰▰▰▰▰▰

TOMATO CORN SALAD

Mary Relyea, Canastota, New York

The lightly dressed salad and the pretty presentation in the tomato shell make this a great summer side dish that is sure to bring on the raves. The basil essence is compatible with all the ingredients and the salad is especially tasty with a barbecued entree.

     4 medium tomatoes
     1 large ear sweet corn, husk removed
 1/4 cup chopped red onion
 1/4 cup loosely packed fresh basil leaves,
         chopped
     2 teaspoons olive oil
 1-1/2 teaspoons balsamic *or* white wine vinegar
 1/4 teaspoon garlic salt
 1/4 teaspoon pepper

Cut a thin slice off the top of each tomato. Scoop out pulp, leaving 1/2-in. shells. Seed and chop enough of the pulp to equal 1 cup (discard any

remaining pulp or save for another use). Place chopped tomato and tomato cups, inverted, on paper towels to drain.

In a large saucepan, cook the corn in boiling water for 3-5 minutes or until tender. Drain and immediately place corn in ice water; drain. Cut corn off cob.

In a small bowl, combine the corn, chopped tomato, onion and basil. In another bowl, whisk the oil, vinegar, garlic salt and pepper. Pour over the corn mixture and toss to coat. Cover and refrigerate for 30 minutes. Spoon into tomato cups. **Yield:** 4 servings.

▰▰▰▰▰▰▰▰▰▰▰▰

MUSHROOM BARLEY SOUP

Rebekah White, Seaside, Oregon

After tinkering with three different recipes, I came up with this warming rich, dark brown broth with hearty mushrooms, barley and onions. It's a beefy tasting soup for my meat-loving husband and healthy for both of us. It can simmer all day in a slow cooker or be served up right after preparation. To make it vegetarian or vegan, use vegetable broth instead of chicken broth.

     1 large onion, chopped
     1 tablespoon olive oil
     2 cups sliced fresh mushrooms
     2 garlic cloves, minced
     7 cups reduced-sodium chicken broth
     2 cups water
 1/2 cup medium pearl barley
     2 tablespoons reduced-sodium soy sauce
     1 teaspoon dried thyme
 1/4 teaspoon pepper

In a large saucepan, saute onion and mushrooms in oil until vegetables are tender. Add garlic; cook 1 minute longer.

Stir in the remaining ingredients. Bring to a boil. Reduce the heat; simmer, uncovered, for 45-50 minutes or until the barley is tender. **Yield:** 7 servings.

▰▰▰▰▰▰▰▰▰▰▰▰

HONEY-OAT GRANOLA BARS

Jean Boyce, New Ulm, Minnesota

I found this recipe on one of our monthly Brown County REA newsletters. My husband and I eat a few of these bars each day. It's a basic recipe to which you can add any of your favorite add-ins…coconut, chocolate chips, nuts or dried fruits.

4 cups quick-cooking oats
1 cup packed brown sugar
1 cup chopped salted peanuts
1 cup (6 ounces) semisweet chocolate
  chips
1/2 cup sunflower kernels
3/4 cup butter, melted
2/3 cup honey
1 teaspoon vanilla extract

In a large bowl, combine the oats, brown sugar, peanuts, chocolate chips and sunflower kernels. Stir in the butter, honey and vanilla until combined (mixture will be crumbly). Press into a greased parchment paper-lined 15-in. x 10-in. x 1-in. baking pan.

Bake at 350° for 15-20 minutes or until browned and bubbly. Cool for 15 minutes on a wire rack; cut into squares. Cool completely before removing from pan. **Yield:** 3 dozen.

SOFTENING BROWN SUGAR

To soften brown sugar, place a slice of bread or an apple wedge with the brown sugar in a covered container for a few days. If you're in a hurry, microwave on high for 20-30 seconds. Repeat if necessary, but watch carefully, because the sugar will begin to melt.

General Recipe Index

A

APPETIZERS & SNACKS

Cold Appetizers
Caesar Salsa Baguette Slices, 10
Cream Cheese Deviled Eggs, 12

Dips & Spreads
Creamy Feta-Spinach Dip, 12
Olive Zucchini Spread, 8
Pumpkin Pie Dip, 6
Salsa Bean Dip, 79
Spinach & Artichoke Dip, 16
Veggie Cheese Spread, 9
Zesty Cheese Spread, 164

Hot Appetizers
Appetizer Chicken Kabobs, 5
Asparagus Snack Squares, 7
Blue Cheese Heart Tarts, 17
Chicken Taco Ring, 13
Crab Crescent Loaf, 10
Crab-Stuffed Mushrooms, 15
Crab Wonton Cups, 7
Garlic-Onion Appetizer
    Rounds, 17
Mushroom Cheese Bread, 14
Onion Swiss Loaf, 89
Parmesan Onion Wedges, 15
Saucy Meatballs, 5
Smoky Onion Biscuit Squares, 90

Snacks
Iced Almonds, 8
Nutty Caramel Corn, 14

APPLES
Apple Butter Pumpkin Pie, 133
Apple Dumplings, 111
Candy Apple Walnut Pie, 131
Caramel-Glazed Apple Cake, 123
Cranberry Apple Crisp, 167
Creamy Waldorf Salad, 33
Fruited Poppy Seed Coleslaw, 148

Lemon Cider, 12
Squash-Stuffed Baked Apples, 74
Warm Percolator Punch, 5
Yogurt Fruit Salad, 28

APRICOTS
Apricot Crisp, 159
Apricot-Pistachio Chicken Salad
    Sandwiches, 148
Apricot Sweet Potato Bake, 78
Mustard-Apricot Pork Chops, 154
Peachy Cookies, 102

ARTICHOKES
Artichokes with Tarragon
    Butter, 77
Olive Zucchini Spread, 8
Spinach & Artichoke Dip, 16
Sweet Pasta Salad, 22

ASPARAGUS
Asparagus Snack Squares, 7
Asparagus with Almonds, 154
Caesar Asparagus, 73
Chicken Asparagus Pasta, 150
Herbed Asparagus Salad, 33

AVOCADO
Avocado Tomato Wraps, 26
Festive Cabbage Salad, 36
Hearty Veggie Sandwiches, 142

B

BANANAS
Banana Split Ice Cream Cake, 130
Green Grape Salad, 143
Moist Banana Bread, 92
Sweet Potato Banana Bake, 79

BARLEY
Italian Sausage Bean Soup, 30
Mushroom Barley Soup, 170
Scotch Broth, 38

BARS & BROWNIES
Brownie Chunk Ice Cream, 116
Caramel Candy Bars, 99
Carrot Cake Bars, 106
Cherry Pineapple Bars, 100
Chocolate-Cherry Cheesecake
    Bars, 108
Chocolate Chip Cheese Bars, 107
Chocolate Raspberry Squares, 169
Coconut Brownies, 109
Honey-Oat Granola Bars, 170
Raspberry Oat Bars, 100
Strawberry Almond Bars, 99

BEANS & LENTILS
Black-Eyed Pea Soup, 166
Cream of Lentil Soup, 34
Creole Black Beans 'n'
    Sausage, 69
Italian Sausage Bean Soup, 30
Moroccan Chickpea Stew, 40
Salsa Bean Dip, 79
Veggie Bean Casserole, 82

BEEF & VEAL (also see
Ground Beef)
Bavarian Stew, 145
Blue Cheese-Topped Steaks, 45
Burgundy Beef, 54
Chipotle-Rubbed Beef
    Tenderloin, 50
Cranberry Short Ribs, 140
French Canadian Meat Pie, 61
Irish Beef Stew, 43
Mushroom Beef Tenderloin, 152

C

CABBAGE & SAUERKRAUT

CAKES & COFFEE CAKES

CANDIES

CARROTS

CASSEROLES

Main Dishes

Side Dishes

CAULIFLOWER

CHEESE

Appetizers

Breads, Rolls & More

Desserts

Main Dishes

Salads & Dressing

Side Dishes

Soup & Sandwich

CHEESECAKES

CHERRIES

CHICKEN & CORNISH HENS

Appetizer

Main Dishes

Alphabetical Recipe Index